Canon 7D:
From
Snapshots to
Great Shots

Nicole S. Young

Peachpit
Press

Canon 7D: From Snapshots to Great Shots
Nicole S. Young

Peachpit Press
1249 Eighth Street
Berkeley, CA 94710
510/524-2178
510/524-2221 (fax)

Find us on the Web at www.peachpit.com
To report errors, please send a note to errata@peachpit.com
Peachpit Press is a division of Pearson Education

Acquisitions Editor: Ted Waitt
Associate Editor: Valerie Witte
Copyeditor: Scout Festa
Proofreader: Erfert Fenton
Production Editor: Lisa Brazieal
Composition: WolfsonDesign
Indexer: Valerie Haynes Perry
Cover Image: Nicole S. Young
Cover Design: Aren Howell
Back Cover Author Photo: Rich Legg

ISBN-13   978-0-321-62482-6
ISBN-10   0-321-62482-3

9 8 7 6 5 4 3 2

Printed and bound in the United States of America

DEDICATION

To my mom and dad, for always believing in me and reminding me that I can accomplish anything I put my mind to.

I love you!

ACKNOWLEDGMENTS

Before writing this book I never really considered myself a writer. Photography is my passion, and my writing was always limited to photography articles and posts on my blog. When I was asked to write the Canon 7D book for the *From Snapshots to Great Shots* series I was floored! Me… an *author?* Well, I made it through the entire process, and the experience was an opportunity that I am so happy to have had. But I didn't finish the project on my own—I can honestly say that I couldn't have completed this book without the help of my family, friends, and peers.

First and foremost, I want to thank my parents. You guys have always been there for me and are 100 percent supportive of anything I put my mind to. Thank you for being my biggest fans.

I also want to thank my friend, Rich, for his help throughout this entire process— for listening, photographing, and just being there when I needed someone to talk to. Also to my mentors, Scott and Rick—thank you for your advice and wisdom.

I'd also like to thank Ace, Amy, Araya, and Prince for supporting me when the dream I'm now experiencing was just a small glimmer in my eye. You were there in the beginning and are a big reason I'm here today. I'll never forget you guys.

Last, but definitely not least, I'd like to thank Scott, Ted, Valerie, Lisa, Sara, and the rest of the Peachpit team, who were an essential part of putting the pieces of this book together. Thanks for your patience and for giving me the opportunity to live my dream.

Contents

Introduction

If you are reading this book, there's a pretty good chance that you have read other "how-to" photography books. Many of those books will be either camera-specific (how to use the settings on your camera) or will be about the methods and techniques used to create specific types of images (landscape, portrait, HDR, etc.). In this book you get the best of both worlds—you learn how to use your 7D and its specific features as well as the different methods and photography techniques to capture those images.

Here is a quick Q&A about the book to help you understand what you'll see in the following pages:

Q: WHAT CAN I EXPECT TO LEARN FROM THIS BOOK?

A: My goal in writing this book is to help owners of the Canon 7D learn more about the specific settings and features of their camera and put that knowledge to use to make great images. You'll also find a ton of general and advanced photography tips and tricks in each of the chapters to push your photography to the next level.

Q: IS EVERY CAMERA FEATURE GOING TO BE COVERED?

A: No. I wrote about what I feel are some of the most important features on your 7D, but don't worry! There's a *lot* of information in here. This is more than just a book on simple steps to get you started… I really dig into some of the advanced features to make sure that you get as much out of your 7D as possible.

Q: SO, IF I ALREADY OWN THE MANUAL, WHY DO I NEED THIS BOOK?

A: Your manual does a great job of explaining *how* to use the features in your camera, but it doesn't necessarily tell you *why* or *when* to use them. I tried my best to do both so that you not only know about the knobs, buttons, and settings in your 7D but also what the best situations are to make use of the features and settings on your camera.

Q: WHAT ARE THE CHALLENGES ALL ABOUT?

A: At the end of each chapter I list a few exercises you can do to practice and solidify some of the techniques and settings you learned about in that chapter. Feel free to try them out if you like, and if you do, be sure to check out the Flickr group and share what you've learned!

Q: SHOULD I READ THE BOOK STRAIGHT THROUGH OR CAN I SKIP AROUND FROM CHAPTER TO CHAPTER?

A: Well, both! The first few chapters are going to give you a lot of basics behind your 7D and digital photography in general, so if you don't quite have a grasp on either of those yet, it's a good idea to read through them before heading on to the rest of the book.

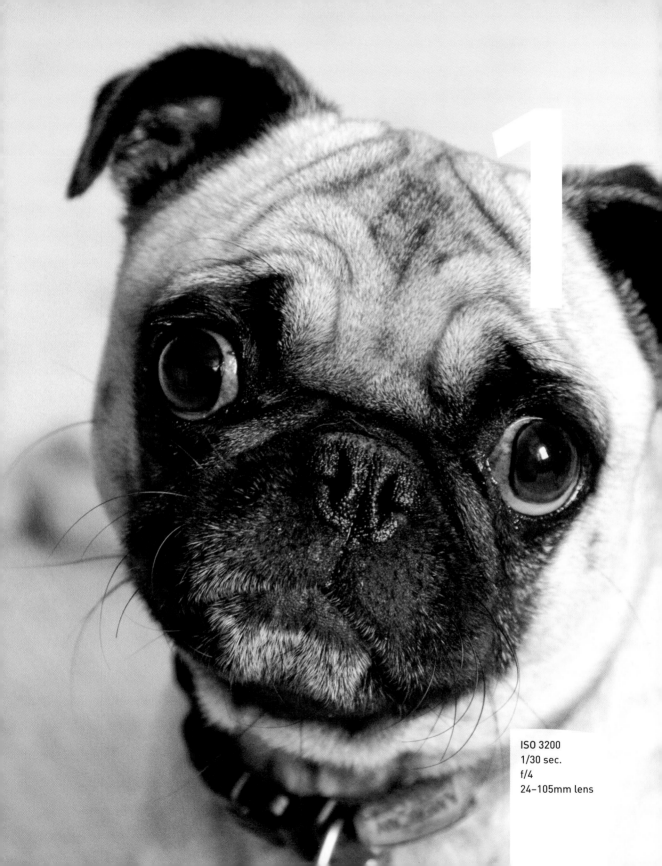

ISO 3200
1/30 sec.
f/4
24–105mm lens

The 7D Top Ten List

TEN TIPS TO MAKE YOUR SHOOTING MORE PRODUCTIVE RIGHT OUT OF THE BOX

When I get a new camera, it is so much fun to open the box, dig in for the camera itself, attach the strap (or not), and run outside to start taking some photos. That's always my first instinct, but what I should do is pull out the manual, sit down on the couch, and start reading and learning about all of the new features that my camera has to offer. Sounds boring, right? Well, maybe it is, but it ends up saving me time in the long run if I know more about my camera from the start.

If this is your first DSLR then you might be a little bit overwhelmed by all of the different features in the 7D. Manuals tend to tell you a lot of "how," but not a lot of "why," and jumping straight into the manual may initially do more harm than good if you're not sure where to start. If you don't have a grasp of the general settings, then some of the information in the manual won't really have any meaning.

To help you understand more about your camera, in this first chapter I'll be discussing the top ten things that you should know before beginning any major photo-taking endeavors.

PORING OVER THE CAMERA

CAMERA FRONT

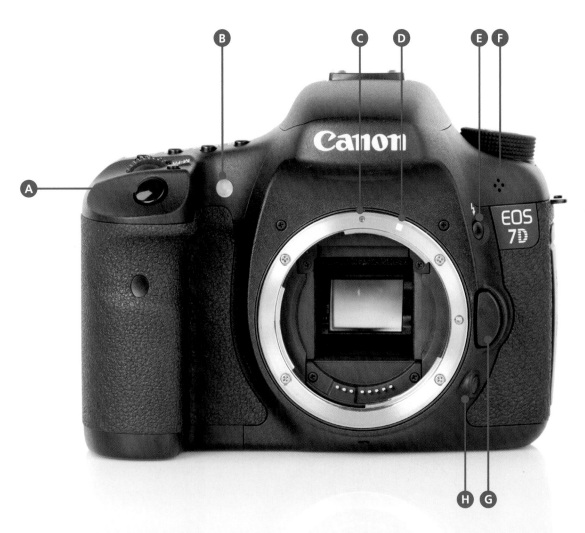

A Shutter Button
B Red-Eye Reduction/Self-Timer Lamp
C EF Lens Mount
D EF-S Lens Mount

E Flash Button
F Microphone
G Lens Release Button
H Depth-of-Field Preview Button

CAMERA BACK

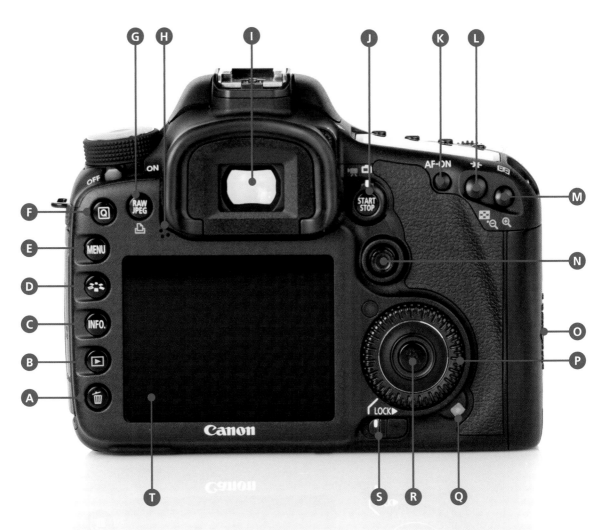

A Erase Button
B Playback Button
C Info Button
D Picture Style Selection Button
E Menu Button
F Quick Control Button
G One-Touch RAW+JPEG Button

H Speaker
I Viewfinder
J Live View and Movie
   Shooting Button
K AF Start Button
L AE Lock/Reduce Button
M AF Point Selection/Magnify Button

N Multi-Controller
O CF Card Slot
P Quick Control Dial
Q Card Busy Indicator
R Set Button
S Quick Control Dial Switch
T LCD Monitor

CAMERA TOP

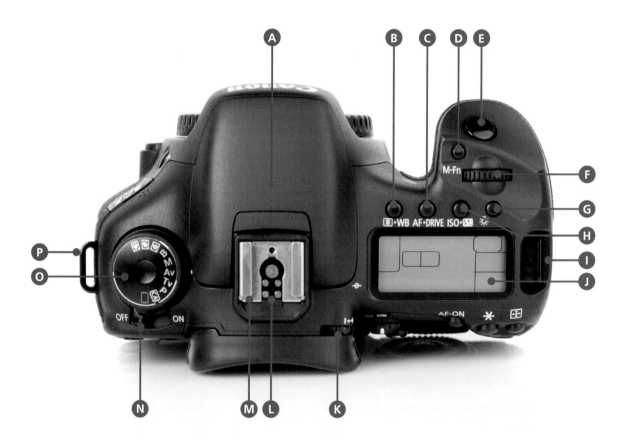

A   Built-In Flash
B   Metering Mode/White-Balance Button
C   AF Mode/Drive Mode Button
D   Multi-Function Button
E   Shutter Button
F   Main Dial
G   LCD Panel Illumination Button
H   ISO/Flash Exposure Compensation Button

I   Strap Mount
J   LCD Panel
K   Dioptric Adjustment Knob
L   Flash-Sync Mounts
M   Hot Shoe
N   Power Switch
O   Mode Dial
P   Strap Mount

1. CHARGE YOUR BATTERY

This might sound obvious, but it's important to give your battery a full charge before you begin taking photos. If you insert the battery into your camera right away, you will find that it has a little bit of juice in it, but plugging it in with the battery charger will give you more shooting time and will get the battery off to a good start.

Once you've got a fully charged battery in your camera, you can register it from the setup menu. This is extremely helpful when you have more than one battery, because it will tell you information about each individual battery, such as the remaining charge, the number of photos you have taken with that battery since its last charge, and the recharge performance (**Figure 1.1**).

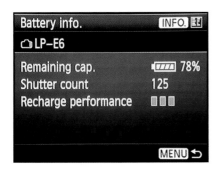

FIGURE 1.1
The LCD shows how much charge is left on your battery.

REGISTERING YOUR CAMERA'S BATTERY

1. Turn the camera on.

2. Press the Menu button on the back of the camera to bring up the menu list.

3. Use the Multi-Controller to select the last setup menu tab (third tab from the right).

4. Select the Battery Info option using the Set button (**A**).

5. Press the Info button on the left side of your camera.

6. Select Register, on the bottom left, to register your battery (**B**).

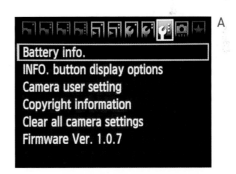

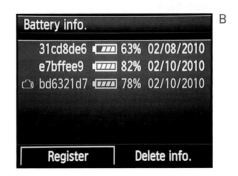

EXTRA BATTERIES AND BATTERY GRIPS

It's wise to have at least one spare battery with your camera at all times. You never know when you will need it—maybe you find that you are doing more shooting than anticipated, or you realize that you forgot to charge the one that's in your camera. Another option is to use a battery grip, which is an optional accessory available for most DSLRs. While not essential, it is very useful for battery life since it holds up to two batteries at a time. It's also beneficial for shooting in general if you don't mind the extra bulk. What I like most about it is the ability to shoot vertically and make use of the extra shutter release and buttons on the grip (**Figure 1.2**).

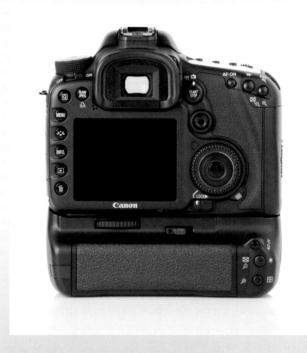

FIGURE 1.2
The BG-E7 battery grip stores and utilizes two LP-E6 batteries and has separate camera buttons to make vertical shooting more convenient.

2. TURN OFF THE RELEASE SHUTTER WITHOUT CARD SETTING

Immediately after I've inserted a battery in my new camera, I ensure that I won't accidentally take a photo without a memory card by turning off the Release Shutter Without Card setting. This step is so important that if I happen to be holding a friend's camera and notice that they don't have this feature disabled, I go ahead and do it for them (they usually don't seem to mind). The benefit to doing this is that if you forget to put your card in and you start shooting, the camera won't let you take a photo. There's nothing worse than spending several hours photographing something only to realize that you didn't have any of those images saved, especially when the mishap could have easily been avoided. This feature has prevented me from losing photos on several occasions, securing it a spot on this Top Ten list.

TURNING OFF THE RELEASE SHUTTER WITHOUT CARD SETTING

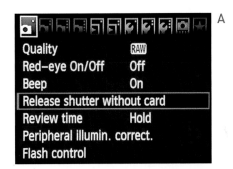
A

1. Turn the camera on.

2. Press the Menu button on the back of the camera to bring up the menu list.

3. Use the Multi-Controller to select the far-left menu tab.

4. Now scroll down to the Release Shutter Without Card option using the Quick Control dial and press the Set button (A).

5. Use the Quick Control dial to select the Disable option, and then press the Set button once again (B).

6. Press the Menu button again to return to shooting mode.

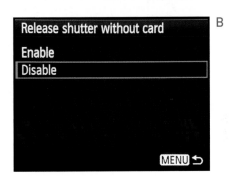
B

Now when you try to take a photo without a memory card inserted in the camera, you will see a message at the bottom of your viewfinder that flashes the words "no CF" (which stands for no Compact Flash card). This is your clue that you need to insert your memory card before the camera will fire. The top LCD Panel will also display the "no CF" message if you activate the Shutter button.

For an in-depth discussion of memory cards and proper formatting, see Chapter 2.

3. SET YOUR RAW/JPEG IMAGE QUALITY

If you are upgrading from a digital point-and-shoot camera to the 7D, then you are already familiar with the JPEG file format. With DSLR cameras you also have the option of using the RAW format. In this section I will discuss the basics of the two file types, and in Chapter 2 you'll find much more detailed information on their differences, benefits, and disadvantages.

Let's start with the JPEG file format. JPEG stands for Joint Photographic Experts Group. It was developed as a method of shrinking digital images in order to reduce large file sizes while retaining the original information. (Technically, JPEG is a mathematical equation for compressing a file format, but we'll refer to it as a file format to keep things simple.) Your camera will embed all information into the photograph at the time of exposure. When you shoot in JPEG you have smaller file sizes, but that also means that each image has less information and lower quality, and making any extreme enhancements or edits to the image could degrade the image quality even more. However, using JPEG you can fit many more images on your memory card, and the images will write to the card faster, which can make this type of file format desirable to many wedding and sports photographers.

RAW files, on the other hand, retain much more information than JPEG files, are not compressed, and offer a lot more "wiggle room" during your editing process (things like exposure and white balance can easily be adjusted without extreme loss of image quality). The downside to this format is that your file sizes will be much larger, and you won't be able to fit as many images on your memory card as you could using JPEG. You'll also need to have a good understanding of photo editing, along with the corresponding software, to edit and share your images.

The 7D has several options for shooting modes. You have the choice to shoot in JPEG only, RAW only, or a combination of the two. If you are new to digital photography and don't know much about shooting RAW and using sophisticated editing software, I recommend you stick with JPEG for now. If you aren't sure what you want to do, and you happen to have a lot of card space, then you can always shoot in both RAW and JPEG at the same time. But for now let's focus on setting up your camera to shoot in JPEG.

When shooting in JPEG format, you need to make some decisions that will determine the file size and quality of your images. There are three different sizes—Large, Medium, and Small—which indicate the actual physical size of your image in pixels. When picking the quality setting, you have two choices: Fine (high quality) and Normal (lower or normal quality). My recommendation, if you prefer to shoot in

JPEG, is to select the highest image size and quality setting—*Large* size and *Fine* quality. It's always best to start with the highest-quality image possible, right?

SETTING THE JPEG IMAGE QUALITY

1. Turn the camera on.

2. Press the Menu button on the back of the camera to bring up the menu list.

3. Use the Multi-Controller to select the far-left menu tab.

4. At the top of this menu tab, locate the Quality option (**A**).

5. Press the Set button to bring up the Quality options screen.

6. Use the Main dial to select your RAW quality; you will move the dial all the way to the left to shoot only in the JPEG format.

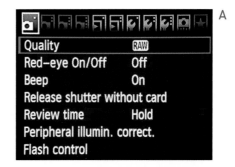

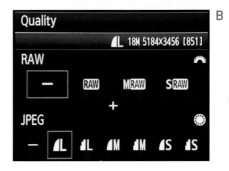

7. Use the Quick Control dial to select the first L on the far left (this will render an 18-megapixel image with a dimension of 5184 pixels by 3456 pixels) (**B**).

8. Press the Set button to lock in this change.

As you will see when scrolling through the quality settings, the higher the quality, the fewer pictures you will be able to fit on your card. If you have a 1-GB memory card, the quality setting we have selected will allow you to shoot about 147 photographs before you fill it. Always try to choose quality over quantity. Your pictures will be the better for it.

Manual Callout

For a complete chart that shows the image quality settings with the number of possible shots for each setting, turn to page 59 in your user manual.

ONE-TOUCH RAW+JPEG BUTTON

If your image quality is set to shoot only in RAW or JPEG quality, you have the option of quickly shooting in RAW+JPEG quality mode for a single image by using the One-Touch RAW+JPEG button (**Figure 1.3**). If you are shooting in JPEG and you decide that your next photo could use some additional processing and want to shoot it in RAW, press the RAW/JPEG button on the top-left part of the back of your camera and take a photo. You will then have both a RAW and a JPEG file of the same image. Once you take a photo, this button reverts to its previous setting.

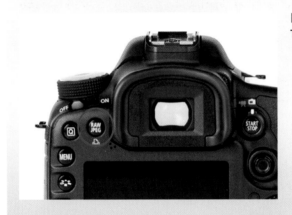

FIGURE 1.3
The One-Touch RAW+JPEG button.

4. SET YOUR ISO

Digital photography has opened up a whole new world when it comes to setting the ISO speed on your camera. With a film camera you were bound to whatever film speed you loaded in your camera or carried with you in your camera bag, but with a digital camera you can adjust the ISO on the fly, depending on your lighting conditions.

The ISO setting in your camera is the baseline that helps determine your aperture and shutter speed settings. It allows you to choose the camera sensor's level of sensitivity to light. It also makes a big difference in image quality. With a film camera, the ISO is also called "film speed," and the higher the ISO number, the grainier your images will be. With digital photography, that grain is referred to as "digital noise," but the principle is the same—the higher the ISO number, the more digital noise you will see in your image. As I mentioned earlier, digital cameras offer an amazing amount of flexibility when it comes to setting your ISO. This is very useful, but it can affect the quality of your images if you set the ISO too high.

Which ISO you choose depends on your level of available, or ambient, light. For sunny days or very bright scenes, use a low ISO such as 100 or 200. As the level of light is reduced, raise the ISO level. Cloudy days or indoor scenes might require you to use ISO 400. For low-light scenes, such as nighttime shots, you'll need to bump up that ISO to 1600. The thing to remember is to shoot with the lowest setting possible for maximum quality.

There is also the option to set your ISO using the Auto ISO feature. I use this from time to time, but I don't recommend new photographers use this feature until they have a strong grasp of how aperture, shutter speed, and ISO work together to produce a proper exposure. While quite powerful at times, Auto ISO can be confusing if you are not sure what your camera is doing.

SETTING THE ISO

1. Activate the camera by lightly pressing the Shutter button.
2. Press the ISO button on the top of the camera (**Figure 1.4**).

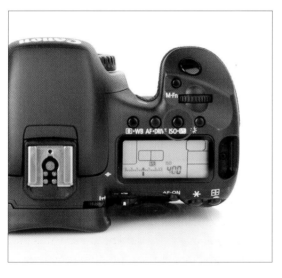

FIGURE 1.4
The ISO button above the top LCD Panel.

3. Use the Main dial to select an ISO between 100 and 6400.
4. Lightly press the Shutter button again to lock in your change.

SET YOUR ISO ON THE FLY

You can also change the ISO without taking your eye from the viewfinder by following the same steps as above. When you press the ISO button, you will see all of the camera settings in the viewfinder disappear, leaving just the ISO information viewable. Once you press the Set button, your new ISO setting will display along with the regular shooting data. This will get easier to do as you become more familiar with the camera buttons.

You can also take advantage of the camera's Quick Control button. This feature allows you to change settings, such as shutter speed, aperture, and ISO (**Figure 1.5**), while looking at the LCD Monitor on the back of the camera.

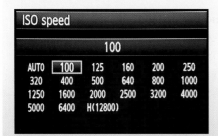

FIGURE 1.5
Using the Quick Control button you can change your ISO speed by viewing the settings on the rear LCD Monitor.

NOISE

Noise is the enemy of digital photography, but it has nothing to do with the loudness of your camera operation. It refers to the electronic artifacts that appear as speckles in your image. They generally appear in darker shadow areas and are a result of the camera trying to amplify the signal to produce visible information. The more the image needs to be amplified—raising the sensitivity through higher ISOs—the greater the amount of noise will be.

5. SET THE CORRECT WHITE BALANCE

White balance refers to the process of balancing the color temperature of the lights in the location where you are shooting, so that the colors appear "normal." Our eyes have the ability to adjust to these changes so quickly that we don't even realize that certain lights give off different colors.

Most of the film used in traditional film photography was daylight balanced, meaning that the color in photos taken outdoors or with a flash looks correct. Another option, tungsten, balanced film for indoor use. But anything beyond that had to be adjusted with colored filters to match the light. With the advances in digital photography, we are able to input any color temperature we want to balance the images with the surrounding light.

It's extremely important to set the white balance in your images correctly, especially if you are shooting in JPEG mode. (With RAW images you can adjust the white balance in editing software, but the color information in a JPEG image is permanently embedded into the file, so trying to bring the image back to its correct color temperature is an impossible task.)

The 7D can perform this task automatically, and it usually does a pretty good job, but your goal should be to maintain as much control as possible with your images. You don't need to have a deep understanding of color temperature to find the correct white balance. Your camera comes with easy-to-understand presets, and even an option to customize or pre-set your white balance in the camera. Your white balance choices are:

- **Auto:** The default setting for your camera. It is also the setting used by all of the Automatic modes (see Chapter 3).

- **Daylight:** Most often used for general daylight/sun-lit shooting.

- **Shade:** Used when working in shaded areas that are still using sunlight as the dominant light source.

- **Cloudy, twilight, sunset:** The choice for overcast or very cloudy days. This and the Shade setting will eliminate the blue colorcast from your images.

- **Tungsten light:** Used for any occasion when you are using regular household-type bulbs as your light source. Tungsten is a very warm light source and will result in a yellow/orange cast if you don't correct for it.

- **White fluorescent light:** Used to get rid of the green-blue cast that can result from using regular fluorescent lights as your dominant light source. Some fluorescent lights are actually balanced for daylight, which would allow you to use the Daylight white balance setting.

- **Flash:** Used whenever you're using the built-in flash or using a flash on the hot shoe. You should select this white balance to adjust for the slightly cooler light that comes from using a flash. (The hot shoe is the small bracket located on the top of your camera, resting just above the viewfinder.)

- **Custom:** This setting gives you the option of photographing something that is pure white and using it as the baseline for your color temperature. The camera will balance its color temperature settings with that particular photograph.

- **Color temperature:** Here you have the option to actually dial in the Kelvin temperature that matches the light in your setting (from 2500-10,000).

SETTING THE WHITE BALANCE

1. After turning on or waking the camera, select one of the shooting modes, such as P (you can't choose anything other than Auto white balance when using either of the Fully Automatic modes).

2. Press the WB button on the top of the camera to bring up the white balance menu (**Figure 1.6**).

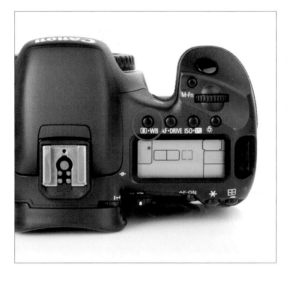

FIGURE 1.6
The White-Balance button above the top LCD Panel.

3. Use the Quick Control dial to select the proper white balance for your shooting situation. The selected white balance icon will appear in the upper-left portion of the top LCD Panel.

4. Press the Shutter button to lock in your selection.

5. Check the camera display to ensure that the proper white balance is selected.

LIVE VIEW AND WHITE BALANCE

One really cool feature of the 7D is the ability to shoot in Live View. This feature can also come in handy when changing settings such as the white balance. To give it a try, make sure the Live View switch is set to the "white camera" position (**Figure 1.7**) and click on the Start/Stop button to activate Live View. Then follow the steps above to scroll through the different white balance settings. You will see an immediate change in the colors of your image as you set it on different white balance settings (**Figure 1.8**).

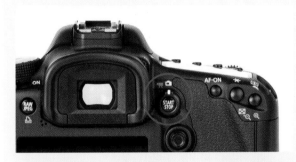

FIGURE 1.7

With Live View shooting activated you can change your white balance and view the changes to the image on the rear LCD Monitor.

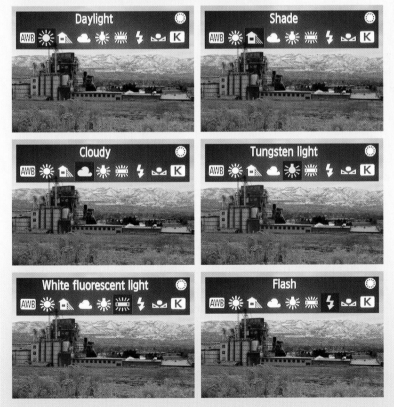

FIGURE 1.8

These six images are examples of what it looks like to use the Live View feature to preview white balance settings for your image. It is easy to identify which setting will give you the correct color temperature even before taking your photograph.

WHITE BALANCE AND THE TEMPERATURE OF COLOR

When you select different white balances in your camera, you will notice that underneath several of the choices is a number, for example, 5200K, 7000K, or 3200K. These numbers refer to the Kelvin temperature of the colors in the visible spectrum. The visible spectrum is the range of light that the human eye can see (think of a rainbow or the color bands that come out of a prism). The visible spectrum of light has been placed into a scale called the Kelvin temperature scale, which identifies the thermodynamic temperature of a given color of light. Put simply, reds and yellows are "warm," and greens and blues are "cool." Even more confusing can be the actual temperature ratings. Warm temperatures are typically lower on the Kelvin scale, ranging from 3000 degrees to 5000 degrees, while cool temperatures run from 5500 degrees to around 10,000 degrees. Take a look at this list for an example of Kelvin temperature properties.

KELVIN TEMPERATURE PROPERTIES

Flames	1700K–1900K	Daylight	5000K
Incandescent bulb	2800K–3300K	Camera flash	5500K
White fluorescent	4000K	Overcast sky	6000K
Moonlight	4000K	Open shade	7000K

The most important thing to remember here is how the color temperature of light will affect the look of your images. If something is "warm," it will look reddish-yellow, and if something is "cool," it will have a bluish cast.

A LITTLE COLOR THEORY

The visible spectrum of light is based on a principle called *additive color,* which involves three primary colors: red, green, and blue. When you add these colors together in equal parts, you get white light. By combining different amounts of them, you can achieve all the different colors of the visible spectrum. This is a completely different process than printing, where cyan, magenta, and yellow are combined to create various colors. This method is called *subtractive color* and has to do with the reflective properties of pigments or inks as they are combined.

6. SET YOUR COLOR SPACE

The color space deals with how your images will ultimately be used. It is basically a set of instructions that tells your camera how to define the colors in your image and then output them to the device of your choice, be it your monitor or a printer. Your camera has a choice of two color spaces: sRGB and Adobe RGB.

The first choice, sRGB, was developed by Hewlett-Packard and Microsoft as a way of defining colors for the Internet. This space was created to deal with the way that computer monitors actually display images using red, green, and blue (RGB) colors. Because there are no black pixels in your monitor, the color space uses a combination of these three colors to display all of the colors in your image.

In 1998, Adobe Systems developed a new color space, Adobe RGB, which was intended to encompass a wider range of colors than was obtainable using traditional cyan, magenta, yellow, and black colors (called CMYK), but doing so using the primary colors red, green, and blue. It uses a wider-defined palette of colors than the sRGB space and, therefore, looks better when printed.

When selecting your color space, base your choice on whether you intend to use your photographs for prints or for online applications. Remember that the color space does not directly affect the color information of your images. It simply embeds the color space profile into the image file as instructions for your computer so that your output device (monitor or printer) can correctly interpret the colors.

SETTING THE COLOR SPACE

1. With the camera turned on, press the Menu button.

2. Use the Multi-Controller to select the second menu tab and then scroll down to Color Space using the Quick Control dial (**A**).

3. Press the Set button, and then highlight your desired color space and press the Set button once again (**B**).

4. Press the Menu button to leave the menu and begin shooting with your new color space.

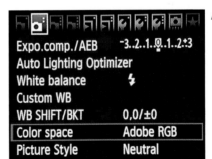

A

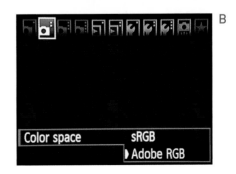

B

There will be no future indication of which space you have selected, so it's important to set this early and make adjustments if your output intentions change. I typically use the Adobe RGB space when shooting because I'm not sure of the end-usage of my images, and if I decide to use them online, I can use image software to change the color space to sRGB. It is always better to go from a larger color space to a smaller one.

7. SET YOUR AUTOFOCUS

Autofocus (AF) on the Canon 7D is extremely sophisticated and very easy to work with. It's important to understand how to use all of the different autofocus modes in order to increase your chances of producing sharp, well-focused images. Here are the descriptions of each of the autofocus modes:

- **One Shot:** Use this setting to focus on a subject that is not moving, like a person posing for a portrait.

- **AI Focus:** Use this feature to focus on something that is not moving, and the focusing system will track the subject if it starts to move (pets or small children, for example).

- **AI Servo:** Use this setting for subjects that are in motion. The focusing system will track the subject that falls in the focus area.

The best way to prompt your camera to focus is to press the shutter down halfway, just enough to activate the camera and the focusing system but not enough to actually take a photo. With the One Shot focus mode, you can set the focus point by half-pressing the shutter, and as long as you leave the shutter pressed halfway your focus point will remain the same (regardless of where you point the camera). However, half-pressing the shutter while using the AI Servo mode will tell the camera to keep searching for something to focus on and will continuously find a new focus point.

SETTING THE FOCUS MODE

1. Wake the camera (if necessary) by lightly pressing the Shutter button.

2. Press the AF mode button, located above the LCD Panel on the top of the camera (**Figure 1.9**).

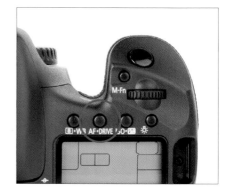

FIGURE 1.9
The AF mode button, located above the top LCD Panel.

3. Using the Main dial, change the focus mode to the desired setting.

4. Lightly press the Shutter button once more to set your new focus mode.

Next you'll decide where you want your camera to find the focus in the viewfinder. The 7D has three separate types of focus areas:

- **Single-Point AF:** Choose where you want the focus to be from one of the 19 focus points within the viewfinder. This focus mode is good for still subjects when using One Shot AF.

- **Zone AF:** Choose this if you know the general area in your viewfinder where you want to find focus. This is an excellent focus mode for photographing sports or fast-moving objects in conjunction with AI Servo AF.

- **Auto select:** With this option, the camera selects one of the 19 focus points for you. This feature can be very useful with the AI Servo AF mode as well.

SETTING THE FOCUS AREA

1. Wake the camera (if necessary) by lightly pressing the Shutter button.

2. Press the AF Point selection button, located on the upper-right part of the back of your camera (**A**).

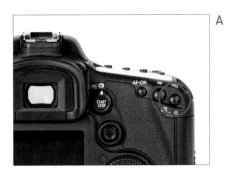
A

3. While looking through the viewfinder, press the M-Fn button (located next to the Shutter button) until you have selected your desired focus area (I recommend Single-Point AF so that you can control your precise focus point rather than letting the camera decide for you) (**B**).

4. Use any of the dials on the camera to change the focus point. You can do this at any time while looking through the viewfinder by pressing the AF Point selection button and moving the point with the dials.

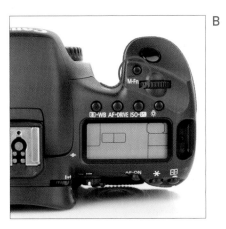
B

5. Lightly press the Shutter button once more to set your new focus area.

MANUAL FOCUSING

If you find that the autofocus system won't find your image, it's really easy to switch over to manual focusing. On each lens there is a switch; just change it from AF (autofocus) to MF (manual focus) and use the focus ring to adjust focus by hand (**Figure 1.10**). If you half-press your shutter during manual focusing, just as you would if you were auto-focusing, and you are focusing in the same area as the autofocus point, then you will hear a beep when the camera senses the image is in focus.

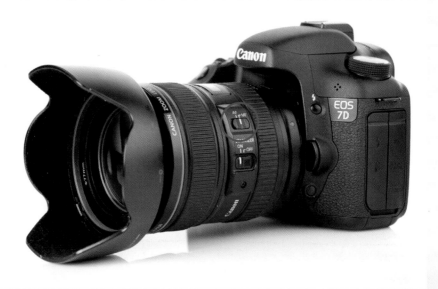

FIGURE 1.10
You can set the focusing mode on your lens to switch from autofocus to manual focus.

8. SET THE PICTURE STYLE

Picture styles on the 7D will allow you to enhance your images in-camera depending on the type of photo you are taking. There are six styles to choose from, along with three additional user-defined styles:

- **Standard:** This general-purpose style is used to create crisp images with bold, vibrant colors. It is suitable for most scenes.

- **Portrait:** This style enhances the colors in skin tone, and is used for a softer-looking image.

- **Landscape:** This style enhances blues and greens, two colors that are typically visible in a landscape image.

- **Neutral:** This style creates natural colors and subdued images and is a good choice if you want to do a lot of editing to your photos on the computer.

- **Faithful:** This picture style is similar to the neutral style but creates better color when shooting in daylight-balanced light (color temperature of 5200K). It's also a good option if you prefer to edit your photos on the computer.

- **Monochrome:** This style creates black and white images. It's important to note that if you use Monochrome style and shoot in JPEG, you cannot revert the image to color.

SETTING THE PICTURE STYLE

1. Wake the camera (if necessary) by lightly pressing the Shutter button.

2. Press the Picture Style Selection button on the back of the camera (**A**).

3. Use either the Main dial or the Quick Control dial to scroll through the styles (**B**).

4. Press the Set button to lock in this change.

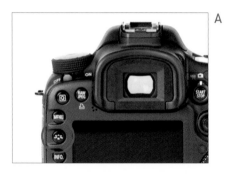

A

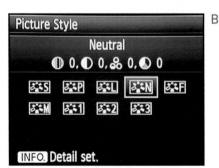

B

You are also able to edit the existing picture styles by clicking the INFO button on the back of the camera and adjusting each individual setting (sharpness, contrast, saturation, and color tone). One other important note is that you cannot change your picture style when using the Full Auto camera mode (it will automatically be set to the Standard picture style).

9. ENABLE HIGHLIGHT ALERT

The LCD on the back of the camera provides wonderful feedback on image exposure and color quality, but if your screen happens to be set too bright or too dark, then the image you are seeing may be deceptive. When you take a photograph, you usually want to keep detail in the highlight areas of the image and don't want to "blow out" anything. That is, you don't want certain areas of your image to be completely white. For example, if you were to use your flash while photographing a person, and the image is overexposed, the light could flood her face. One way to prevent this loss of detail is by enabling Highlight Alert.

ENABLING THE HIGHLIGHT ALERT SETTING

1. Press the Menu button and use the Multi-Controller to select the center menu tab (second playback tab).

2. Select Highlight Alert, and then press the Set button (**A**).

3. Use the Quick Control dial to select Enable, and then press the Set button (**B**).

4. Press the Menu button to leave the menus and continue shooting.

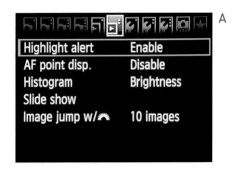

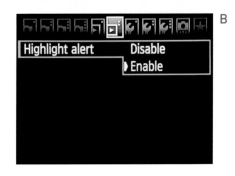

Now that you have enabled Highlight Alert, you will see a difference in your images while you review them. If you photograph something that is pure white (255, 255, 255 on the RGB color model), then that part of the image will blink red on the LCD when you review your shot. At first you might find this a bit annoying, but trust me, it's extremely useful. This feedback will help you properly expose your images. It's very difficult to pull in detail from the areas that blink red, so if it's blinking somewhere you don't want it to (someone's face, for example), you should probably dial down your exposure a bit.

10. REVIEW YOUR PHOTOS

Digital cameras are amazing because of the immediate feedback you get after taking a photo. You can make changes to the exposure and white balance and see the results on the LCD Monitor to instantly tell if you got the shot you wanted.

Your camera, out of the box, will have a very short review time—that is, when you take a photo and it shows up on the LCD Monitor you will only see it for a few seconds. I like shots to stay on until I decide to keep shooting or turn off the camera, so I have it set to the Hold setting. This setting allows you to review the image you photographed for as long as you like (lightly pressing the shutter will get you back into shooting mode and turn off the LCD Monitor). Note that this option will drain your batteries faster than the default setting.

CHANGING YOUR REVIEW TIME SETTING

1. Press the Menu button and use the Main dial to select the leftmost menu tab.

2. Using the Quick Control dial, scroll down to Review Time and press the Set button (**A**).

3. Scroll down to Hold and then press the Set button once again (**B**).

4. Press the Menu button to leave the menus and continue shooting.

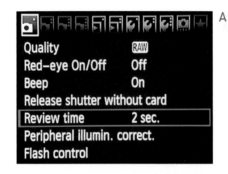

A

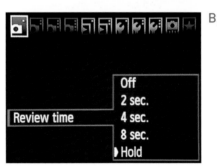

B

Now that you have the image display set, let's check out some of the other visual information that will really help you when shooting.

When you press the Playback button on the back of the camera, you will see the default screen, also called the Single Image Display (**Figure 1.11**). This screen shows you information such as shutter speed, aperture, and file number.

If you press the Info button while in the Single Image Display, then you will also see your image quality (JPEG and/or RAW) and the number of images you have on your card (**Figure 1.12**).

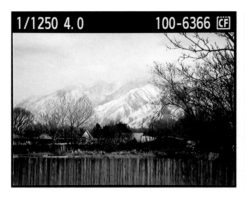

FIGURE 1.11
The default display mode on the 7D.

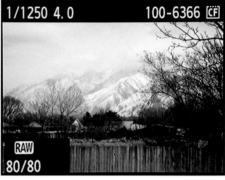

FIGURE 1.12
By pressing the Info button you can scroll through the camera's four display modes.

ERASING IMAGES

Deleting, or erasing, images is a fairly simple process that is covered on page 179 of your manual. To quickly get you on your way, simply press the Playback button and spin the Quick Control dial until you find the picture that you want to delete. Then press the Erase button just below the Playback button (to the left of the LCD Monitor). Use the Quick Control dial to select Erase, and then press the Set button (**Figure 1.13**).

Caution: Once you have deleted an image, it is gone for good. Make sure you don't want it before you drop it in the trash.

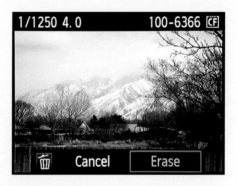

FIGURE 1.13
Erasing an image on the Canon 7D.

The third display, which appears after you press the Info button again, will take you to the Shooting Information Display. This shows you more details, such as your white balance, camera mode, and file size, and offers more information about your image than any of the other display settings (**Figure 1.14**).

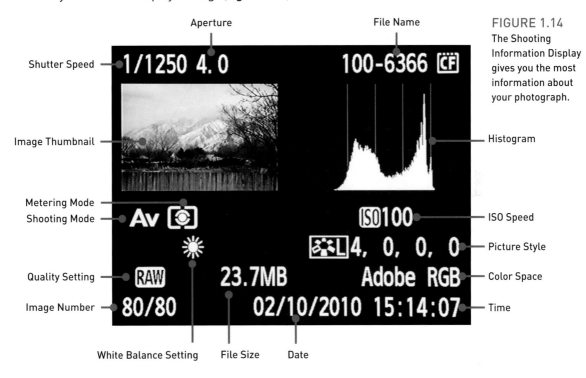

Aperture

File Name

Shutter Speed

Image Thumbnail

Histogram

Metering Mode
Shooting Mode

ISO Speed

Picture Style

Quality Setting

Color Space

Image Number

Time

White Balance Setting   File Size   Date

FIGURE 1.14
The Shooting Information Display gives you the most information about your photograph.

The last display will give you detailed histogram information (**Figure 1.15**). This is useful if you need to see each individual color channel, but I find that the basic histogram display in the Shooting Information Display is sufficient for most images.

If you prefer one display mode to another, press the Info button until you reach the display mode you like best; if you leave it in that mode, you will see your images in that display mode every time you press the Playback button. I usually use the default display (Single Image Display) and will sometimes click through the display modes if I need to view more information about a specific shot.

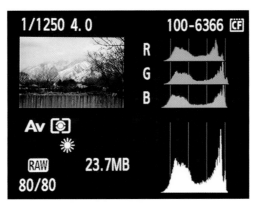

FIGURE 1.15
The fourth display option shows you a color histogram.

THE VALUE OF THE HISTOGRAM

Simply put, histograms are two-dimensional representations of your images in graph form. There are two different histograms that you should be concerned with: the luminance and the color histograms. Luminance is referred to in your manual as "brightness" and is most valuable when evaluating your exposures. In **Figure 1.16**, you see what looks like a mountain range. The graph represents the entire tonal range that your camera can capture, from the whitest whites to the blackest blacks. The left side represents black, all the way to the right side, which represents white. The heights of the peaks represent the number of pixels that contain those luminance levels (a tall peak in the middle means your image contains a large amount of medium-bright pixels). Looking at this figure, I can see that the largest peak of the graph is in the middle and trails off as it reaches the edges. In most cases, you would look for this type of histogram, indicating that you captured the entire range of tones, from dark to light, in your image. Knowing that is fine, but here is where the information really gets useful.

When you evaluate the histogram that has a spike or peak riding up the far left or right side of the graph, it means that you are clipping detail from your image. In essence, you are trying to record values that are either too dark or too light for your sensor to accurately record. This is usually an indication of over- or underexposure. It also means that you need to correct your exposure so that the important details will not record as solid black or white pixels (which is what happens when clipping occurs). There are times, however, when some clipping is acceptable. If you are photographing a scene where the sun will be in the frame, you can expect to get some clipping because the sun is just too bright to hold any detail. Likewise, if you are shooting something that has true blacks in it—think coal in a mineshaft at midnight—there are most certainly going to be some true blacks with no detail in your shot.

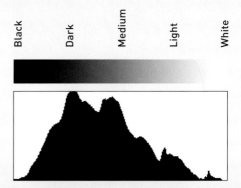

FIGURE 1.16

This is a typical histogram, where the dark to light tones run from left to right. The black to white gradient above the graph demonstrates where the tones lie on the graph and would not appear above your camera's histogram display.

The main goal is to ensure that you aren't clipping any "important" visual information, and that is achieved by keeping an eye on your histogram. Take a look at **Figure 1.17**. The histogram displayed on the image shows a heavy skew toward the left with almost no part of the mountain touching the right side. This is a good example of what an underexposed image histogram looks like. Now look at **Figure 1.18** and compare the histogram for the image that was correctly exposed. Notice that even though there are two distinct peaks on the graph, there is an even distribution across the entire histogram.

FIGURE 1.17
This image is about three stops under-exposed. Notice the histogram is skewed to the left.

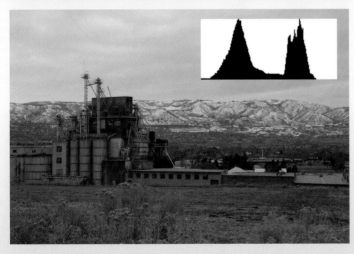

FIGURE 1.18
This histogram reflects a properly exposed image.

Chapter 1 Challenges

Let's begin our shooting assignments by setting up and using all of the elements of the Top Ten list. If you're not yet familiar with the shooting modes (more information on them will be covered in Chapter 3), then go ahead and set your camera to the P (Program) mode. This will allow you to interact with the various settings and menus that have been covered thus far.

Basic camera setup

Charge your battery to 100 percent and register it in the camera. Next, go ahead and set up your camera to address the following: Shooting without a card, image quality, ISO, and color space.

Selecting the proper white balance

Take your camera outside into a daylight environment and photograph the same scene using different white balance settings. Pay close attention to how each setting affects the overall colorcast of your images. Next, try moving inside and repeat the exercise while shooting in a tungsten lighting environment. Finally, find a fluorescent light source and repeat one more time.

Focusing with Single Point and One Shot

Change your camera setting so that you are focusing using the Single-Point focus mode. Try using all of the different focus points to see how they work in focusing your scene. Then set your focus mode to One Shot and practice focusing on a subject and then recomposing before actually taking the picture. Try doing this with subjects at varying distances.

Discovering the Manual focus mode

Change your focus mode from Autofocus to Manual focus and practice a little manual-focus photography. Get familiar with where the focus ring is and how to use it to achieve sharp images.

Playing with the picture styles

Find one thing to photograph and take six different photos—one for each picture style. Compare the images to see how the style changes the colors and tones.

Enabling Highlight Alert and reviewing your images

Enable Highlight Alert and set up your image display properties, and then review some of your previous images using the different display modes. Watch how the Highlight Alert will flash in some areas on your LCD, especially when an image is overexposed.

Share your results with the book's Flickr group!

Join the group here: flickr.com/groups/canon7dfromsnapshotstogreatshots

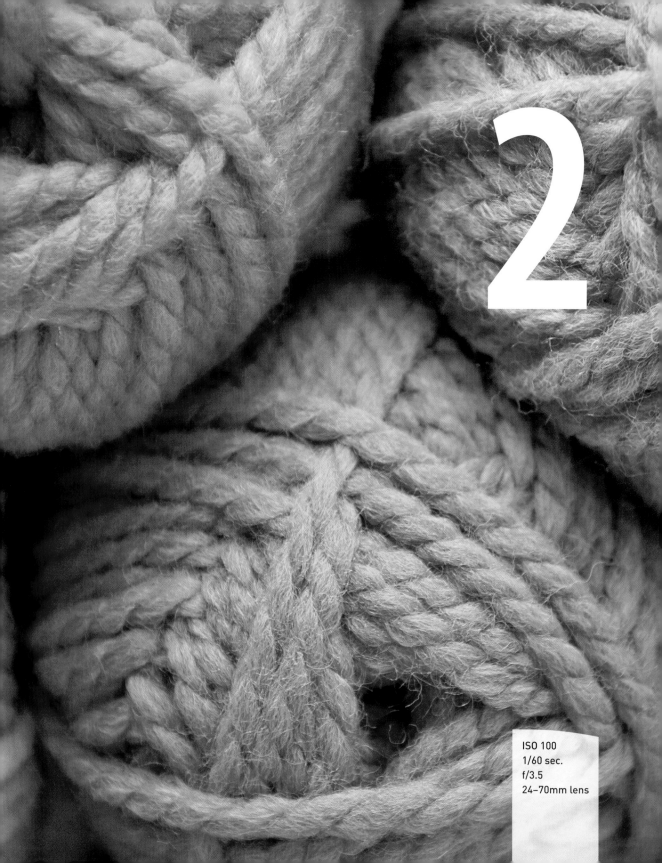

2

ISO 100
1/60 sec.
f/3.5
24–70mm lens

First Things First

A FEW THINGS TO KNOW AND DO BEFORE YOU BEGIN TAKING PICTURES

So you now have a basic grasp of the top ten tips to get you started shooting with your 7D, but there are still a few important details that need mentioning before you can take full advantage of your camera. In this chapter we'll review some 7D basics on lenses and exposure and get you started formatting your memory card and preparing the camera for use. Let's start with the very first thing you will need before you can run out and take photos: a memory card.

The camera was placed on a tripod to allow the use of a slow shutter speed when shooting in diffused natural light.

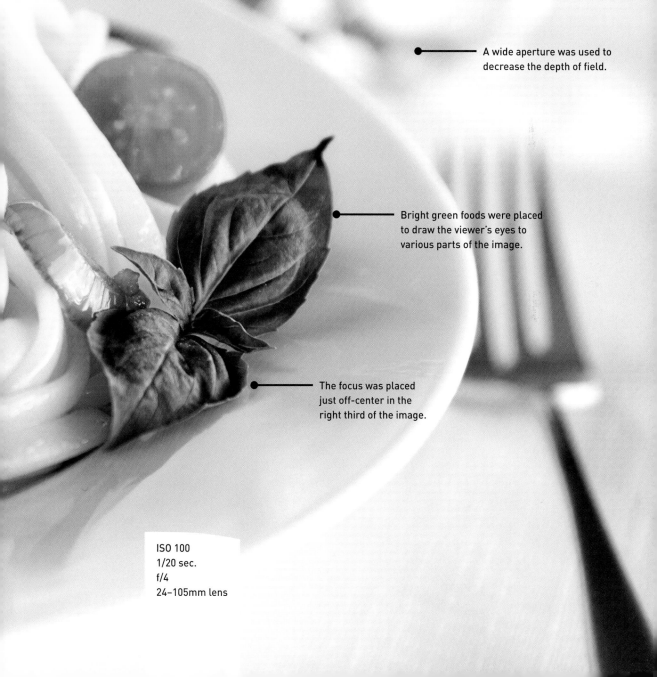

Food is one of my favorite subjects to photograph. I not only have fun taking the photo but I also enjoy the process of creating the dish and making something look good enough to eat right off the page. For this image, I chose to use my favorite lens (24-105mm f/4 L IS) along with a wide-open aperture to achieve the blurry background and make the pasta the center of attention.

A wide aperture was used to decrease the depth of field.

Bright green foods were placed to draw the viewer's eyes to various parts of the image.

The focus was placed just off-center in the right third of the image.

ISO 100
1/20 sec.
f/4
24–105mm lens

PORING OVER THE PICTURE

It was a cold day in Utah and we had the first tiny snowfall of the winter season. The snow quickly melted, and as I was standing outside with another photographer, he pointed out some water drops on the roof of his car. We both ended up getting some really neat photos—and I just love the way the water droplets have a "metallic," surreal feel about them.

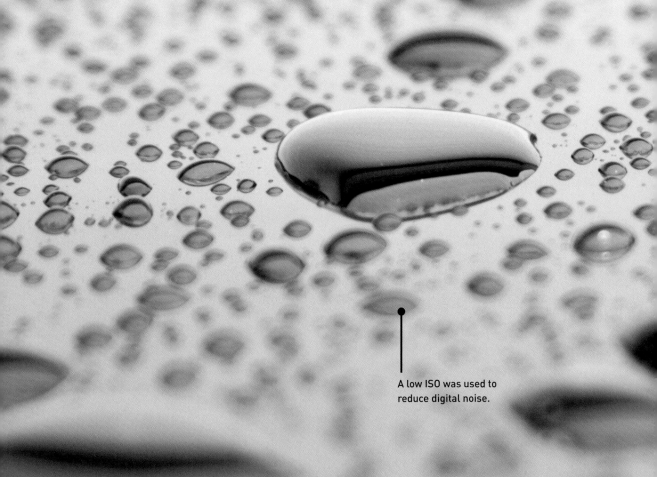

A low ISO was used to reduce digital noise.

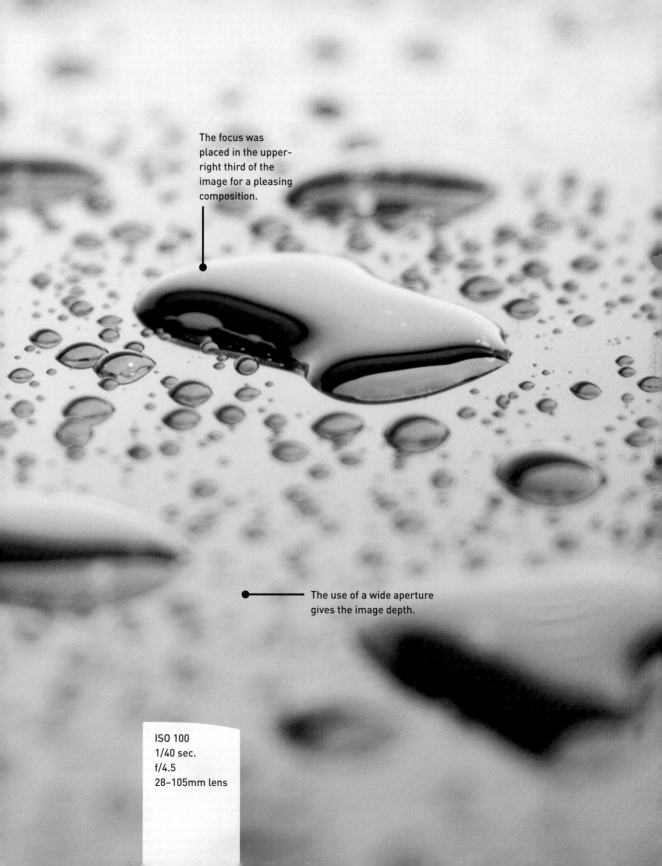

The focus was placed in the upper-right third of the image for a pleasing composition.

The use of a wide aperture gives the image depth.

ISO 100
1/40 sec.
f/4.5
28–105mm lens

CHOOSING THE RIGHT MEMORY CARD

The memory card is where you will store all of the images you photograph until you off-load them to your computer or hard drive. It's a very important accessory to own, since you can't create any images until you have one in your camera. If you own a digital point-and-shoot camera, you are most likely already familiar with Secure Digital (SD) cards. The 7D uses CompactFlash (CF) cards, a larger and sturdier version of the SD card (**Figure 2.1**).

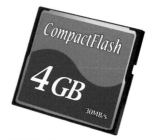

FIGURE 2.1
Make sure you select a CF card that has enough capacity to handle your photographic needs.

There are many different brands and sizes to choose from, and there's a lot to consider when buying CF cards for your camera. Here are some tips to help you make your purchase:

- The size of your card is very important, especially since the 7D can shoot up to 18 megapixels in both RAW and JPEG file formats. You can find CF cards in many sizes, but you will probably not want anything smaller than 4 GB per card. It's also a good idea to have more than one card tucked away in your camera bag to use as backup.

- Consider buying Ultra Direct Memory Access (UDMA) cards. These cards are generally much faster, both when writing images to the card as well as when transferring the files to your computer. If you are planning to use the continuous shooting mode (see Chapter 6) for capturing fast action, you can gain huge boosts in performance just by using a UDMA card.

- Don't skimp on quality because of a good price. Remember, the card is the only place that your image files are stored until you can transfer them to a computer. A high-quality card might cost a few more dollars but will be more reliable and will last much longer than a less expensive one. You don't always know that something is wrong with a card until it's too late, and having a reliable card is one step to help prevent that.

Along with a CF card, it's also a good idea to have a CompactFlash card reader. It is possible to connect your camera to the computer to retrieve the files, but over time you will unnecessarily drain your camera's battery. Some card readers can also be connected to the computer via FireWire, making transfer time much faster than using the USB cord from your camera.

FORMATTING YOUR MEMORY CARD

The first thing to do when you have a new card is format it. When you format a card, the camera creates a layout for the images to be written more easily and saved properly. Formatting also "cleans" your card, making it a blank slate to write new images to, and is the recommended way of deleting data from the card. You should always format the card within the camera itself, because formatting it from the computer could render the card useless. You also want to be certain that your images and files on the card have been safely transferred over to another source before formatting your card.

I try to re-format my card before each use and after I have uploaded the images to my hard drive. I also format my card if it's brand-new or has been used in a different camera. I like to start with a fresh card each time I shoot to simplify my workflow when I'm taking a lot of photos, so I can keep them organized and separated from my other images.

FORMATTING YOUR MEMORY CARD

1. Insert the memory card into your camera.

2. Press the Menu button, and navigate to the first setup menu tab (the fifth from the right).

3. Rotate the Quick Control dial on the back of the camera to highlight the Format option, and press Set (**A**).

4. The default selection for the Format screen is Cancel, just in case you didn't really want to format the card (**B**). Turn the Quick Control dial to highlight OK. The screen will warn you that you will lose any data by formatting your card, so make sure that you have saved any images that you want onto your computer or elsewhere before formatting.

5. Press the Set button to finalize the formatting of the card.

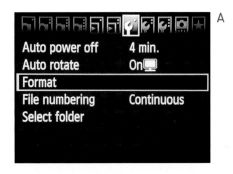
A

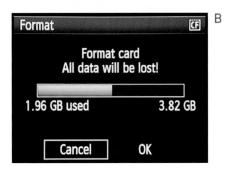
B

UPDATING THE 7D'S FIRMWARE

The great thing about digital cameras is that they are operated by internally running software, called firmware, that can improve operation or fix problems that might arise. The 7D is no exception, and the Canon Firmware Update page (www.canon.com/eos-d/) provides all of the data you need to make sure your camera is up to date. It's a good idea to check your camera's firmware against this Web site to make sure you have the most recent version.

CHECKING THE CAMERA'S CURRENT FIRMWARE VERSION NUMBER

1. Rotate the Mode dial to select P (it will not work in the Creative Auto or Full Auto modes).

2. Press the Menu button to display the menu.

3. Turn the Main dial to get to the third camera setup menu tab (third menu tab from the right), and you will see the currently installed firmware version number at the bottom of the settings (**Figure 2.2**). If this version is not the latest one listed on the Canon Web site, follow the steps in the next section to load the latest version.

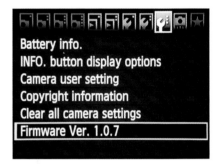

FIGURE 2.2

The firmware menu item on the 7D will tell you which version your camera has.

UPDATING THE FIRMWARE DIRECTLY FROM YOUR COMPUTER

1. Go to the Canon Web site's digital camera page (www.canon.com/eos-d/) and find the link to the Canon 7D. This will take you to the camera-specific Web page (**A**).

2. From the "Drivers and Downloads" section, download the firmware update file that matches your operating system (Windows or Mac) (**B**).

3. Extract the downloaded firmware file as per your operating system (**C**). (The firmware will automatically be extracted if you are using Mac OS.)

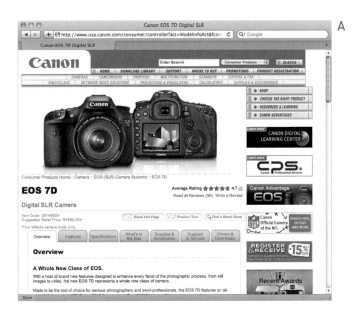

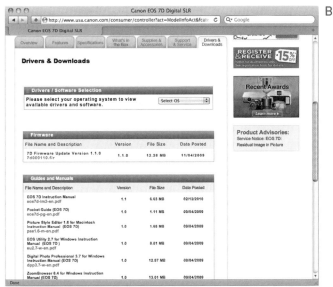

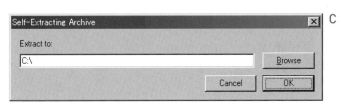

4. Attach your camera to the computer via USB and turn the camera on (**D**). Make sure there is a CF card inserted in your camera.

5. Open the EOS Utility program and select the Camera Settings/Remote Shooting option (**E**). (This program was included on the CD in your camera box. You will need to install it prior to performing this operation.)

D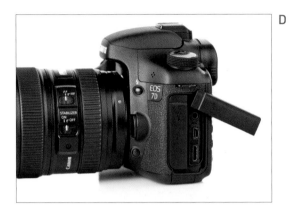

E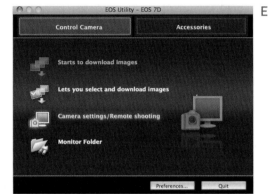

6. When the panel opens, click the Set-Up icon and then click the Firmware button at the bottom of the panel (**F**).

7. Click OK and then locate the extracted firmware file to begin the update.

8. Click Yes on the confirmation screen to begin the update (**G**). Note that the software will not allow you to continue the update unless the camera is plugged into the AC power adapter or the battery is fully charged.

F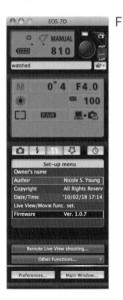

G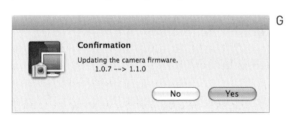

USING THE RIGHT FORMAT: RAW VS. JPEG

The 7D gives you the option to shoot and save your images to your memory card in RAW, JPEG, or both. Most people are already familiar with JPEG since it's one of the most common file formats for anyone using a digital camera. This topic was briefly discussed in Chapter 1, so you already have a basic understanding of RAW and JPEG.

You may want to set your camera to JPEG and start shooting, never bothering with the other settings. After all, a JPEG is a very simple file to work with! It's ready to go right out of the camera and you can store a lot more JPEG files on your memory card than you can RAW files. JPEG will also write to the card much faster, making it a good choice for photographers who do a lot of high-speed photography (such as sports photographers or photojournalists). So what's the drawback of JPEG? There's really nothing wrong with it if you can create your photos in-camera exactly how you want them to look (proper exposure, white balance, and so on).

However, as I mentioned in Chapter 1, JPEG is not actually an image format. It is a compression standard, and compression is where things go bad. When you have your camera set to JPEG, you are telling the camera to process the image however it sees fit and then throw away enough image data to make it shrink into a smaller space. In doing so, you give up subtle image details that you will never get back in postprocessing.

SO WHAT DOES RAW HAVE TO OFFER?

The RAW format is an uncompressed file that stores as much data as it can possibly collect from each image you take. Unlike JPEG, it is lossless compression, which means that it loses no image data when it writes to the memory card. Photographing with the RAW format means that you have a lot of room to edit the photo, but it also requires the use of software in order for you to share or print the image.

RAW images have a greater dynamic range than JPEG-processed images. This means that you can recover image detail in the highlights and shadows that just isn't available in JPEGs.

There's more color information in a RAW image because it is a 14-bit image, meaning it contains more color information than a JPEG, which is almost always an 8-bit image. More color information means more to work with and smoother changes between tones, and it will preserve the quality of your image while you edit.

Regarding sharpening, a RAW image offers more control because you are the one applying the sharpening according to the effect you want to achieve. Once again, JPEG processing applies a standard amount of sharpening that you cannot change after the fact. Once it is done, it's done.

Finally, and most importantly, a RAW file is your negative. No matter what you do to it, you won't change it unless you save your file in a different format. This means that you can come back to that RAW file later and try different processing settings to achieve differing results and never harm the original image. By comparison, if you make a change to your JPEG and accidentally save the file, guess what? You have a new original file, and you will never get back to that first image. That alone should make you sit up and take notice.

ADVICE FOR NEW RAW SHOOTERS

If you are used to only using the JPEG format, moving to RAW is a big step but a very worthwhile one. Using the RAW format means more work at your computer, but don't give up just because it takes a few extra minutes to process each image. It will also take up more space on your CF card, but that's an easy fix—go buy more cards, or get them in larger sizes (I like to use 16 GB CF cards when I shoot with my 7D). Also, don't worry about needing to purchase expensive software to work with your RAW files; you already own a program that allows you to work with them. Canon's Digital Photo Professional software comes bundled in the box with your camera and gives you the ability to work directly on the RAW files and then output the enhanced results.

SELECTING A RAW FORMAT

The 7D has the ability to capture different-sized RAW files. This means you can now have all of the benefits of a RAW file in a smaller image size. The standard RAW file uses the full sensor resolution of 5184 x 3456 pixels. If you want the flexibility and power of using the RAW format but don't necessarily need an image that large, you can select one of the smaller RAW files: mRAW (3888 x 2592) or sRAW (2592 x 1728). These smaller RAW files will also take up less space on your memory card, allowing you to shoot more images.

IMAGE RESOLUTION

When discussing digital cameras, image resolution is often used to describe pixel resolution, or the number of pixels used to make an image. This can be displayed as a dimension such as 5184 × 3456. This is the physical number of pixels in width and height of the image sensor. Resolution can also be referred to in megapixels (MP), such as 18 MP. This number represents the number of total pixels on the sensor and is commonly used to describe the amount of image data that a digital camera can capture.

SELECTING YOUR IMAGE QUALITY SETTING

1. Press the Menu button and use the Main dial to select the first shooting menu tab.

2. Use the Quick Control dial to highlight the Quality setting and press the Set button to enter the Quality setting page (**A**).

3. Use the Main dial to change the RAW setting and the Quick Control dial to change the JPEG setting (**B**).

4. Press the Menu button to lock in your changes.

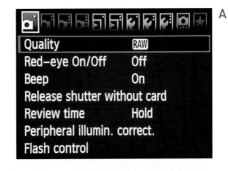

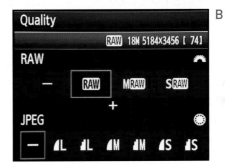

If you are uncomfortable shooting in RAW, that is perfectly OK. My recommendation is to use what works best for your photography, but don't be afraid to try new things. One great feature of the 7D is that you don't have to pick one or the other—the camera gives you the option to shoot in both RAW and JPEG simultaneously (**Figure 2.3**). This will take up a significant amount of space on your memory card, but it's a good way to transition over, or to just give RAW a chance.

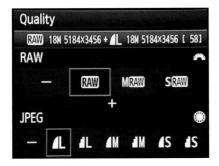

FIGURE 2.3
To shoot in both RAW and JPEG simultaneously, follow the steps above to change your quality setting and use the Main dial and Quick Control dial to select both a RAW and JPEG image. Then press Set to lock in your changes.

CROP SENSOR VS. FULL FRAME

The 7D is what we consider a "crop sensor" camera. Many digital SLR cameras have one of two different types of sensors: full-frame or crop sensor. The sensor is the area in the camera that converts the image you see through the viewfinder into the digital file that writes to the memory card. All **full-frame** sensors have an area of 36 × 24 mm (the same size as a 35mm negative). The **crop sensor** on the 7D is slightly smaller at 22.3 × 14.9 mm (**Figure 2.4**). This will increase your focal length by a crop-factor of 1.6, so if you have a 50mm lens attached to your 7D, then you are actually seeing the equivalent of 80mm when you look through the viewfinder.

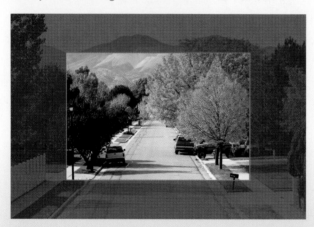

FIGURE 2.4
The center square in this image shows the visible area that the 7D will capture in relation to what a full-frame sensor would photograph with the same setup.

LENSES AND FOCAL LENGTHS

If you ask most photographers what they believe to be their most critical piece of photographic equipment, they would undoubtedly tell you that it's their lens (also referred to as "glass"). The technology and engineering that goes into your camera is a marvel, but it isn't worth much if it can't get the light from the outside onto the sensor. Most photographers will happily put their resources into purchasing high-quality lenses before they get a new camera body, since lenses can be passed on from one camera to the next and are a huge factor in the overall quality of the image.

The 7D, as a digital single lens reflex (DSLR) camera, uses the lens for a multitude of tasks, from focusing on a subject, to metering a scene, to delivering and focusing the light onto the camera sensor. The lens is also responsible for the amount of the scene that will be captured (the frame). With all of this riding on the lens, let's take a more in-depth look at the camera's eye on the world.

Lenses are composed of optical glass that is both concave and convex in shape. The alignment of the glass elements is designed to focus the light coming in from the front of the lens onto the camera sensor. The amount of light that enters the camera is also controlled by the lens, the size of the glass elements, and the aperture mechanism within the lens housing. The quality of the glass used in the lens will also have a direct effect on how well the lens can resolve details and the contrast of the image (the ability to deliver great highlights and shadows). Most lenses now include things like the autofocus motor and, in some cases, an image-stabilization mechanism.

There is one other aspect of the camera lens that is often the first consideration of the photographer: lens length. Lenses are typically divided into three or four groups depending on the field of view they deliver.

Wide-angle lenses cover a field of view from around 110 degrees to about 60 degrees (**Figure 2.5**). There is a tendency to get some distortion in your image when using extremely wide-angle lenses. This will be apparent toward the outer edges of the frame. As for which lenses would be considered wide angle, anything 35mm or smaller could be considered wide.

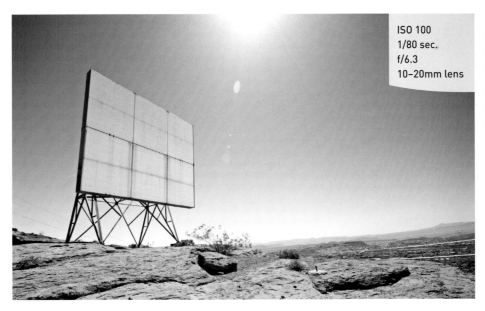

ISO 100
1/80 sec.
f/6.3
10–20mm lens

FIGURE 2.5
A very wide-angle lens allowed me to photograph this billboard and include a large amount of the surrounding area.

Wide-angle lenses can display a large depth of field, which allows you to keep the foreground and background in sharp focus. This makes them very useful for landscape photography. They also work well in tight spaces, such as indoors, where there isn't much elbow room available. They can also be handy for large group shots but, due to the amount of distortion, not so great for close-up portrait work (**Figure 2.6**).

FIGURE 2.6
While a wide-angle lens works for this unique perspective, it is not ideal for a traditional portrait due to the extreme distortion near the edges of the frame.

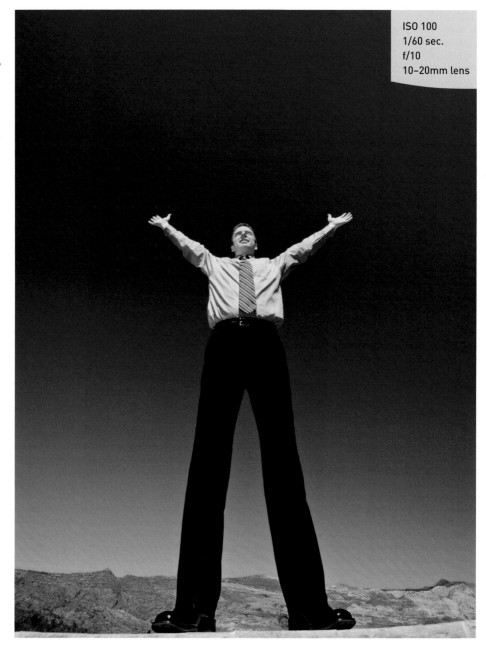

ISO 100
1/60 sec.
f/10
10–20mm lens

A *normal* lens has a field of view that is about 45 degrees and delivers approximately the same view as the human eye. The perspective is very natural and there is little distortion in objects. A normal lens will have a focal length between 35 and 80mm. (**Figure 2.7**).

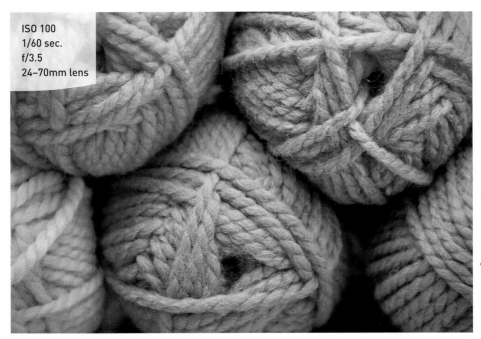

ISO 100
1/60 sec.
f/3.5
24–70mm lens

FIGURE 2.7
Using a normal focal length will produce very little distortion in your images.

Normal focal length lenses are useful for photographing people and architecture, and for most other general photographic needs. They have very little distortion and offer a moderate range of depth of field (**Figure 2.8**).

Most longer focal length lenses are referred to as *telephoto* lenses. They can range in length from 135mm up to 800mm or longer and have a field of view that is about 35 degrees or smaller. These lenses have the ability to greatly magnify the scene, allowing you to capture details of distant objects, but the angle of view is greatly reduced (**Figure 2.9**).

Telephoto lenses are most useful for sports photography or any application where you just need to get closer to your subject. They can have a compressing effect—making objects look closer together than they actually are—and a very narrow depth of field when shot at their widest apertures.

FIGURE 2.8
Normal lenses are great for close-up portrait work.

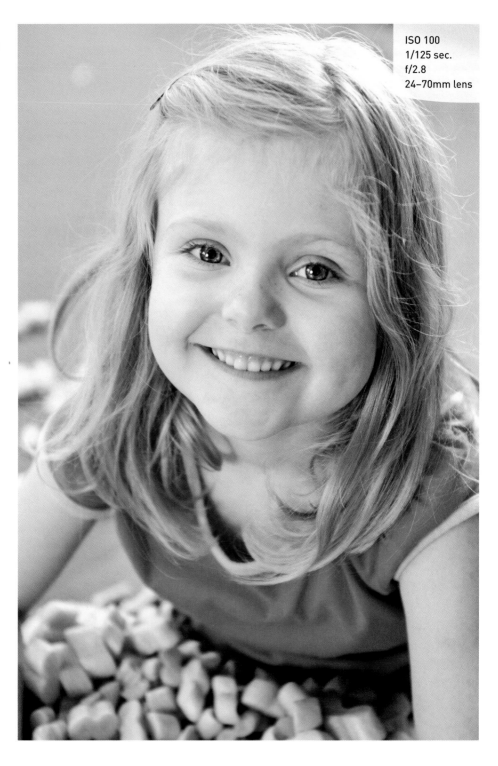

ISO 100
1/125 sec.
f/2.8
24–70mm lens

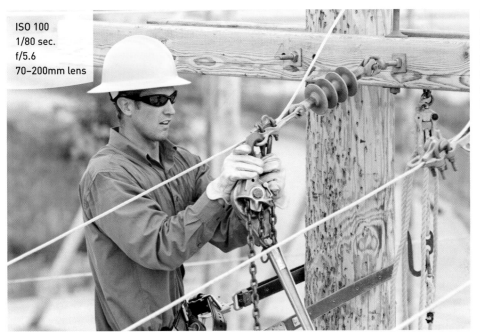

ISO 100
1/80 sec.
f/5.6
70–200mm lens

FIGURE 2.9
A telephoto zoom lens combined with a fairly large aperture helps to create a compressed and blurred background.

A *zoom* lens is a great compromise to carrying a bunch of single focal length lenses (also referred to as "prime" lenses). Zoom lenses can cover a wide range of focal lengths because of the configuration of their optics. However, because it takes more optical elements to capture a scene at different focal lengths, the light must pass through more glass on its way to the image sensor. The more glass, the lower the quality of the image sharpness. The other sacrifice that is made is in aperture. Zoom lenses typically have smaller maximum apertures than prime lenses, which means they cannot achieve a narrow depth of field or work in lower light levels without the assistance of image stabilization, a tripod, or higher ISO settings (**Figure 2.10**). (We'll discuss all this in more detail in later chapters.)

The 7D can be purchased with the body only, but many folks will purchase it with a kit lens, especially if this is their first DSLR camera. The most common kit lenses are the 28–135mm IS f/3.5–5.6 and the 18–135mm IS f/3.5–5.6. Both lenses are great all-purpose "walkaround" lenses that will give you a lot of flexibility with your shooting. The lens I use almost exclusively with my 7D is the 24–105mm f/4L IS lens—the "L" series of Canon lenses is their top-of-the-line glass, but also comes at a much higher price than the other lenses.

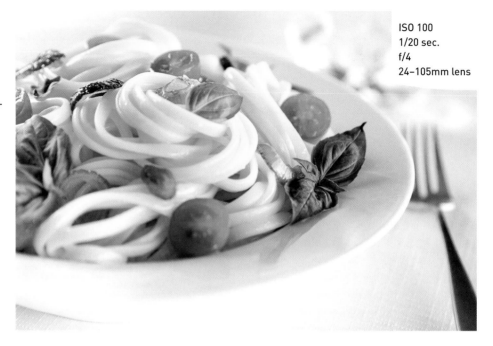

ISO 100
1/20 sec.
f/4
24–105mm lens

UNDERSTANDING APERTURE, SHUTTER SPEED, AND ISO

Proper exposure is crucial to creating a good image, and if you're not sure what's going on inside the camera it can be difficult to grasp many of the concepts you will read about in this book. Your camera can, and will, make a lot of decisions during the shooting process, and it's important that you understand what it is doing and why. Here I'll cover some of the basic principles of exposure, so you have the tools to move forward and improve your photography.

Exposure is the process whereby the light reflecting off a subject reflects through an opening in the camera lens for a defined period of time onto the camera sensor. The combination of the lens opening, shutter speed, and sensor sensitivity is used to achieve a proper exposure value (EV) for the scene. The EV is the sum of the components necessary to properly expose a scene. A relationship exists between these factors that is sometimes referred to as the "Exposure Triangle."

At each point of the triangle lies one of the factors of exposure:

- **ISO:** Determines the sensitivity of the camera sensor. ISO stands for the International Organization for Standardization, but the acronym is used as a term to describe the sensitivity of the camera sensor to light. The higher the sensitivity, the less light is required for a good exposure. These values are a carryover from the days of traditional color and black and white films.

- **Aperture:** Also referred to as the f-stop, this determines how much light passes through the lens at once.

- **Shutter speed:** Controls the length of time that light is allowed to hit the sensor.

Here's how it works. The camera sensor has a level of sensitivity that is determined by the ISO setting. To get a proper exposure—not too much, not too little—the lens needs to adjust the aperture diaphragm (the size of the lens opening; think of it as the pupil in your eye increasing and decreasing in size) to control the volume of light entering the camera. Then the shutter is opened for a relatively short period of time to allow the light to hit the sensor long enough for it to record on the sensor.

ISO numbers for the 7D start at 100 and then double in sensitivity as you double the number. So 200 is twice as sensitive as 100. The camera can be set to use 1/2- or 1/3-stop increments, but for ISO just remember that the base numbers double: 100, 200, 400, 800, and so on. There are also a wide variety of shutter speeds that you can use. The speeds on the 7D range from as long as 30 seconds to as short as 1/8000 of a second. When using the camera, you will not see the "1" over the number, so you will need to remember that anything shorter than a second will be a fraction. Generally speaking, for handheld photography you should stay at 1/60 of a second for the slowest speed (or 1/30 if you have steady hands), so you will most likely be working with a shutter speed range from around 1/30 of a second to about 1/2000. These numbers will change depending on your circumstances and the effect that you are trying to achieve. The lens apertures will vary slightly depending on which lens you are using. This is because different lenses have different maximum apertures. The typical apertures that are at your disposal are f/4, f/5.6, f/8, f/11, f/16, and f/22.

When it comes to exposure, a change to any one of these factors requires changing one or more of the other two. This is referred to as reciprocal change. If you let more light in the lens by choosing a larger aperture opening, you will need to shorten the amount of time the shutter is open. If the shutter is allowed to stay open for a longer period of time, the aperture needs to be smaller to restrict the amount of light coming in.

HOW IS EXPOSURE CALCULATED?

We now know about the exposure triangle—ISO, shutter speed, and aperture—so it's time to put all three together to see how they relate to one another and how you can change them as needed.

When you point your camera at a scene, the light reflecting off your subject enters the lens and is allowed to pass through to the sensor for a period of time as dictated by the shutter speed. The amount and duration of the light needed for a proper exposure depends on how much light is being reflected and how sensitive the sensor is. To figure this out, your camera utilizes a built-in light meter that looks through the lens and measures the amount of light. That level is then calculated against the sensitivity of the ISO setting and an exposure value is rendered. Here's the catch: There is no single way to achieve a perfect exposure because the f-stop and shutter speed can be combined in different ways to allow the same amount of exposure. Deciding which combination to use is one of the fun, creative parts of being a photographer.

Here is a list of reciprocal settings that would all produce the same exposure result. Let's use the "sunny 16" rule, which states that, when using f/16 on a sunny day, you can use a shutter speed that is roughly equal to your ISO setting to achieve a proper exposure. For simplification purposes, we will use an ISO of 100.

RECIPROCAL EXPOSURES: ISO 100

F-STOP	2.0	2.8	4.0	5.6	8	11	16	22
SHUTTER SPEED	1/8000	1/4000	1/2000	1/1000	1/500	1/250	1/125	1/60

If you were to use any one of these combinations, they would each have the same result in terms of the exposure (that is, how much light hits the camera's sensor). Also take note that every time we cut the f-stop in half, we reciprocated by doubling our shutter speed. For those of you wondering why f/5.6 is half of f/8, it's because those numbers are actually fractions based on the opening of the lens in relation to its focal length. This means that a lot of math goes into figuring out just what the total area of a lens opening is, so you just have to take it on faith that f/5.6 is half of f/8 but twice as much as f/4. A good way to remember which opening is larger is to think of your camera lens as a pipe that controls the flow of water. If you had a pipe that was 1/2" in diameter (f/2) and one that was 1/8" (f/8), which would allow more water to flow through? It would be the 1/2" pipe. The same idea works here with the camera f-stops; f/2 is a larger opening than f/4 or f/8 or f/16.

Now that we know this, we can start using this information to make intelligent choices in terms of shutter speed and f-stop. Let's bring the third element into this by changing our ISO by one stop, from 100 to 200.

RECIPROCAL EXPOSURES: ISO 200

F-STOP	2.0	2.8	4.0	5.6	8	11	16	22
SHUTTER SPEED	–	1/8000	1/4000	1/2000	1/1000	1/500	1/250	1/125

Notice that, since we doubled the sensitivity of the sensor, we now require half as much exposure as before. We have also reduced our maximum aperture from f/2 to f/2.8 because the camera can't use a shutter speed that is faster than 1/8000 of a second.

So why not just use the exposure setting of f/16 at 1/250 of a second? Why bother with all of these reciprocal values when this one setting will give us a properly exposed image? The answer is that the f-stop and shutter speed also control two other important aspects of our image: motion and depth of field.

STOP

You will hear the term *stop* thrown around all the time in photography. It relates back to the f-stop, which is a term used to describe the aperture opening of your lens. When you need to decrease the exposure, you might say that you are going to "stop down." This doesn't just equate to the aperture; it could also be used to describe the shutter speed or even the ISO. So when your image is too light or dark or you have too much movement in your subject, you will probably be changing things by a stop or two.

MOTION AND DEPTH OF FIELD

There are distinct characteristics that are related to changes in aperture and shutter speed. Shutter speed controls the length of time the light has to strike the sensor; consequently, it also controls the blurriness (or lack of blurriness) of the image. The less time light has to hit the sensor, the less time your subjects have to move around and become blurry. This can let you control things like freezing the motion of a fast-moving subject (**Figure 2.11**) or intentionally blurring subjects to give the feel of energy and motion (**Figure 2.12**).

FIGURE 2.11
This little boy was waving the flag back and forth very quickly, so I used a faster shutter speed to freeze the action.

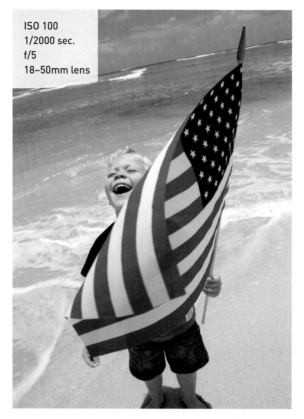

ISO 100
1/2000 sec.
f/5
18–50mm lens

FIGURE 2.12
Using a slow shutter speed with a fast-moving subject will intensify the feeling of movement in an image.

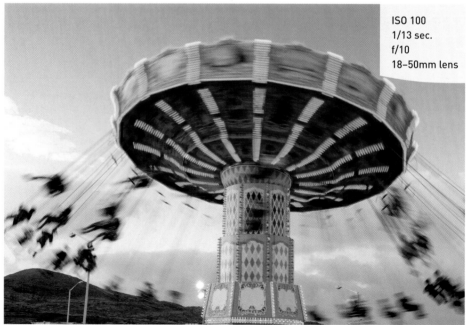

ISO 100
1/13 sec.
f/10
18–50mm lens

The aperture controls the amount of light that comes through the lens, but also determines what areas of the image will be in focus. This is referred to as depth of field, and it is an extremely valuable creative tool. The smaller the opening (the larger the number, such as f/22), the greater the sharpness of objects from near to far (**Figure 2.13**).

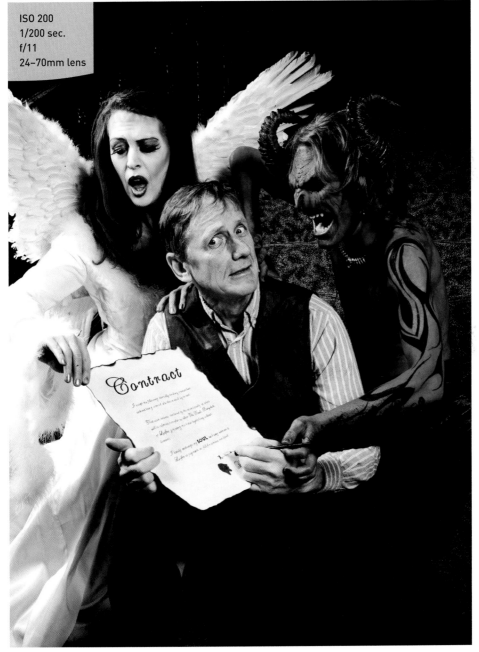

ISO 200
1/200 sec.
f/11
24–70mm lens

FIGURE 2.13
I wanted all three people in this photo to be in focus, so I chose to use a small aperture.

A large opening (or small number, like f/2.8) means more blurring of objects that are not at the same distance as the subject you are focusing on (**Figure 2.14**).

As we further explore the features of the camera, we will learn not only how to utilize the elements of exposure to capture properly exposed photographs, but also how to make adjustments to enhance the outcome of your images. It is the manipulation of these elements—motion and focus—that will take your images to the next level.

FIGURE 2.14
A wide-open aperture created a shallow depth of field for this photograph.

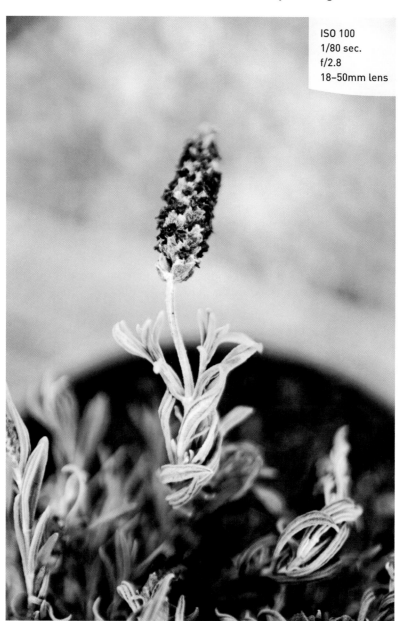

ISO 100
1/80 sec.
f/2.8
18–50mm lens

Chapter 2 Challenges

Formatting your card

Even if you have already begun using your camera, make sure you are familiar with formatting the CompactFlash card. If you haven't done so already, follow the directions given earlier in the chapter and format as prescribed (make sure you save any images that you may have already taken). Then perform the format function every time you have downloaded or saved your images or use a new card.

Checking your firmware version

Using the most up-to-date version of the camera firmware will ensure that your camera is functioning properly. Use the menu to find your current firmware version and then update as necessary using the steps listed in this chapter.

Exploring your image formats

Take a look at all of the image formats in your menu settings and become familiar with what your options are. If you are not yet familiar with the RAW file format, take a few photos and try opening them up in the Canon software supplied with your camera.

Exploring your lens

If you are using a zoom lens, spend a little time shooting with all of the different focal lengths, from the widest to the longest. See just how much of an angle you can cover with your widest lens setting. How much magnification will you be able to get from the telephoto setting? Try shooting the same subject with a variety of different focal lengths to note the differences in how the subject looks, and also the relationship between the subject and the other elements in the photo.

Share your results with the book's Flickr group!

Join the group here: flickr.com/groups/canon7dfromsnapshotstogreatshots

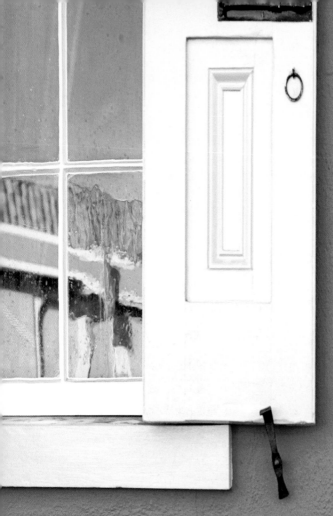

3

ISO 100
1/125 sec.
f/2.8
50mm lens

Camera Shooting Modes

USING THE CAMERA'S MODE SETTINGS

The Canon 7D has several different shooting modes located on the Mode dial on the top of your camera. Each setting is unique, and they allow you to have as much or as little control as you would like when taking pictures. It might be tempting to turn to the mode that you're most familiar with and start shooting without ever learning about the other settings, but what fun would that be? If you've never used an SLR camera before, some of these settings may be new to you and maybe even a bit confusing. My goal is to introduce these settings so you can decide which ones best suit your photography style.

We're going to start with the mode that gives you the least amount of control, and work our way through the settings to the more advanced modes. By the end of this chapter, you should have enough information to start taking your photography to the next level by harnessing control over your camera's features and developing a better grasp of the fundamental principles of photography.

PORING OVER THE PICTURE

Photographing with a long lens can be challenging, and this little bird didn't make it easy. I followed him around a bit and he finally decided to pause and lift up one of his legs so he was balancing on just one foot. I was using a very low ISO to keep as much detail in the shot as possible, and doing so required me to use a slower shutter speed. Luckily this fellow stayed still long enough for me to get a nice shot.

A large aperture and long focal length helped to give the image very shallow depth of field.

ISO 100
1/60 sec.
f/4
400mm lens

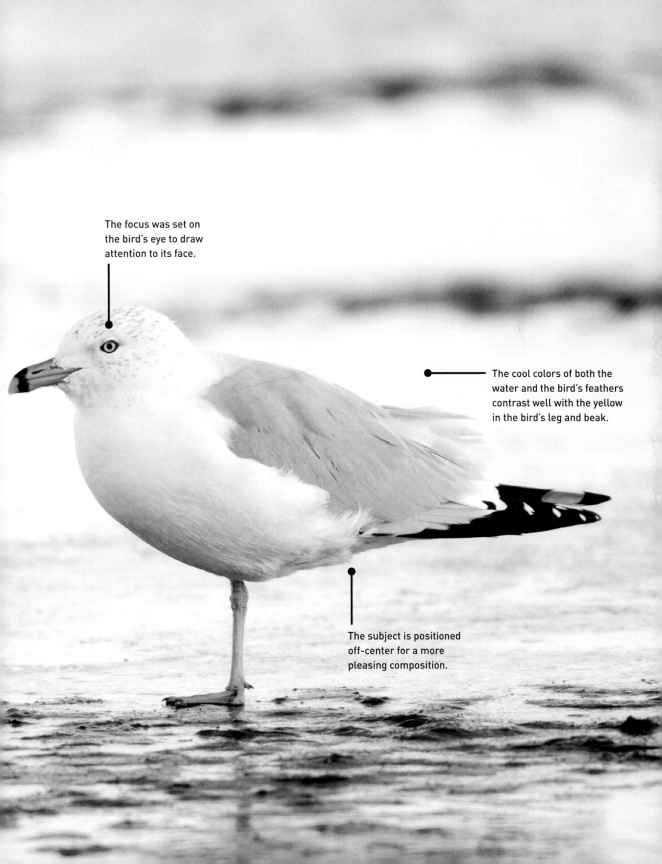

The focus was set on the bird's eye to draw attention to its face.

The cool colors of both the water and the bird's feathers contrast well with the yellow in the bird's leg and beak.

The subject is positioned off-center for a more pleasing composition.

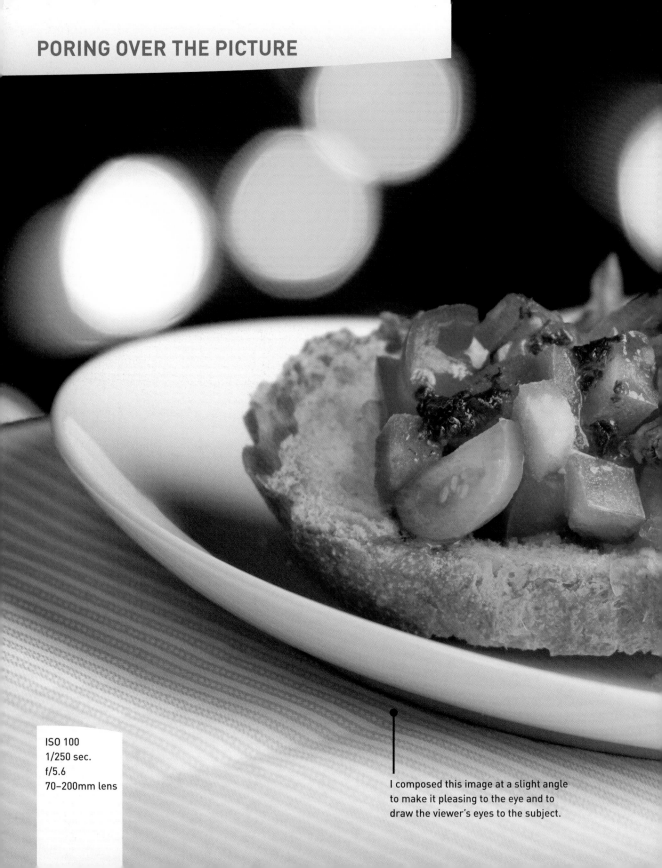

ISO 100
1/250 sec.
f/5.6
70–200mm lens

I composed this image at a slight angle
to make it pleasing to the eye and to
draw the viewer's eyes to the subject.

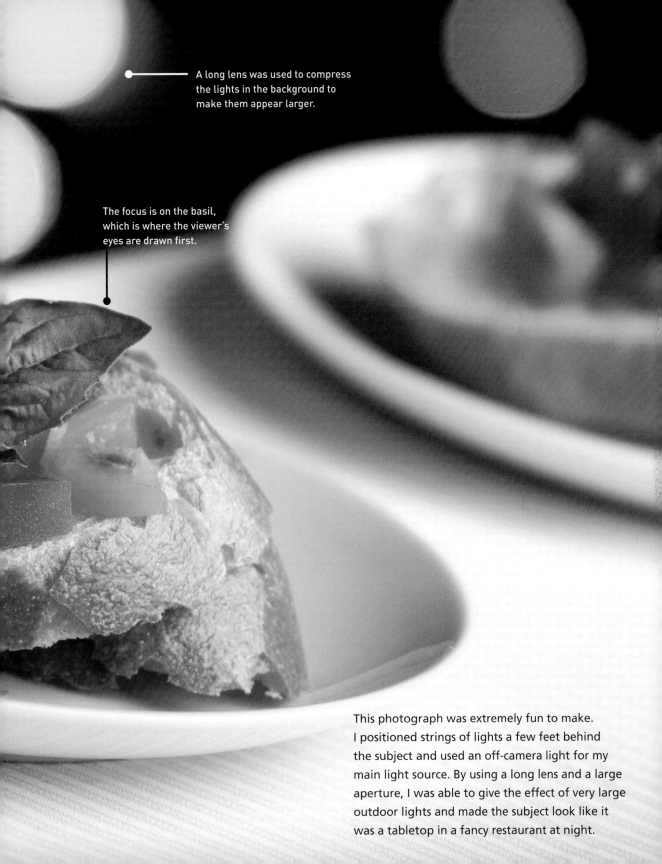

A long lens was used to compress the lights in the background to make them appear larger.

The focus is on the basil, which is where the viewer's eyes are drawn first.

This photograph was extremely fun to make. I positioned strings of lights a few feet behind the subject and used an off-camera light for my main light source. By using a long lens and a large aperture, I was able to give the effect of very large outdoor lights and made the subject look like it was a tabletop in a fancy restaurant at night.

FULL AUTO MODE

 Full Auto mode, indicated on the Mode dial by a green square, is exactly what it sounds like—fully automatic shooting. This means that the camera decides all of your in-camera settings. It chooses the ISO, shutter speed, aperture, white balance, and whether or not you will need more light with the pop-up flash. You only control the quality settings (RAW or JPEG) and drive mode setting (where you can choose between single or self-timer shooting).

You might be wondering when you would use the Full Auto mode, right? Well, my answer is pretty simple: never! OK, that may be a little extreme, but you have this incredible camera to take great photos with, and letting the camera decide how to do it defeats the purpose of your investment. If you are very new to photography, my hope is that you want to expand beyond the full automatic mode and use your 7D as a powerful tool. It's OK if you need to switch to this mode every once in a while, but do your best to learn the other modes to get as much out of your camera as you possibly can.

SETTING UP AND SHOOTING IN FULL AUTO MODE

1. Turn your camera on and then turn the Mode dial to align the green square with the indicator line.
2. Make sure your image quality setting is selected (RAW or JPEG—see Chapter 2 for more information on quality settings).
3. Point the camera at your subject and press the shutter to take a photo. The camera will set both your color and exposure settings for you.

CA: CREATIVE AUTO MODE

 One good alternative for new photographers is to start out in the Creative Auto (CA) mode. It's very similar to Full Auto, so it's something you might want to use in moderation, but you do have a bit more control over some of the settings. You have the ability to change the brightness, background blurriness (aperture), and Picture Style of each image, along with your quality setting and drive mode. The camera will decide the rest for you. It's a good option if you know what you want your image to look like but are still not familiar with how aperture and shutter speed function to properly expose your image. For example, if you know that you want to photograph a person with a blurred background, you can do this very easily in the Creative Auto setting (**Figure 3.1**). The camera will know where to set the aperture to give you the effect you want.

This mode is still limited because you are not able to change your white balance, ISO, focus point, and shutter speed. Keep reading to explore the more advanced shooting modes—this will ultimately give you full control over the images you create.

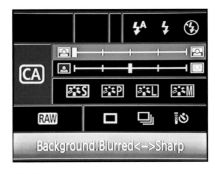

FIGURE 3.1
The display on the LCD gives you the ability to adjust some of the settings while in the CA mode. This is an example of changing the setting so that your background is blurry.

SETTING UP AND SHOOTING IN CREATIVE AUTO MODE

1. Turn your camera on and turn the Mode dial to align "CA" with the indicator line.

2. The display on the LCD will automatically turn on, allowing you to change some of your settings. To make changes, press the Quick Control button and use the Multi-Controller to toggle between the settings. Then use the Quick Control dial to make your adjustments.

3. When you've finalized your settings, point the camera at your subject and press the Shutter button to take a photo.

MENU ITEMS IN AUTOMATIC MODES

One important detail to know when using the Full Auto and Creative Auto modes is that your menu tabs are limited. Only seven out of the eleven tabs that are normally visible when shooting in all other mode settings will display (**Figure 3.2**). Because in fully automatic modes the camera decides the majority of the exposure and color settings, the information in some menu tabs is not necessary.

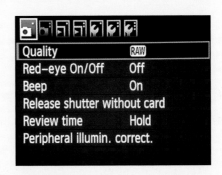

FIGURE 3.2
The menu tabs are limited in the automatic shooting modes.

P: PROGRAM MODE

 Next up on the dial is the Program mode (P). This mode is similar to the Full and Creative Auto modes in that it gives the camera control over some of the settings, but it opens up the rest of the decisions to the user (that's you!).

So what are the differences between the Auto modes and the Program mode? It's actually quite simple. In Program mode the only settings that the camera determines are shutter speed and aperture. You choose the ISO, white balance, focus point, and so on, so you will still have a lot of control over the quality of your images. The camera is just making some of the last, yet still very important, decisions for you.

WHEN TO USE PROGRAM (P) MODE INSTEAD OF THE AUTOMATIC MODES

- When shooting in a casual environment where quick adjustments are needed

- When you want control over the ISO

- If you want to make corrections to the white balance

Now, just because the camera chooses a starting point with an aperture and shutter speed doesn't mean that you are stuck with its first choice. The Canon 7D has a feature called "Program AE" that allows you to adjust the aperture and shutter speed on the fly while maintaining the same amount of light that is coming through the lens. Do you remember the Reciprocal Exposures chart in Chapter 2? That's the same principle applied here—if the camera wants the settings to be 1/250 of a second (shutter speed) at f/5.6 (aperture), you can turn the dial to a reciprocal exposure of 1/60 of a second at f/11. You will get the same exposure in your image, but your depth of field will vary because of the different aperture settings.

The key to using the Program AE function is understanding what you want the overall image to look like. If you are photographing a fast-moving subject and need to freeze the action, then you will turn the Main dial to the right to be sure that your shutter speed is fast enough to capture the movement. This also increases the size of the aperture, which can result in a blurred background, or shallow depth of field. Turning the Main dial to the left will do just the opposite—it will slow your shutter speed, possibly increasing the likelihood of motion in the image, and it will shrink the size of the aperture, which will result in a more focused image, or greater depth of field.

Let's set up the camera for Program mode and Program AE and see how we can make all of this come together.

SETTING UP AND SHOOTING IN PROGRAM MODE

1. Turn your camera on and then turn the Mode dial to align the P with the indicator line.

2. Make sure that your ISO, white balance, picture style, and focus point are all set appropriately (this is where you get to make the decisions!).

3. Point the camera at your subject and then activate the camera meter by depressing the Shutter button halfway.

4. View the exposure information while looking through the viewfinder (underneath the focusing screen) or at the LCD Panel on the top of the camera.

5. With the Shutter button still pressed halfway, use your index finger to roll the Main dial left and right to see the changed exposure values.

6. Select the exposure that is right for you and start shooting. (Don't worry if you aren't sure what the right exposure is. We will start working on making the right choices for those great shots beginning with the next chapter.)

STARTING POINTS FOR ISO SELECTION

There is a lot of discussion concerning ISO in this and other chapters, but it might be helpful if you know where your starting points should be for your ISO settings. The first thing you should always try to do is use the lowest possible ISO setting. That said, here are good starting points for your ISO settings:

- 100: Bright sunny day

- 200: Hazy or outdoor shade on a sunny day

- 400: Indoor lighting at night or cloudy conditions outside

- 800: Late night, low-light conditions or sporting arenas at night

These are just suggestions, and your ISO selection will depend on a number of factors that we will discuss later in the book. You might have to push your ISO even higher as needed, but at least now you know where to start.

TV: SHUTTER PRIORITY MODE

The Shutter Priority mode, referred to on your Mode dial as Tv (which stands for "Time Value"), is where you select the shutter speed and the camera adjusts the aperture accordingly. Use this mode to push yourself toward the more advanced modes with your camera. This will allow you an enormous amount of control with your final image.

Before we go any further, let me briefly explain the mechanics of the camera shutter. The shutter is like a curtain that opens and closes to allow light to hit the sensor. The speed is calculated in seconds and fractions of a second (which is what you will likely use most often), and the longer the shutter stays open the more light will reach the sensor. Using a very fast shutter speed is ideal for capturing fast-moving subjects (think of a football player jumping in the air to receive a pass), while a slow shutter speed can show movement in an image (like creating a soft effect on the water in a flowing stream or waterfall). These settings are offset by a larger aperture for fast shutter speeds and a smaller aperture for slow shutter speeds.

It's important to understand that if the shutter speed gets too low you won't be able to handhold the camera to take the photo. Doing so might introduce "camera shake" in your image, which often makes an image appear out of focus. A good rule of thumb is to keep your shutter speed the same as your lens's focal length. For example, if you are using a 200mm lens, try to keep the slowest handheld shutter speed no slower than 1/200 of a second. Because the 7D has a 1.6 crop-factor, the number might be slightly off, but sticking to that basic principle will help you keep your images sharp and free of camera shake.

WHEN TO USE SHUTTER PRIORITY (TV) MODE

- When working with fast-moving subjects where you want to freeze the action (**Figure 3.3**); there is much more on this in Chapter 6

- When you want to emphasize movement in your subject with motion blur (**Figure 3.4**)

- When you want to create that silky-looking water in a waterfall or stream (**Figure 3.5**)

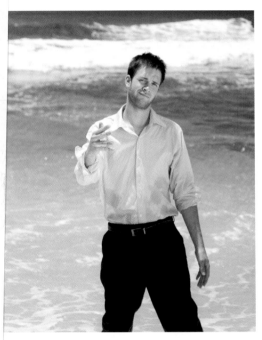

FIGURE 3.3
To freeze the laptop mid-air and reduce motion blur, I used a very fast shutter speed to photograph this image.

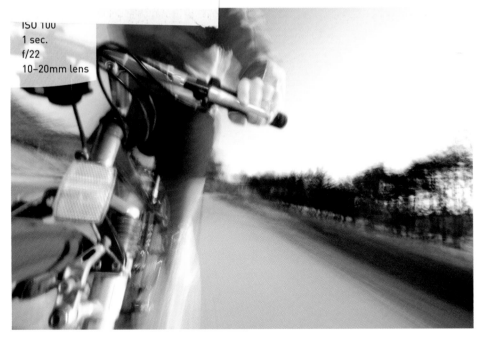

ISO 100
1 sec.
f/22
10–20mm lens

FIGURE 3.4
A slow shutter speed was used to emphasize the movement of the biker.

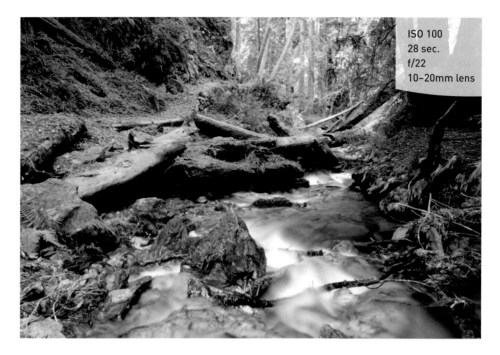

ISO 100
28 sec.
f/22
10–20mm lens

As you can see, the subject of your photo usually determines whether or not you will use Tv mode. It is important that you be able to visualize the result of using a particular shutter speed. The great thing about shooting with digital cameras is that you get instant feedback by checking your shot on the LCD screen. But what if you only have one chance to catch the shot? Such is often the case when shooting sporting events. It's not like you can go ask the quarterback to throw that winning touchdown pass again because your last shot was blurry from a slow shutter speed. This is why it's important to know what those speeds represent in terms of their capabilities to stop the action and deliver a blur-free shot.

First, let's examine just how much control you have over the shutter speeds. The 7D has a shutter speed range from 1/8000 of a second all the way up to 30 seconds. With that much latitude, you should have enough control to capture almost any subject. The other thing to think about is that Tv mode is considered a "semiautomatic" mode. This means that you are taking control over one aspect of the total exposure while the camera handles the other. In this instance, you are controlling the shutter speed and the camera is controlling the aperture. This is important, because there will be times that you want to use a particular shutter speed but your lens won't be able to accommodate your request.

For example, you might encounter this problem when shooting in low-light situations. If you are shooting a fast-moving subject that will blur at a shutter speed slower than 1/125 of a second but your lens's largest aperture is f/3.5, you might find that the aperture display in your viewfinder and on the top LCD panel will begin to blink. This is your warning that there won't be enough light available for the shot—due to the limitations of the lens—so your picture will be underexposed.

Another case where you might run into this situation is when you are shooting moving water. To get that look of silky, flowing water, it's usually necessary to use a shutter speed of at least 1/15 of a second. If your waterfall is in full sunlight, you may get that blinking aperture display once again because the lens you are using only stops down to f/22 at its smallest opening. In this instance, your camera is warning you that you will be overexposing your image. There are workarounds for these problems, which we will discuss later (see Chapter 5), but it is important to know that there can be limitations when using Tv mode.

SETTING UP AND SHOOTING IN TV MODE

1. Turn your camera on and then turn the Mode dial to align the Tv with the indicator line.

2. Select your ISO by pressing the ISO button on the top of the camera and then turning the Main dial (the ISO selection will appear in the top LCD Panel).

3. Point the camera at your subject and then activate the camera meter by depressing the Shutter button halfway.

4. View the exposure information in the bottom area of the viewfinder or by looking at the top LCD Panel.

5. While the meter is activated, use your index finger to roll the Main dial left and right to see the changed exposure values. Roll the dial to the right for faster shutter speeds and to the left for slower speeds.

SHUTTER SPEEDS

A *slow* shutter speed refers to leaving the shutter open for a long period of time—like 1/30 of a second or longer. A *fast* shutter speed means that the shutter is open for a very short period of time—like 1/250 of a second or less.

IMAGE STABILIZATION LENSES

Some Canon lenses come with a feature called Image Stabilization (IS) (**Figure 3.6**). It's a mechanism that's built directly into the lens and helps reduce motion blur due to camera shake when photographing at slower shutter speeds.

If you have this option on your lens, it's a good idea to leave it turned on when doing any handheld photography. Because the IS mechanism in the lens moves when turned on, you'll want to turn it off when using a tripod. It could introduce camera shake in your images if the camera is perfectly still on a tripod, so it is typically only recommended for handheld photography.

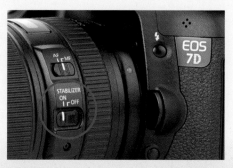

FIGURE 3.6

AV: APERTURE PRIORITY MODE

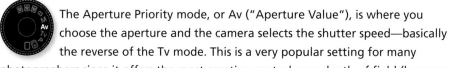

The Aperture Priority mode, or Av ("Aperture Value"), is where you choose the aperture and the camera selects the shutter speed—basically the reverse of the Tv mode. This is a very popular setting for many photographers since it offers the most creative control over depth of field (how much of your image appears in focus). This is my favorite setting when I'm not shooting in the Manual mode, and I have a feeling that you will find it just as useful.

In Chapter 2 I discussed the basics of how the aperture works, so you should know that a large aperture (smaller number) equates to more light coming through the lens, and vice versa. The Av mode allows the camera to select the shutter speed. When you use a large aperture, you will end up with a faster shutter speed, and since a smaller aperture allows less light in through the lens, the camera will give a slower shutter speed to compensate. Once you have a solid understanding of how aperture and shutter speed work together, you will have taken a giant leap toward gaining complete control over your photography.

The greatest benefit of using the Av mode is that the photographer can control the depth of field in the image. Photographing something with a large aperture will decrease the depth of field and blur the background, while a small aperture will increase the depth of field so that more of the image is in focus (**Figures 3.7** and **3.8**).

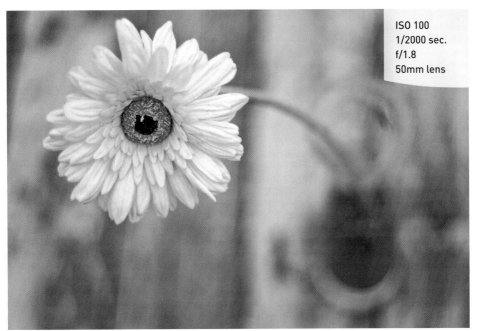

ISO 100
1/2000 sec.
f/1.8
50mm lens

FIGURE 3.7
This image of a flower was photographed with a large aperture of f/1.8, allowing me to significantly blur the background. This is an example of shallow depth of field.

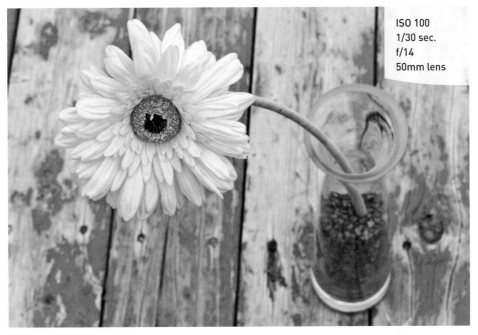

ISO 100
1/30 sec.
f/14
50mm lens

FIGURE 3.8
For this image I reduced the size of the aperture to f/14. The focus is set on the flower, but you are still able to make out a lot of detail in the background. This is an example of great depth of field.

WHEN TO USE APERTURE PRIORITY (AV) MODE

- When shooting portraits or wildlife (**Figure 3.9**)

- When shooting most landscape photography (**Figure 3.10**)

- When shooting macro, or close-up, photography (**Figure 3.11**)

It's important to note that because the aperture is physically located inside the lens (not the camera), your lens will determine how large an opening you can use. Lenses with a large maximum aperture are considered "fast" lenses, and tend to be much more expensive. Canon's fastest glass goes to an f-stop of 1.2, which allows you to shoot at faster shutter speeds in lower light situations. The largest aperture available for the majority of lenses on the market ranges from f/2.8 to f/4, which still allows a lot of light through to the sensor. The lens I use with my 7D for most of my work will only go to f/4, but I tend to work in brighter, more controlled lighting situations. Photographers who shoot weddings or events with uncontrollable lighting generally find that they need faster lenses with an opening of f/2.8 or larger.

FIGURE 3.9
A large aperture gave this image a blurry background.

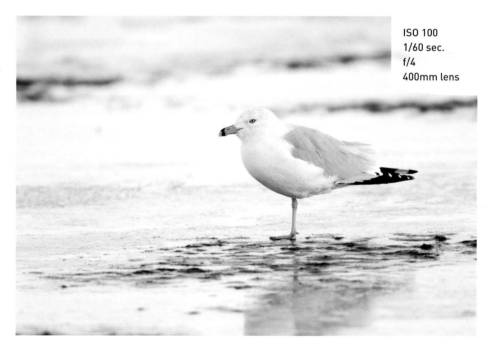

ISO 100
1/60 sec.
f/4
400mm lens

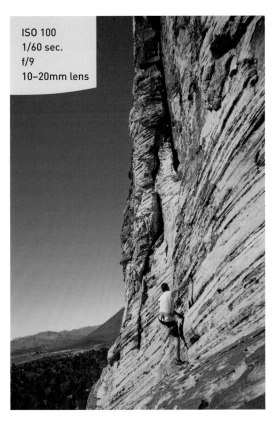

ISO 100
1/60 sec.
f/9
10–20mm lens

FIGURE 3.10
A small aperture kept both the foreground and background in focus.

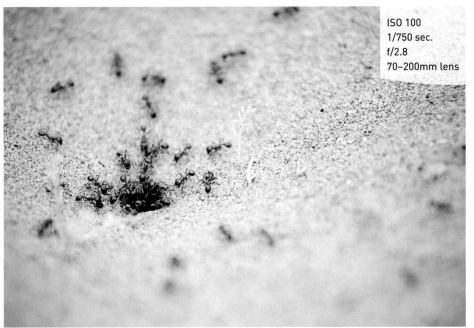

ISO 100
1/750 sec.
f/2.8
70–200mm lens

FIGURE 3.11
A macro lens in combination with a large aperture helped to show more detail and focus the attention on the ants in this image.

SETTING UP AND SHOOTING IN AV MODE

1. Turn your camera on and then turn the Mode dial to align the Av with the indicator line.

2. Select your ISO by pressing the ISO button on the top of the camera and then turning the Main dial (the ISO selection will appear in the top LCD Panel).

3. Point the camera at your subject and then activate the camera meter by depressing the Shutter button halfway.

4. View the exposure information in the bottom area of the viewfinder or by looking at the top display panel.

5. While the meter is activated, use your index finger to roll the Main dial left and right to see the changed exposure values. Roll the dial to the right for a smaller aperture (higher f-stop number) and to the left for a larger aperture (smaller f-stop number).

F-STOPS AND APERTURE

As discussed earlier, the numeric value of your lens aperture is described as an *f-stop*. The f-stop is one of those old photography terms that, technically, relates to the focal length of the lens (for example, 200mm) divided by the effective aperture diameter. These measurements are defined as "stops" and work incrementally with your shutter speed to determine proper exposure. Older camera lenses used one-stop increments to assist in exposure adjustments, such as 1.4, 2, 2.8, 4, 5.6, 8, 11, 16, and 22. Each stop represents about half as much light entering the lens iris as the larger stop before it. Today, most lenses don't have f-stop markings since all adjustments to this setting are performed via the camera's electronics. The stops are also now typically divided into 1/3-stop increments to allow much finer adjustments to exposures, as well as to match the incremental values of your camera's ISO settings, which are also adjusted in 1/3-stop increments.

ZOOM LENSES AND MAXIMUM APERTURES

Some zoom lenses (like the 18–55mm kit lens) have a variable maximum aperture. This means that the largest opening will change depending on the zoom setting. In the example of the 18–55mm zoom the lens has a maximum aperture of f/3.5 at 18mm and only f/5.6 when the lens is zoomed out to 55mm.

EXPOSURE COMPENSATION

One of my favorite features of Canon cameras is that they allow you to change the exposure compensation very quickly using the Quick Control dial on the back of your camera. Exposure compensation is a way to trick the camera into thinking that there is more or less light coming through the lens than its light meter actually reads. This meter wants to balance the exposure so that it is equal to a neutral gray shade. For example, if you were to photograph in an all-white environment, such as in the snow, your camera would want to make all of the white areas look gray and your image would end up dark and underexposed. You can compensate for this by telling the camera to overexpose the image so that your white snow will look white in your photograph (**Figure 3.12**).

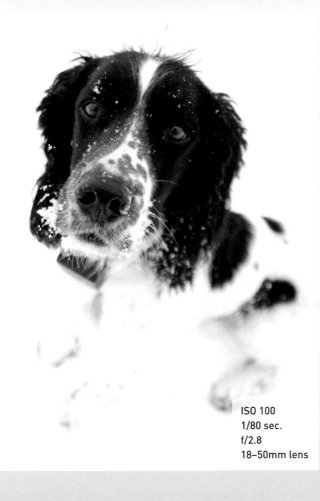

ISO 100
1/80 sec.
f/2.8
18–50mm lens

FIGURE 3.12
The white color of both the snow and the dog fooled my camera meter to underexpose the image, so I over-exposed the image by 2/3 stop to add more light and keep the white areas white.

SETTING EXPOSURE COMPENSATION

1. On the back of your camera, make sure that the Quick Control Dial switch is pushed all the way to the left.

2. Use your thumb to scroll the Quick Control dial to the left or right. Moving the dial to the left will tell your camera to underexpose the image (**A**), and moving it to the right will tell it to overexpose the image (**B**).

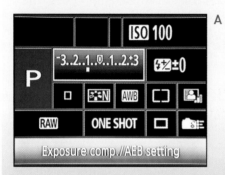

A

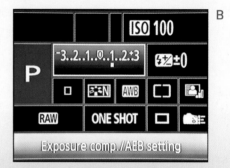

B

3. This setting will stay in place until you change it back. If you want to lock it in to prevent further changes, then set the Quick Control Dial switch to the right (**C**).

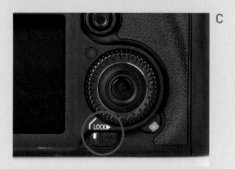

C

Using the Quick Control dial to change your exposure compensation will expand the flexibility of using the P, Tv, and Av modes on your camera so that you won't always have to rely on the camera to make the final decision.

M: MANUAL MODE

Before cameras had shooting modes such as Aperture Priority, Program, and so on, all exposures were set manually. This means that the photographer chose all of the settings, and since both the ISO and white balance were already decided depending on the kind of film loaded into the camera, the photographer was only responsible for selecting the proper aperture and shutter speed. As technology advanced and automatic features were added to cameras, many photographers discovered new ways of capturing their images. However, the "old-fashioned" method of taking pictures was never set aside or forgotten about. You will find that using the Manual (M) mode on the 7D will give you total control over your images.

When shooting in Manual mode, you choose both the aperture and shutter speed and the camera

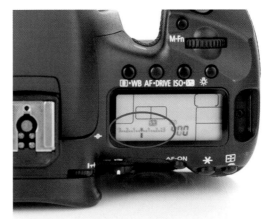

FIGURE 3.13
The light meter located on the top LCD Panel ranges from -3 stops (underexposed) to +3 stops (overexposed).

will do nothing other than give you its feedback through the internal light meter. You can view how the meter is reading a scene by looking in one of two places: the LCD on the top of the camera (**Figure 3.13**), or underneath the focusing frame while looking through the viewfinder. This meter is what the camera uses when shooting images in all other modes, and its goal is always to find the most balanced exposure. Sometimes, the light meter reads the scene incorrectly or the photographer wants to have full control over the exposure, and in those scenarios using the Manual mode is the best choice.

WHEN TO USE MANUAL (M) MODE

- When learning how each exposure element interacts with the others

- When your environment is fooling your light meter and you need to maintain a certain exposure setting, such as with a silhouette (**Figure 3.14**)

- When using an artificial light source, such as strobes or flashes, in a controlled environment (**Figures 3.15** and **3.16**)

I prefer to use the Manual mode when using strobes or any other type of controlled light source in an unchanging environment. I also use it when I have my camera on a tripod while photographing things such as food or landscapes. The great thing about Manual mode is that it can be used in any circumstance and can yield some amazing results if you know what you are doing.

FIGURE 3.14
Use the Manual mode for silhouettes to obtain proper exposure.

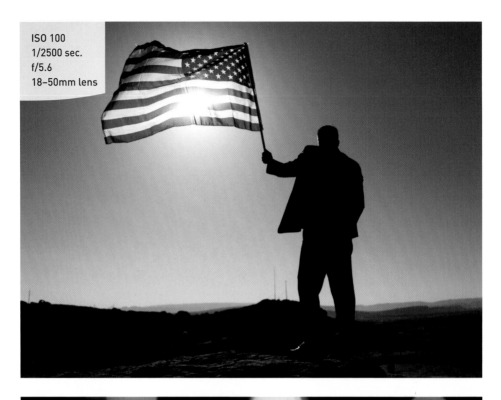

ISO 100
1/2500 sec.
f/5.6
18–50mm lens

FIGURE 3.15
This image was photographed in a studio setting. Because the main light source was a radio-triggered strobe, I used Manual mode in order to get the correct exposure.

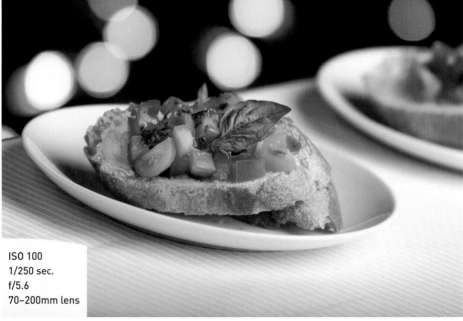

ISO 100
1/250 sec.
f/5.6
70–200mm lens

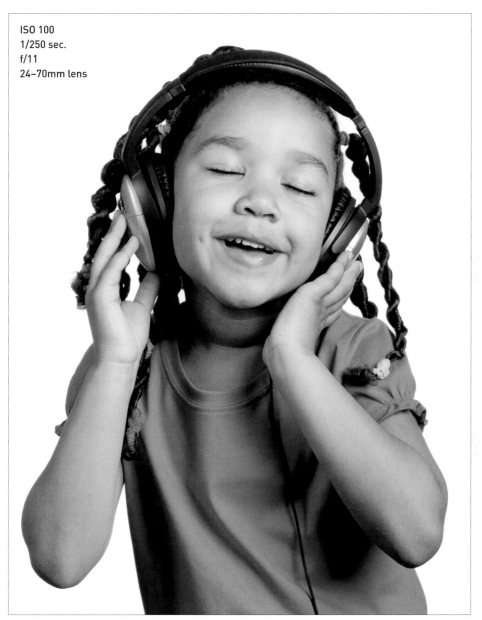

ISO 100
1/250 sec.
f/11
24–70mm lens

FIGURE 3.16
It's necessary to use Manual mode for most studio portrait images when using strobe lights or flash units.

1. Turn your camera on and turn the Mode dial to align the M with the indicator line.

2. Check the Quick Control Dial switch to make sure it is in the "off" position (pushed all the way to the left).

3. Select your ISO by pressing the ISO button on the top of the camera and then turning the Main dial (the ISO selection will appear in the top LCD Panel).

4. Point the camera at your subject and then activate the camera meter by depressing the Shutter button halfway.

5. View the exposure information in the bottom area of the viewfinder or by looking at the display panel on top of the camera.

6. While the meter is activated, use your index finger to roll the Main dial left and right to change your shutter speed value until the exposure mark is lined up with the zero mark. The exposure information is displayed by a scale with marks that run from –3 to +3 stops. The camera will meter a proper exposure when it is lined up with the arrow mark in the middle. As the indicator moves to the left, it is a sign that you will be underexposing (telling you that there is not enough light on the sensor to provide adequate exposure). Move the indicator to the right and you will be providing more exposure than the camera meter calls for. This is overexposure.

7. To set your exposure using the aperture, depress the Shutter button until the meter is activated. Then, using your thumb, scroll the Quick Control dial to change the aperture: clockwise for a smaller aperture (large f-stop number), and counterclockwise for a larger aperture (small f-stop number).

B: BULB MODE

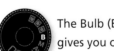 The Bulb (B) mode on your camera is another manual mode setting that gives you complete control over the shutter speed, but instead of choosing a specific setting you are able to leave the shutter open for an indefinite period of time. The word *bulb* comes from the early days of photography when camera shutters were pneumatically activated, meaning a bulb was pressed and the air from it was released through a tube that caused the shutter to open and close. It's a mode that is typically used in dark environments to capture light that is sporadic or changing, such as fireworks or star trails. It can be extremely useful in creating images that need very long shutter speeds.

When using this mode it's essential to use both a tripod and a cable release (**Figure 3.17**). A tripod will keep the camera steady while the shutter is open, and a cable release will open and close the shutter without you having to push the button on the top of the camera, reducing the likelihood of camera shake in your images.

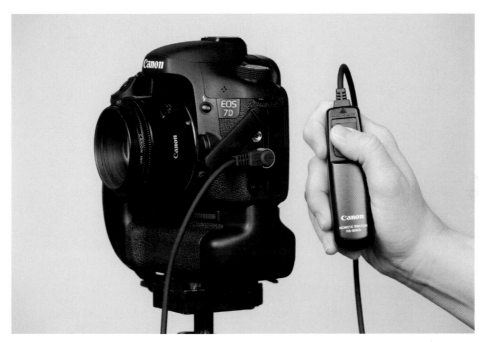

FIGURE 3.17
A tripod and a cable release are essential accessories when photographing in Bulb mode. (Photo by Rich Legg)

WHEN TO USE BULB (B) MODE

- When shooting fireworks displays (**Figure 3.18**)

- When you want to capture trails of lights, such as stars or cars moving down a street at night (**Figure 3.19**)

- When you want to photograph any image in a dark environment at a very small aperture (**Figure 3.20**)

Using the Bulb mode can bring a lot of creativity into your photography, and there are really no limits to what you can create. The wonderful thing about this mode is that you are able to capture images that are so different from what we see with our eyes. When I lived in the Midwest, I used to chase storms and photograph lightning and was always amazed at the results (**Figure 3.21**). We see the bolts of light for only a split second, but by using the Bulb mode we can freeze the lightning and see more than we could with our eyes during the storm.

FIGURE 3.18
A long shutter speed was necessary to capture several bursts of fireworks on one image.

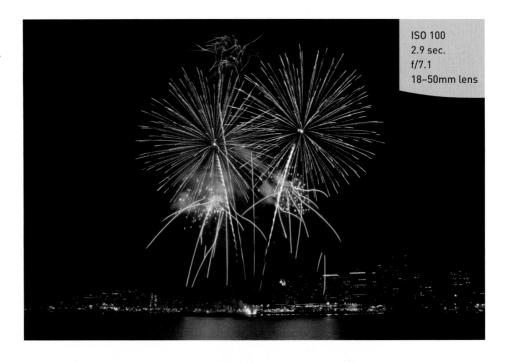

ISO 100
2.9 sec.
f/7.1
18–50mm lens

FIGURE 3.19
I left the shutter open for several seconds to catch the trail of lights created by the Ferris wheel as it was spinning.

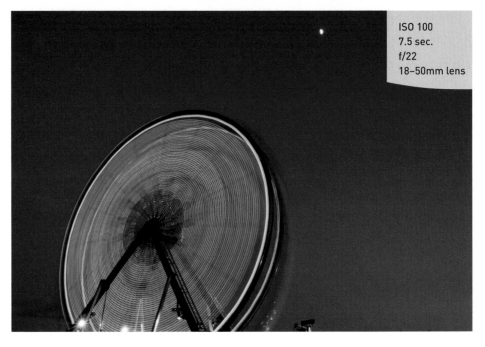

ISO 100
7.5 sec.
f/22
18–50mm lens

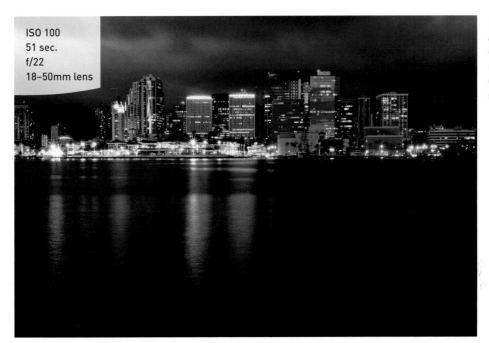

ISO 100
51 sec.
f/22
18–50mm lens

FIGURE 3.20
A very long exposure was required to photograph this skyline scene at night.

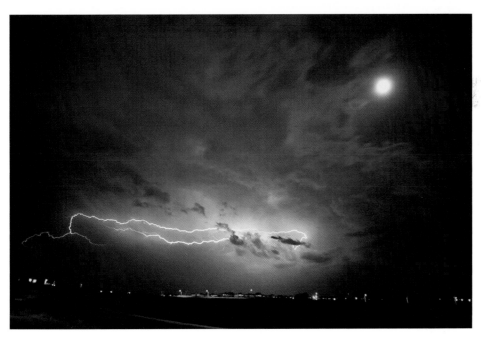

FIGURE 3.21
Although this image was photographed on 35mm film, it's a good example of the types of images you can create digitally using the Bulb mode on your 7D.

SETTING UP AND SHOOTING IN BULB MODE

1. Set your camera on a sturdy tripod and attach a cable release to the Remote Control terminal on the side of your camera.

2. Turn the Mode dial to align the B with the indicator line.

3. Select your aperture by turning the Main dial.

4. Select your ISO by pressing the ISO button on the top of the camera and then turning the Main dial (the ISO selection will appear in the top LCD Panel).

5. Position the camera toward your subject and press the button on the cable release. Hold the button down until you are satisfied with your exposure, and then release the shutter.

6. If you want an extremely long exposure (several minutes or hours), lock the cable release by sliding the button up, which will allow you to lock the shutter in place indefinitely. The only limitation to your exposure is the amount of life left in your battery.

C1, C2, AND C3: CUSTOM MODES

The Canon 7D comes with three custom modes: C1, C2, and C3. These modes allow the photographer to program specific shooting modes or exposure settings and save them as a preset. They are extremely useful if you find yourself photographing the same scene again and again and always using the same settings each time. To learn more about them, please turn to Chapter 10.

DIGITAL NOISE AND LONG EXPOSURES

One issue that arises when making extremely long exposures is that you are likely to introduce more digital noise into your images than with a normal exposure. This is one area in which film still has an advantage over digital (**Figure 3.22**). Digital noise due to long exposures is difficult to prevent, but there are some advanced ways to reduce its effect by using noise-reduction software while editing your images. You can also reduce the amount of noise in-camera by turning on the Long Exposure Noise Reduction setting in your 7D. Please turn to Chapter 7 for more information.

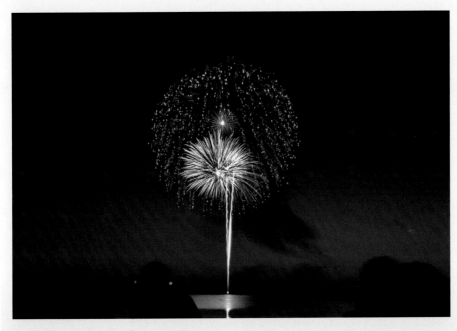

FIGURE 3.22
Long exposures photographed with film, such as this image of fireworks at night, had a high dynamic range (more detail in the darker and brighter areas) and, unlike the digital cameras of today, did not introduce excess noise or grain in the images.

HOW I SHOOT: A CLOSER LOOK AT THE CAMERA SETTINGS I USE

I started my journey with photography before consumer digital cameras were afford-able and available to the general public, so I had the advantage of learning how to photograph and develop film with a fully manual camera. When I finally upgraded to a camera with shooting modes, I had a solid understanding of how aperture and shutter speed worked together and knew how to create the look I wanted using certain settings. Because the majority of my work both then and now involves pho-tographing people, I tend to want to control the depth of field in my images so that I have creative control over what parts are in focus and what areas are blurry. So, as you have probably guessed, the majority of my work is photographed using the Aperture Priority (Av) mode. Since I also do work in a studio or controlled-lighting environment, my second most frequently used mode is Manual (M).

Now don't get me wrong—I play around with the other modes depending on what I'm shooting, but I find that I prefer to have as much control as possible so that I'm creating images that fit my style of photography. If you handed me a camera that had only Av and M and no other modes, I would probably be able to photograph in any environment and capture the images that I wanted without hesitation.

What I love about Canon cameras is the ability to change the exposure compensation quickly when I am using the Av mode. This can make shooting in Av or Tv mode very similar to using the Manual mode because you regain control over your exposure. The internal light meter does an amazing job, but I find that when I'm in a tricky lighting situation the Quick Control dial can work wonders to help bring the expo-sure back to where it should be.

The last thing that I always have enabled on my camera is the Highlight Alert (see Chapter 1 for more information). This tells me when my images are overexposed or whether I have lost detail in an area of a properly exposed image. The ability to quickly adjust the exposure using the Quick Control dial makes it easy to capture as much detail in my images as possible.

As you work your way through the coming chapters, you will see other tips and tricks I use in my daily photography, but the most important tip I can give you is to understand the features of your camera so that you can leverage the technology in a knowledgeable way—and produce better photographs.

Chapter 3 Challenges

These will be more of a mental challenge than anything else, but you should put a lot of work into them because the information covered in this chapter will define how you work with your camera from this point on. Granted, there may be times that you just want to grab some quick pictures and will resort to the automatic modes, but to get serious with your photography you will want to learn what the other modes have to offer.

Familiarize yourself with the Auto modes

While you probably don't want to use these modes too often, it's still a good idea to understand how they work. If you're new to photography, go ahead and turn your camera to the CA mode and play with the settings. See what happens when you take a photo after you increase the blurriness of the background, and then change your settings to make it sharper. Adjust the exposure to make it darker and brighter. After taking a few photos, review your images and pay attention to the shutter speed and aperture and how each setting affected the outcome of your image.

Starting off with Program mode

Set your camera to Program mode and start shooting. Become familiar with the adjustments you can make to your exposure by turning the Main dial. Shoot in bright sun, deep shade, indoors, anywhere that you have different types and intensities of light. While you are shooting, make sure that you keep an eye on your ISO and raise or lower it according to your environment.

Learning to control time with the Tv mode

Find some moving subjects and then set your camera to Tv mode. Have someone ride a bike back and forth, or just photograph cars as they go by. Start with a slow shutter speed of around 1/30 of a second, and then start shooting with faster and faster shutter speeds. Keep shooting until you can freeze the action. Now find something that isn't moving (like a flower), set your shutter speed to something fast (like 1/500 of a second), and then work your way down. Don't brace the camera on a steady surface. Just try to shoot as slowly as possible, down to about 1/4 of a second. The point is to see how well you can handhold your camera before you start introducing camera shake into the image, making it appear soft and somewhat unfocused.

Controlling depth of field with the Av mode

The key with Av mode is depth of field. Set up three items an equal distance from you. I would use chess pieces or something similar. Now focus on the middle item and set your camera to the largest aperture that your lens allows (remember, a large aperture means a small number like f/2.8). Now, while still focusing on the middle subject, start shooting with ever-smaller apertures until you are at the smallest f-stop for your lens. If you have a zoom lens, try doing this exercise with the lens at the widest and then the most telephoto settings. Now move up to subjects that are farther away, like telephone poles, and shoot them in the same way. The idea is to get a feel for how each aperture setting affects your depth of field.

Taking control with Manual mode

Manual mode is not going to require a lot of work, but you should pay close attention to your results. Start by composing your image, then watch the light meter in the viewfinder. Set your aperture and shutter speed until the arrow is in the middle. Take a photo and review your shot. If you still need to make some adjustments to the exposure, then change your settings and take another shot, but this time don't worry about balancing the exposure to the light meter. Try several different settings until you start to get comfortable using the Manual mode.

Using long exposures with Bulb mode

If you have a tripod and cable release, find a location to set up your camera where you can capture moving light. Find a street corner or a carnival at night, or if you have the time and patience to sit outside for a few hours then you could even try photographing star trails on a dark night. Test out different apertures with your exposures to see which ones work best for your subject.

Each time you try something new, make sure that you keep track of your modes and exposures so that you can compare them with the image. If you are using software to review your images, you should also be able to check the camera settings that are embedded within the image's metadata.

Share your results with the book's Flickr group!

Join the group here: flickr.com/groups/canon7dfromsnapshotstogreatshots

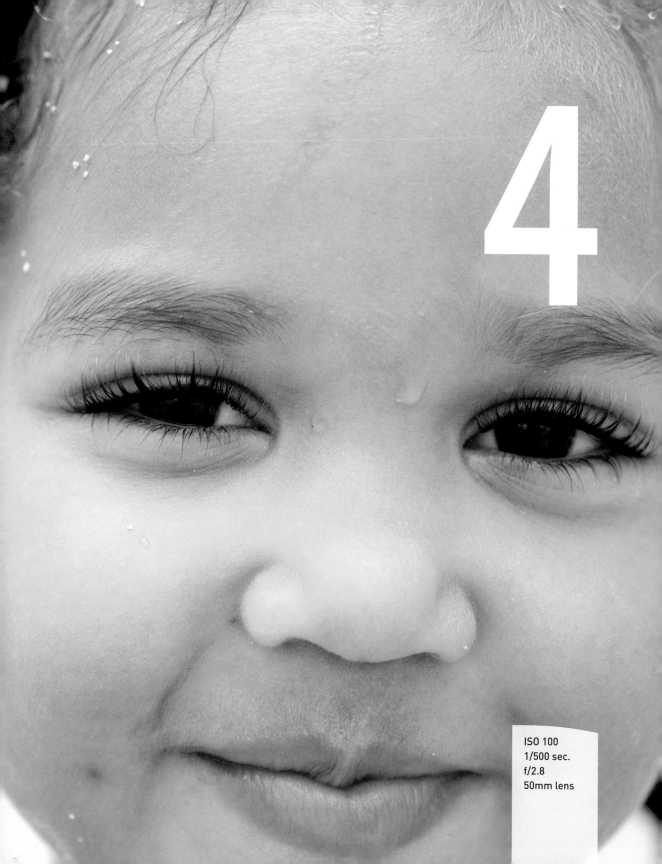

4

ISO 100
1/500 sec.
f/2.8
50mm lens

Say Cheese!

SETTINGS AND FEATURES TO MAKE GREAT PORTRAITS

Photographing people is challenging, rewarding, and fun all at the same time. When you photograph a person, you are capturing a memory, a moment in time. Images of friends and family often become our most cherished possessions. The people you photograph are depending on you to make them look good, and while you can't always change how a person looks, you can control the way you photograph that individual. In this chapter we will explore some camera features and techniques that can help you create great portraits.

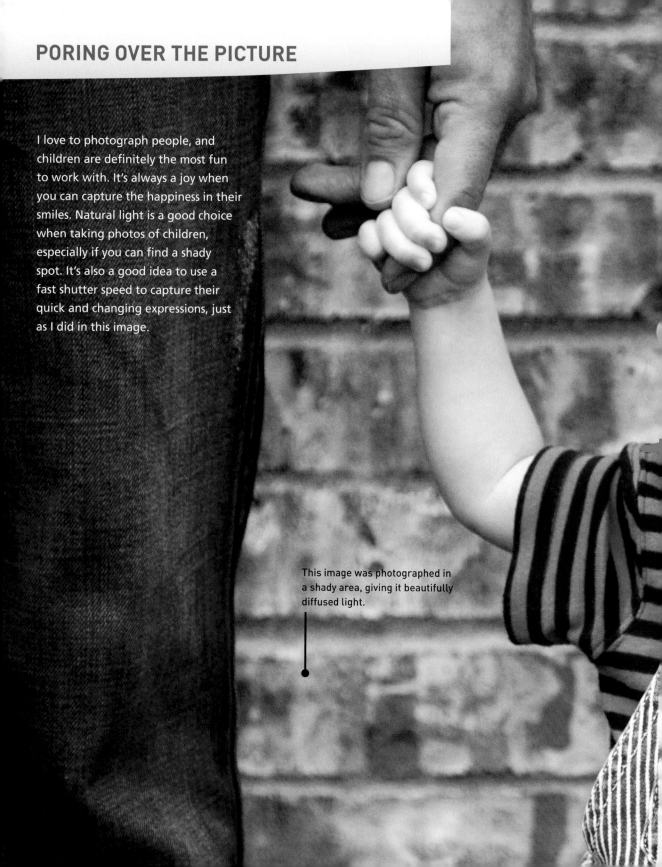

I love to photograph people, and children are definitely the most fun to work with. It's always a joy when you can capture the happiness in their smiles. Natural light is a good choice when taking photos of children, especially if you can find a shady spot. It's also a good idea to use a fast shutter speed to capture their quick and changing expressions, just as I did in this image.

This image was photographed in a shady area, giving it beautifully diffused light.

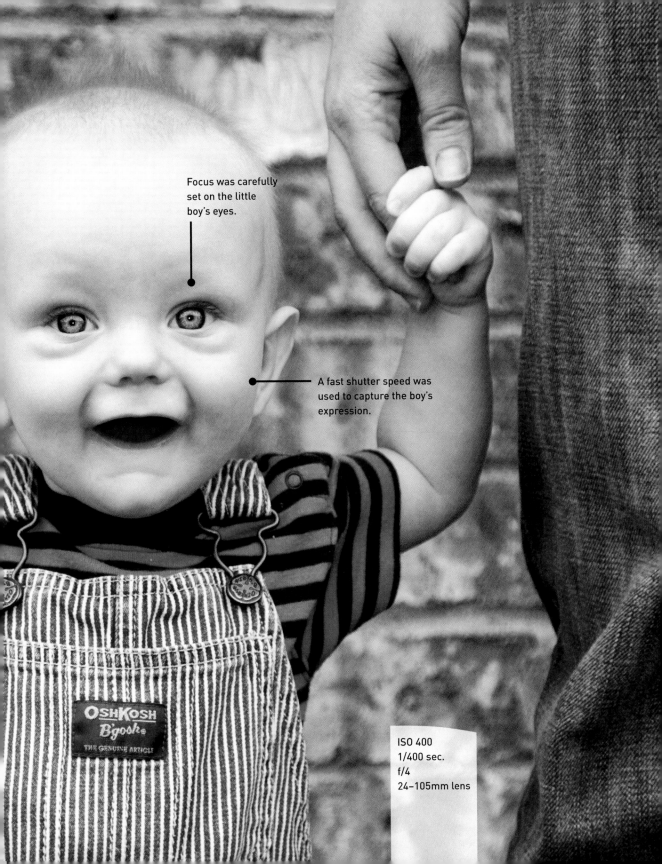

Focus was carefully set on the little boy's eyes.

A fast shutter speed was used to capture the boy's expression.

ISO 400
1/400 sec.
f/4
24–105mm lens

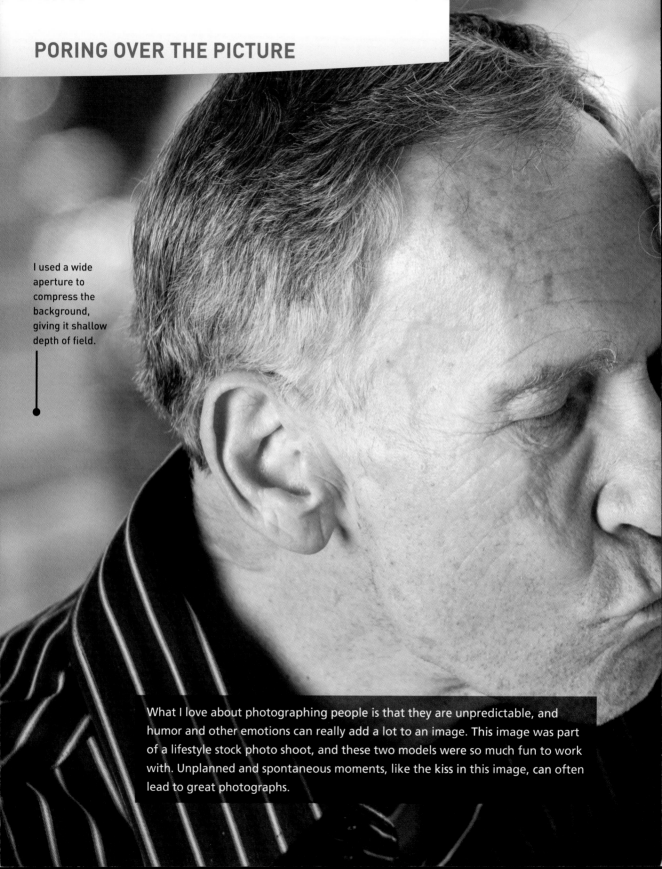

I used a wide aperture to compress the background, giving it shallow depth of field.

What I love about photographing people is that they are unpredictable, and humor and other emotions can really add a lot to an image. This image was part of a lifestyle stock photo shoot, and these two models were so much fun to work with. Unplanned and spontaneous moments, like the kiss in this image, can often lead to great photographs.

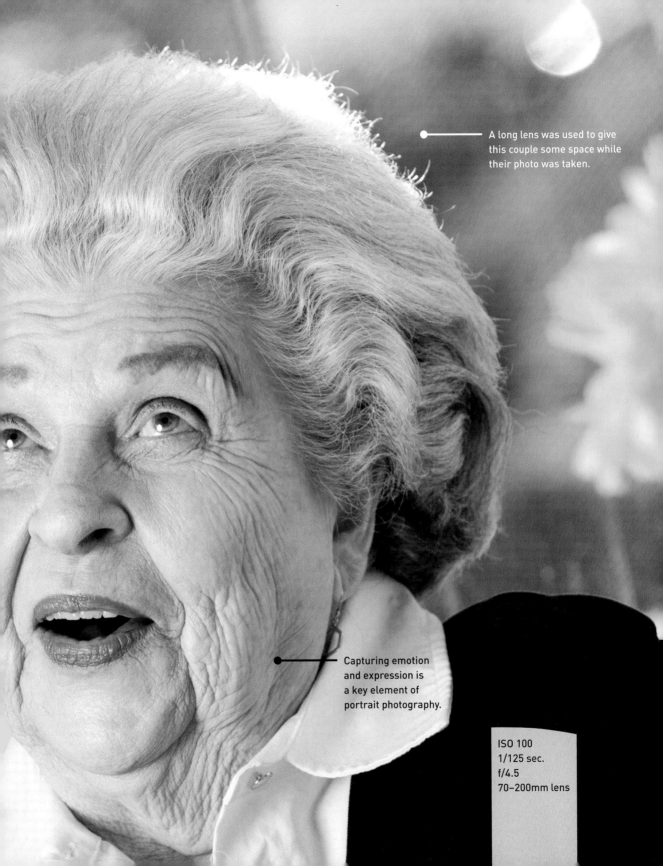

A long lens was used to give this couple some space while their photo was taken.

Capturing emotion and expression is a key element of portrait photography.

ISO 100
1/125 sec.
f/4.5
70–200mm lens

USING APERTURE PRIORITY MODE

In the previous chapter you learned about the different shooting modes, and when photographing people, you're likely to be most successful using the Aperture Priority (Av) mode. With portraits we usually like to see a nice, soft, out-of-focus background, and you can only guarantee that you'll achieve those results if you have full control of the aperture setting (**Figure 4.1**). You'll also be letting more light into your camera, which means that your ISO can be set lower, giving your image less noise and more detail.

Now, don't think that you have to use a crazy-fast lens (such as f/1.2 or f/2.8) to achieve great results and get a blurry background. Often an f-stop of 4.0 or 5.6 will be sufficient, and you might even find that having an extremely wide-open aperture gives you too little depth of field for a portrait, since you want most of the face to be in focus. I shoot the majority of my portrait photographs with a lens that has a maximum aperture of f/4, and I always achieve the results I'm looking for.

FIGURE 4.1
For this image I used a large aperture combined with a long lens to decrease the depth of field and make the background blurry.

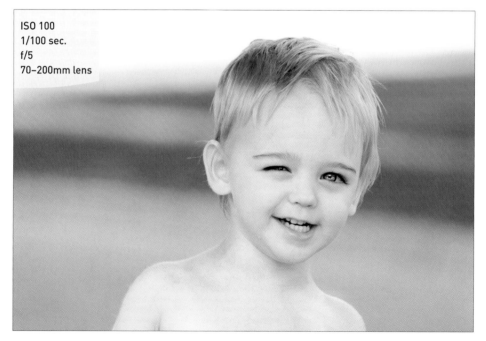

ISO 100
1/100 sec.
f/5
70–200mm lens

GO WIDE FOR ENVIRONMENTAL PORTRAITS

Sometimes you'll find that a person's environment is important to the story you want to tell. When photographing people this way, you will want to use a smaller aperture for greater depth of field so that you can include details of the scene surrounding the subject.

Also keep in mind that in order to capture the person and their surroundings, you'll need to adjust your view and use a wider than normal lens. Wide-angle lenses require less stopping down of the aperture to achieve greater depth of field. This is because wide-angle lenses cover a greater area, so the depth of field appears to cover a greater percentage of the scene.

A wider lens might also be necessary to relay more information about the scenery (**Figure 4.2**). Select a lens length that is wide enough to tell the story but not so wide that you distort the subject. There's nothing quite as unflattering as giving someone a big, distorted nose (unless you are going for that sort of look). When shooting a portrait with a wide-angle lens, keep the subject away from the edge of the frame. This will reduce the distortion, especially in very wide focal lengths.

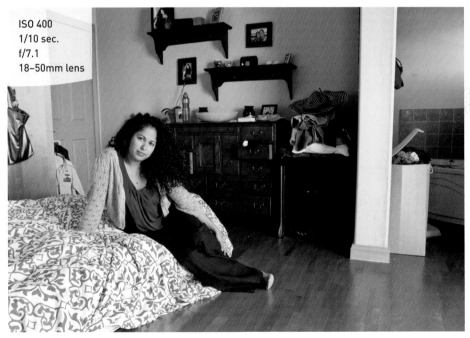

ISO 400
1/10 sec.
f/7.1
18–50mm lens

FIGURE 4.2
A wide-angle lens and a small aperture allowed me to show as much detail as possible in the room.

LIGHTING IS EVERYTHING

Photography is all about capturing light, so the most important thing in all of your images is the quality of the light on your subject. When you photograph people, you typically have a lot of control over when and where the image is taken, so you can manipulate your environment and find the best possible light for your subject.

Before I get into what you should do, let me first talk about what *not* to do. It's a common misconception that bright sunlight is great for portrait photographs. Of course, this is not entirely untrue, since there are some creative and amazing ways to use harsh natural sunlight and make great portraits. The problem is that when the sun is at its highest point, in the middle of the day, it's going to cast some very harsh shadows on your subject and probably make them squinty-eyed as well.

There are several easy ways to achieve beautifully lit portraits in an outdoors setting, and here are my two favorites. The first is to find shade. It might not seem like it at first, but on a sunny day an extraordinary amount of light fills shaded areas, for example, on the side of a building or underneath a covered patio. This light is diffused sunlight and will give a very soft, even light on your subject's face (**Figure 4.3**).

FIGURE 4.3
The light was diffused evenly across the little boy's face in this image, taken in a shady area on the side of a house.

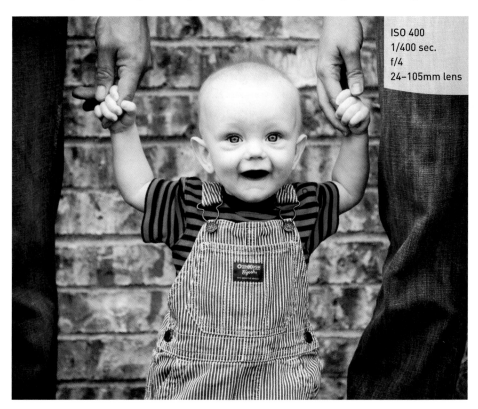

ISO 400
1/400 sec.
f/4
24–105mm lens

The second way to light your images outdoors is to use the light that occurs during the "golden hour" of the day. This is the time period that occurs one hour after sunrise and one hour before sunset (many photographers are more likely to use the evening light since it's more convenient). The quality of this light is soft, warm-toned, and very pleasing for portraits.

WHEN TO USE THE POP-UP FLASH

I'm not usually a big fan of using the pop-up flash or any type of on-axis flash, which is a light source that comes from the same direction as the camera. It usually results in lighting that is very flat, and often adds harsh shadows behind the subject. But you won't always have the perfect lighting situation for each photograph, so keeping an on-camera ready-to-go flash on-hand can be very practical. It's also good for those moments when you just have to get the shot and there's not a lot of light available, for example, if your baby takes his or her first steps in a dark room. You wouldn't want to miss that, and the pop-up flash is a handy tool to help capture those moments.

The flash can also be useful if you are in a situation where the afternoon sunlight is the only light available and you need to use a fill light. A fill light will "fill in" the areas in your subject that are not already lit by the main light, in this case the sun. When photographing people outdoors in the direct sunlight, you don't want them to face directly into the light. Try to position your subject so the sun is off to their side or behind them. This is a good situation in which to use a fill light, such as the pop-up flash on your 7D, to properly expose their face (**Figure 4.4**).

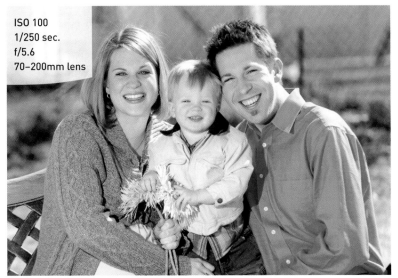

ISO 100
1/250 sec.
f/5.6
70–200mm lens

FIGURE 4.4
I positioned this family with the sun out of their faces and filled in the shadows with a flash.

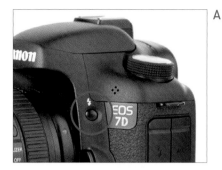

1. Press the Flash button to raise your pop-up flash into the ready position (**A**).

2. Press the ISO/Flash Exposure Compensation button (**B**).

3. Turn the Quick Control dial to change the flash exposure (this is similar to exposure compensation, but you are only affecting the amount of light that your flash will generate for each shot).

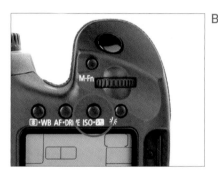

4. Take a photograph and check your LCD Monitor to see if it looks good. If not, try increasing or reducing the flash meter in one-third-stop increments until you get the correct amount of fill-flash for your shot.

There are other options for filling in areas of your image that need additional light. A reflector is a very common and inexpensive accessory that you can use to bounce light back onto your subject (**Figure 4.5**). You can buy these at any camera store, but you could even use a large piece of white foam core or anything that is reflective (like a sun shade for the windshield of your car) to get similar results.

METERING MODE FOR PORTRAITS

Your camera gives you four different metering modes that tell it where and how to meter the light. Each mode has a unique way of reading the scene, and which mode you use will depend on the environment you are shooting in.

I use the Evaluative metering mode for the majority of my work, and this mode is ideal for portraits. However, sometimes you'll run into situations where the background is much darker or lighter than the person you are photographing, which could give you an incorrect exposure. In these cases you'll want to use Partial metering, which will meter a smaller portion of the center of the frame (**Figure 4.6**). The great thing about digital SLRs is that with instant feedback on the LCD, you are able to make adjustments as needed if the metering mode didn't measure the light properly.

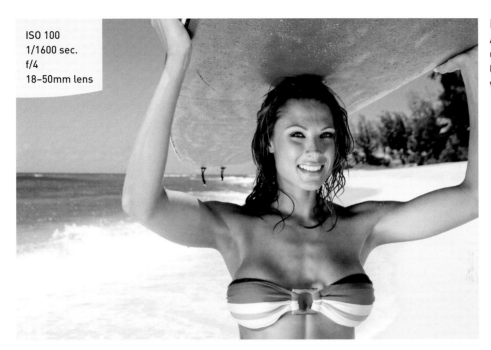

ISO 100
1/1600 sec.
f/4
18–50mm lens

FIGURE 4.5
A reflector was used to bounce light back onto this woman's face.

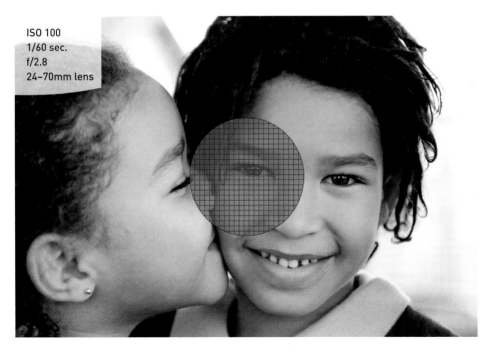

ISO 100
1/60 sec.
f/2.8
24–70mm lens

FIGURE 4.6
The shaded circle in the center represents the area in your image that the Partial metering mode will meter from while you are looking through the viewfinder.

SHOOTING WITH THE AE LOCK FEATURE

Once you select your metering, you can lock that setting in your camera temporarily if you want to recompose your image—for example, if you are in an environment where there is sufficient light on your subject but the background is significantly brighter or darker. The metering in your camera is continuous, meaning it will change depending on where the center of the viewfinder is pointed. If you have composed the image so that the person is off-center, the camera will meter the wrong part of the scene.

To correct this, you can meter for one part of the image (your subject), lock those settings down so they don't change, and then recompose the scene and take your photo. Here's how to use the AE Lock feature on the 7D:

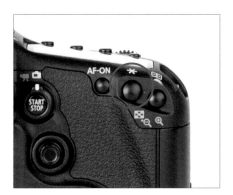

FIGURE 4.7

1. Find the AE Lock button on the back of the camera and place your thumb on it (**Figure 4.7**).

2. While looking through the viewfinder, place the center focus point on your subject.

3. Press and hold the AE Lock button to get a meter reading.

4. Recompose your shot, and then take the photo.

5. To take more than one photo without having to take another meter reading, just hold down the AE Lock button until you are done using the meter setting.

FOCUSING: THE EYES HAVE IT

When you look at a person, probably the very first thing you notice is their eyes—it's just natural to make eye contact with other people, and we even do this with pets and other animals. This is extremely important when taking photographs because you want to be sure that your focus is on your subject's eyes (**Figure 4.8**). Also keep in mind that if the person is positioned at an angle, it's best to focus on the eye that is nearest the camera, since that's where we naturally tend to look first (**Figure 4.9**).

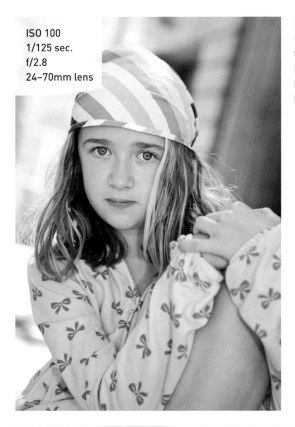

ISO 100
1/125 sec.
f/2.8
24–70mm lens

FIGURE 4.8
It's important to set your focus on a person's eyes when photographing portraits.

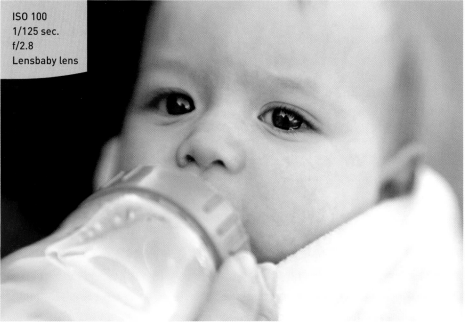

ISO 100
1/125 sec.
f/2.8
Lensbaby lens

FIGURE 4.9
I focused on this little boy's left eye since it was closest to my camera.

In Chapter 1, I discussed the different focusing points you can use with your 7D. In my experience, the best option for portrait work is Single-Point AF. You can move the focus around within your viewfinder to find the eye, ensuring that you are focusing on the proper part of the image before taking your photo. Leaving the focusing decision up to the camera means you could end up with an in-focus nose and blurry eyes, or, even worse, it might try to focus on the background instead of the person.

FOCUSING TIP FOR PORTRAIT WORK

When focusing on your subject's eyes, do your best to focus on the iris—the colored part of the eyeball. This is especially important if you are doing a very close-up portrait where the person's face fills most of the frame, since the focus area will be much more noticeable. Sometimes, if you're shooting with a large aperture and have shallow depth of field, it's easy to miss focus and instead have the eyelash in focus and the eyeball a bit blurry.

SETTING YOUR FOCUS TO A SINGLE POINT

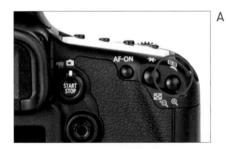

1. Press the AF Point Selection button (**A**) and look in your viewfinder.

2. Press the M.Fn button on the top of your camera, located next to the Shutter button (**B**), until you see the setting with one small red square inside the viewfinder.

3. Use the Main dial, the Multi-Controller, or the Quick Control dial to set the location of your focus point. I prefer to use the Multi-Controller because it acts like a joystick, and it's easier to place the focus point where I need it.

I typically set the focus point location in the middle, find my subject's eye, and press the Shutter button halfway to set focus. With my finger still holding the shutter halfway down, I recompose and take my photo. I find that the "focus and recompose" method is a much quicker way to photograph people. Speed is important because people tend to move around during the shooting process, and keeping the focus point in the middle simplifies my shooting.

CATCHLIGHT

A *catchlight* is that little sparkle that adds life to the eyes (**Figure 4.10**). When you are photographing a person with a light source in front of them, you will usually get a reflection of that light in the eye, be it your flash, the sun, or something else brightly reflecting in the eye. The light reflects off the surface of the eyes as bright highlights and serves to bring attention to the eyes. Larger catchlights from a reflector or studio softbox tend to be more attractive than tiny catchlights from a flash.

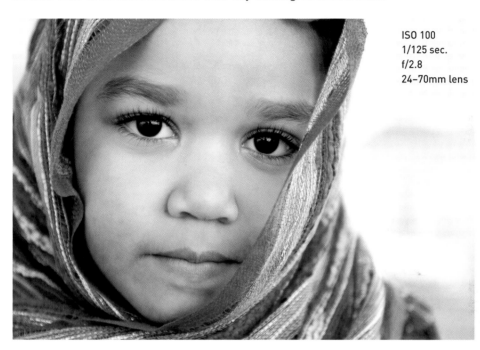

ISO 100
1/125 sec.
f/2.8
24–70mm lens

FIGURE 4.10
The catchlights in this image add a sparkle to the little girl's somber expression.

COMPOSING PEOPLE AND PORTRAITS

When photographing people it can be easy to get carried away with focusing on their expressions and checking your exposure, but it's always crucial to consider how the photo is composed. The placement of the person, as well as the perspective and angle you are using, can make or break the shot. Here are a few simple tips to help you create some amazing portrait compositions.

RULE OF THIRDS

One of the most basic rules of composition, the "rule of thirds" is a very good principle to stick with when photographing people. It states that you should place the subject of your photograph on a "third-line" within the frame of your viewfinder. Imagine a tic-tac-toe board, with two lines spaced evenly down the center of the frame both horizontally and vertically (**Figure 4.11**). Your goal is to place the subject on one of the intersecting lines—you're basically trying to keep the person off-center without pushing them too close to the edge of the frame.

FIGURE 4.11
The woman's face in this photo was positioned on one of the intersecting third-lines for a pleasing composition.

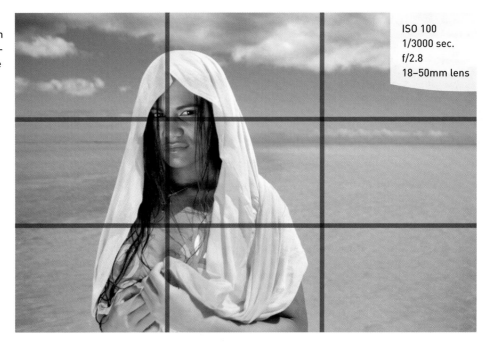

ISO 100
1/3000 sec.
f/2.8
18–50mm lens

Another thing to keep in mind is that you want to fill the frame as much as possible with your subject. This doesn't mean that you should get in so close that you have nothing in the shot but their face, but rather that you should be close enough so that you aren't adding anything to the image that you don't want to see. This is usually done by sticking to the third-line principle of framing the head near the top third of the frame. When I hand my camera to a friend to take my photo, I always chuckle to myself when I look at the image afterwards and my head is completely centered in the frame. I usually just go into editing software and crop out the excess headroom, making it look like it was properly composed. However, it's much easier and more efficient to do as much of the work in-camera as possible.

The great thing about the 7D is that you can add a grid overlay to your viewfinder and LCD (when shooting in Live View) to help you with the composition. You'll need to set up each one individually, but if it's something that you find useful, it's worth taking the extra steps.

SETTING UP THE GRID DISPLAY IN YOUR VIEWFINDER

1. Press the Menu button and go to the second setup menu tab (fourth tab from the right).

2. Use the Quick Control dial and scroll down to the last menu item, labeled VF Grid Display (**A**).

3. Press the Set button and select Enable (**B**). You will now see a grid overlay when you look through your viewfinder.

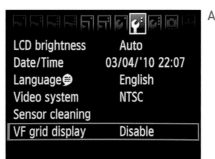

A

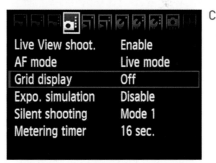

B

SETTING UP THE GRID DISPLAY FOR LIVE VIEW SHOOTING

1. Press the Menu button and go to the fourth shooting menu tab (fourth tab from the left).

2. Use the Quick Control dial and scroll down to the menu item labeled Grid Display (**C**).

3. Press the Set button and select Grid 1 (**D**). I prefer this grid because it clearly shows the third-lines on the frame. Press the Set button to lock in this change.

4. Next, press the Live View shooting button, located on the back of your camera, and you'll see a grid overlay on your LCD Monitor.

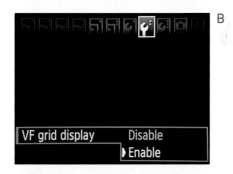

C

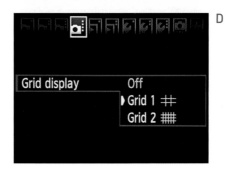

D

PERSPECTIVE

When taking photos, it's very easy to take all of your images from a standing position. This of course will vary in height from person to person, but so will the people you are photographing. I usually carry a small stepladder with me when I go on location so I can vary my height with the people I'm photographing, especially since I'm shorter than most other people. The basic rule to follow is to try to stay eye-level with your subject, which could mean flopping down on your belly to photograph a child or baby (**Figure 4.12**).

FIGURE 4.12
It's often a good idea to get down to a child's level when taking their picture—I got down on my belly in the sand to photograph this adorable baby boy.

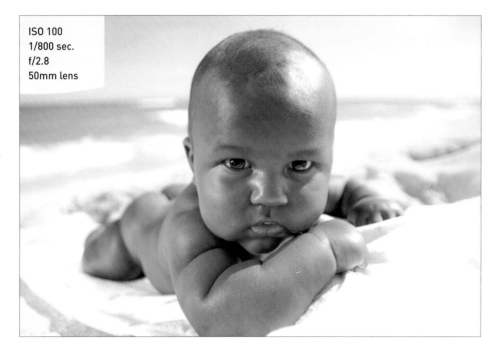

ISO 100
1/800 sec.
f/2.8
50mm lens

Another technique I like to use is to shoot my photos three different ways—vertical, horizontal, and slanted. I will often do one of each with the subject I'm photographing, and these are all very good ways to angle your camera for portraits. Sometimes you don't realize what will make a pleasing image until you try it out, so it's good to experiment a little bit to see what works best. My favorite angle to shoot at is a slanted angle, also referred to as "Dutch angle" (**Figure 4.13**). I find that doing this gives my images a sense of motion and uniqueness, since our eyes want to see things straight up and down.

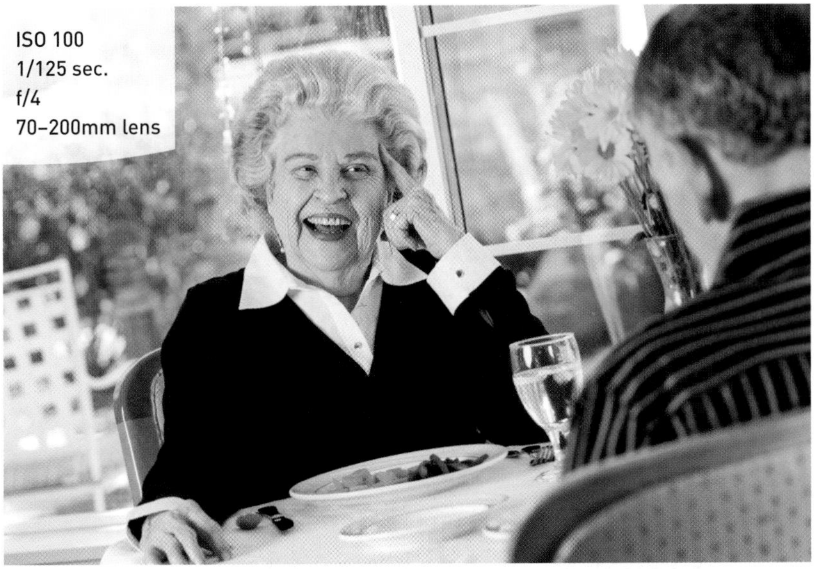

ISO 100
1/125 sec.
f/4
70–200mm lens

FIGURE 4.13
This image was photographed from a position sometimes referred to as "Dutch angle."

BREAK THE RULES!

So now that I've given you all of these great rules to follow when composing your image, the last rule I'm going to tell you is to break all of them! Don't think that you always need to keep an image off-center or that you have to photograph children at their level all the time (**Figure 4.14**). Experiment and find new ways to capture your images—you just might find that breaking the rules was the best thing you could have done for your image.

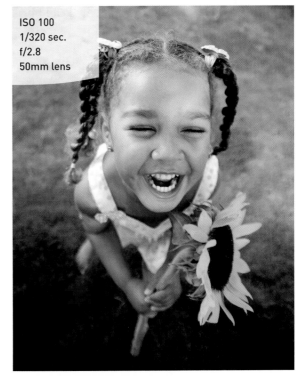

ISO 100
1/320 sec.
f/2.8
50mm lens

FIGURE 4.14
Breaking rules can sometimes yield great results—this image was photographed from high up, a perspective that you usually would not photograph children from.

THE PORTRAIT PICTURE STYLE FOR BETTER SKIN TONES

In Chapter 1 I discussed the different picture styles the 7D has to offer, and as you have probably guessed, the Portrait style is best for photographing people. The default Portrait settings give your images a softer look, but the neat thing about the styles in general is that you have the ability to change the settings to increase or decrease the amount of sharpness, contrast, saturation, and color tone to your preference.

SETTING THE PORTRAIT PICTURE STYLE

1. Wake the camera (if necessary) by lightly pressing the Shutter button.
2. Press the Picture Style Selection button on the back of the camera (**A**).
3. Use either the Main dial or the Quick Control dial to scroll through to the Portrait style (**B**).
4. If you would like to make any changes to the style, press the INFO button and use the Multi-Controller or Quick Control dial to select the setting you would like to adjust (**C**). Then press the Set button and use the same dial to change the setting (**D**).
5. Press the Set button to lock in this change, and then press the Menu button to go back to the Picture Style screen.

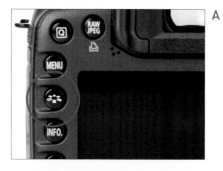

A

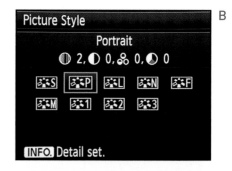

B

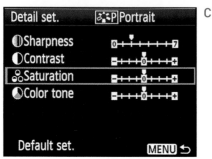

C

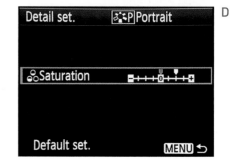

D

BEAUTIFUL BLACK AND WHITE PORTRAITS

Sometimes a portrait just looks better in black and white—we see more of the person and their expression rather than their surroundings or the color of their clothing (**Figure 4.15**). You can change the picture style to Monochrome in your camera so that you are photographing the image in black and white, but when you do this, you are only giving yourself one option. If you decide you liked it better in color, you have no way to change it back.

I prefer to do all of my black and white conversions while editing the photo on my computer, and I encourage you to do the same. You can make black and white conversions, along with many other types of adjustments to your images, by using the Canon Digital Photo Professional software on the disc included with your camera.

ISO 100
1/80 sec.
f/2.8
24–70mm lens

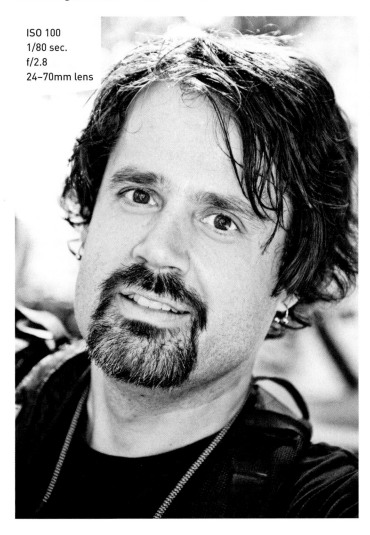

FIGURE 4.15
A black and white portrait eliminates the distraction of color and puts all the emphasis on the subject.

TIPS FOR SHOOTING BETTER PORTRAITS

Before we get to the challenges for this chapter, I thought it might be a good idea to discuss some tips that don't necessarily have anything specific to do with your camera. There are entire books that cover things like portrait lighting, posing, and so on. But here are a few pointers that will make your people photos look a lot better.

AVOID THE CENTER OF THE FRAME

This falls under the category of composition. Place your subject to the side of the frame (**Figure 4.16**)—it just looks more interesting than plunking them smack dab in the middle.

FIGURE 4.16
An off-center image creates a pleasing composition.

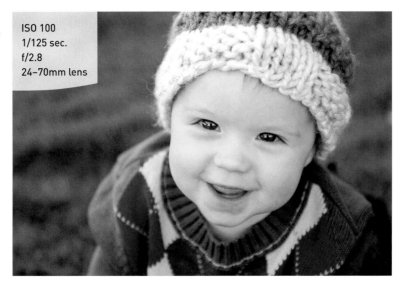

ISO 100
1/125 sec.
f/2.8
24–70mm lens

CHOOSE THE RIGHT LENS

Choosing the correct lens can make a huge impact on your portraits. A wide-angle lens can distort the features of your subject, which can lead to an unflattering portrait. Select a longer focal length if you will be close to your subject (**Figure 4.17**).

USE THE FRAME

Have you ever noticed that most people are taller than they are wide? Turn your camera vertically for a more pleasing composition (**Figure 4.18**).

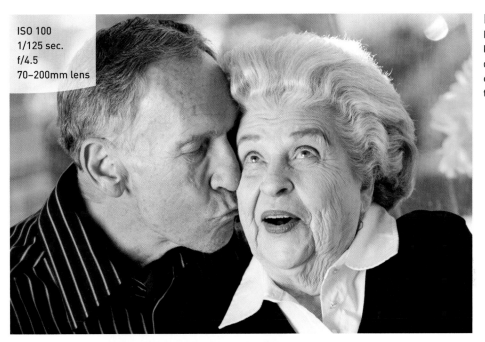

ISO 100
1/125 sec.
f/4.5
70–200mm lens

FIGURE 4.17
I used a long focal length to keep my distance from this couple while taking their picture.

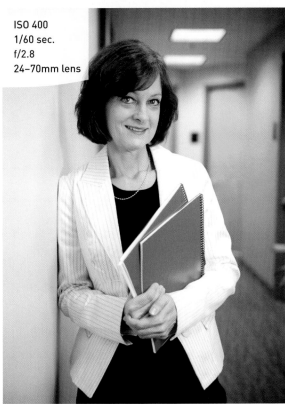

ISO 400
1/60 sec.
f/2.8
24–70mm lens

FIGURE 4.18
A vertically composed image is a good choice for many portraits.

SUNBLOCK FOR PORTRAITS

The midday sun can be harsh and can do unflattering things to people's faces. If you can, find a shady spot out of the direct sunlight (**Figure 4.19**). You will get softer shadows, smoother skin tones, and better detail. This holds true for overcast skies as well. Just be sure to adjust your white balance accordingly.

FIGURE 4.19
A shady area will give you beautiful, diffused lighting for portraits.

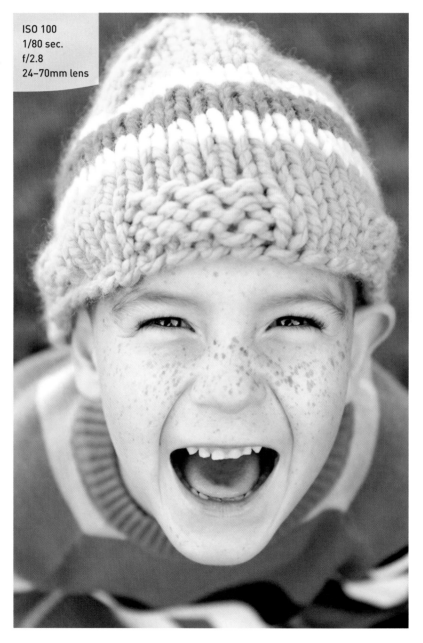

ISO 100
1/80 sec.
f/2.8
24–70mm lens

KEEP AN EYE ON YOUR BACKGROUND

Sometimes it's so easy to get caught up in taking a great shot that you forget about the smaller details. Try to keep an eye on what is going on behind your subject so they don't end up with things popping out of their heads (**Figure 4.20**).

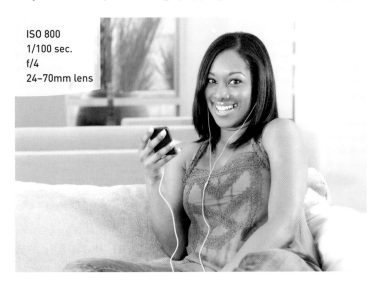

ISO 800
1/100 sec.
f/4
24–70mm lens

FIGURE 4.20
I positioned this model so that there were no distracting elements directly behind her.

MORE THAN JUST A PRETTY FACE

Most people think of a portrait as a photo of someone's face. Don't ignore other aspects of your subject that reflect their personality—hands, especially, can go a long way toward describing someone (**Figure 4.21**).

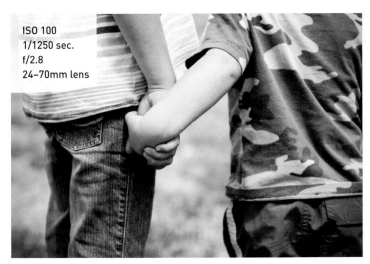

ISO 100
1/1250 sec.
f/2.8
24–70mm lens

FIGURE 4.21
Find other ways to photograph people—this image of children holding hands tells a story without having to show their faces.

GET DOWN ON THEIR LEVEL

If you want better pictures of children, don't shoot from an adult's eye level. Getting the camera down to the child's level will make your images look more personal (**Figure 4.22**).

FIGURE 4.22
Children look their best when photographed from their level.

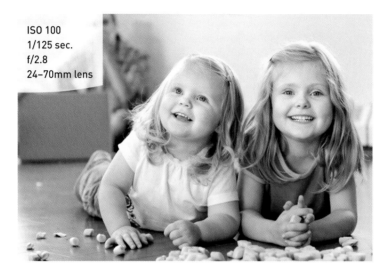

ISO 100
1/125 sec.
f/2.8
24–70mm lens

DON'T BE AFRAID TO GET CLOSE

When you are taking someone's picture, don't be afraid of getting close and filling the frame (**Figure 4.23**). This doesn't mean you have to shoot from a foot away; try zooming in and capturing the details.

FIGURE 4.23
Fill the frame to focus the attention on the person rather than their surroundings.

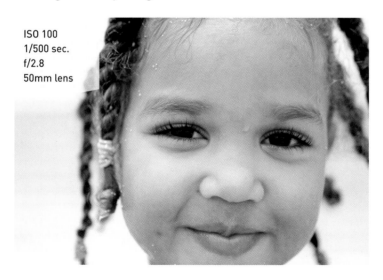

ISO 100
1/500 sec.
f/2.8
50mm lens

FIND CANDID MOMENTS

Sometimes the best images are the ones that aren't posed. Find moments when people are just being themselves (**Figure 4.24**) and use a faster shutter speed to capture expressions that happen quickly (**Figure 4.25**).

ISO 100
1/800 sec.
f/3.2
70–200mm lens

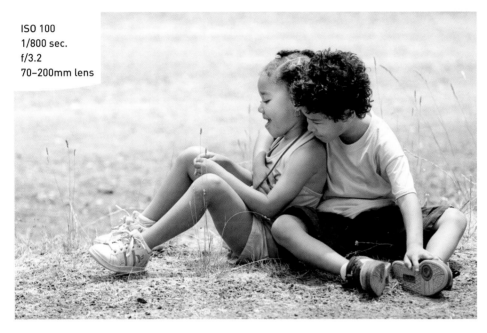

FIGURE 4.24
Sometimes the best photos are the ones that weren't planned—find these moments in your models and you can capture their true selves.

ISO 100
1/320 sec.
f/2.8
70–200mm lens

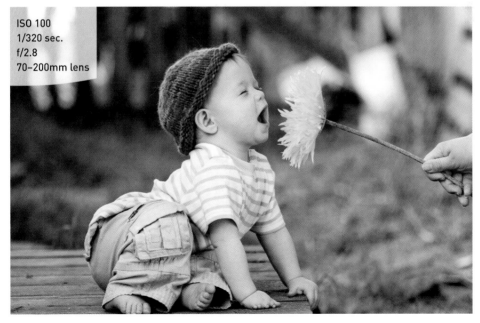

FIGURE 4.25
A fast shutter speed will help to capture moments that pass quickly.

SHOOT HIGH AND LOW

Portraits don't always need to be photographed at eye level. Try moving up, down, and all around. Shooting from a high angle is a flattering way to photograph most people (**Figure 4.26**), and sometimes it can be fun to get down on the ground and shoot up at your subject (**Figure 4.27**).

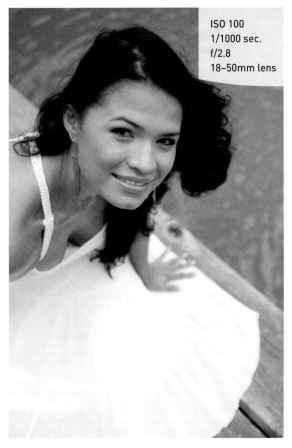

ISO 100
1/1000 sec.
f/2.8
18–50mm lens

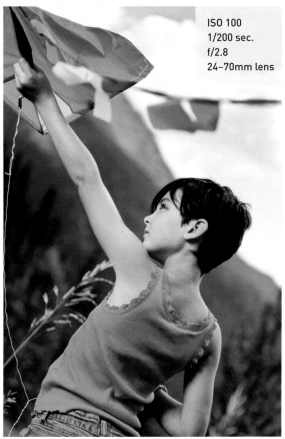

ISO 100
1/200 sec.
f/2.8
24–70mm lens

FIGURE 4.26
Try photographing portraits from different angles and perspectives.

FIGURE 4.27
I shot this from a lower perspective to include the kite in the image without introducing any distracting background elements.

Chapter 4 Challenges

Depth of field in portraits

Let's start with something simple. Grab your favorite person and start experimenting with using different aperture settings. Shoot wide open (the widest your lens goes, such as f/2.8 or f/4) and then really stopped down (like f/22). Look at the difference in the depth of field and the important role it plays in placing the attention on your subject. (Make sure your subject isn't standing directly against the background. Give some distance so that there is a good blurring effect of the background at the wide f-stop setting.)

Discovering the qualities of natural light

Pick a nice sunny day and try shooting some portraits in the midday sun. If your subject is willing, have them turn so the sun is in their face. If they are still speaking to you after blinding them, ask them to turn their back to the sun. Try this with and without the fill flash so you can see the difference. Finally, move them into a completely shaded spot and take a few more.

Picking the right metering method

Find a very dark or light background and place your subject in front of it. Now take a couple of shots, giving a lot of space around your subject for the background to show. Now switch metering modes and use the AE Lock feature to get a more accurate reading of your subject. Notice the differences in exposure between the metering methods.

Picture styles for portraits

Have some fun playing with the different picture styles. Try the Portrait style as compared to the Standard style. Play with the different adjustment settings within the styles to see how they affect skin tones.

Share your results with the book's Flickr group!

Join the group here: flickr.com/groups/canon7dfromsnapshotstogreatshots

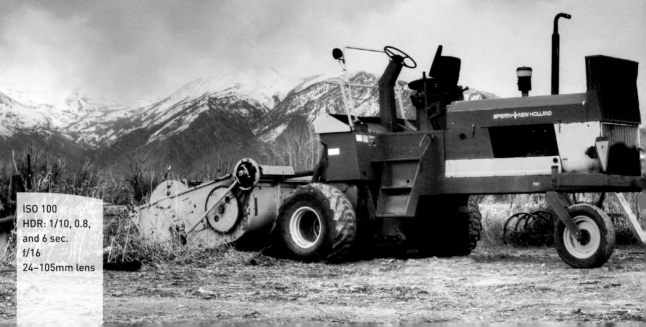

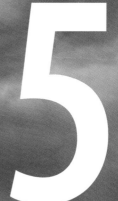

5

ISO 100
HDR: 1/10, 0.8,
and 6 sec.
f/16
24–105mm lens

Landscape Photography

TIPS, TOOLS, AND TECHNIQUES TO GET THE MOST OUT OF YOUR LANDSCAPE PHOTOGRAPHY

There's something fun and challenging about relying on Mother Nature when trying to capture great landscape images, because a scene can change dramatically from moment to moment depending on the weather. I feel that I lose some control over my images, but that's what makes photographing nature so intriguing. Now, I'll be honest—I'm not a huge fan of getting up at 5 a.m., before the sun rises. But on the rare occasions that I've found myself out in the middle of nowhere with a tripod and camera in tow, I have experienced some of my most relaxing and peaceful photographic moments.

In this chapter, we will explore some of the features of the 7D that not only improve the look of your landscape photography, but also make it easier to take great shots. We will also explore some typical scenarios and discuss methods that will bring out the best in your landscape photography.

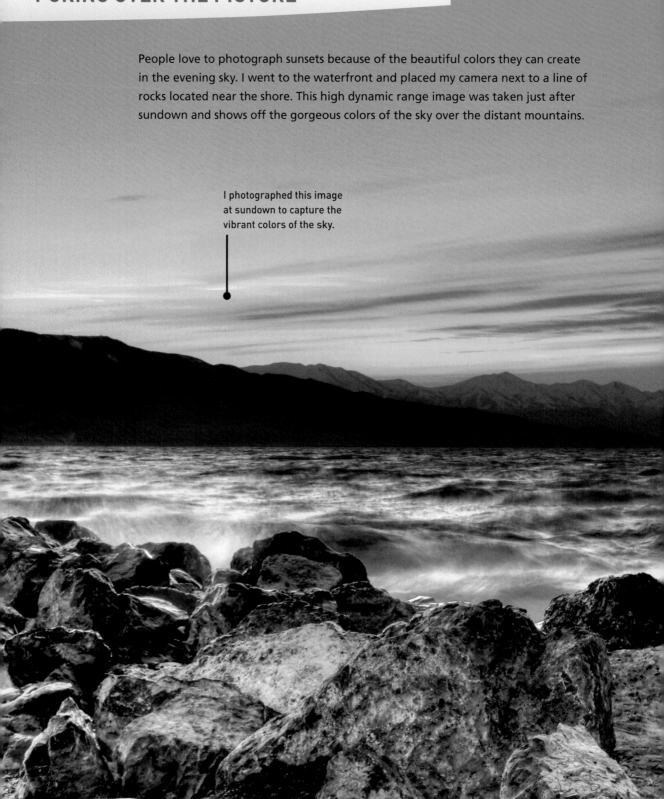

PORING OVER THE PICTURE

People love to photograph sunsets because of the beautiful colors they can create in the evening sky. I went to the waterfront and placed my camera next to a line of rocks located near the shore. This high dynamic range image was taken just after sundown and shows off the gorgeous colors of the sky over the distant mountains.

I photographed this image at sundown to capture the vibrant colors of the sky.

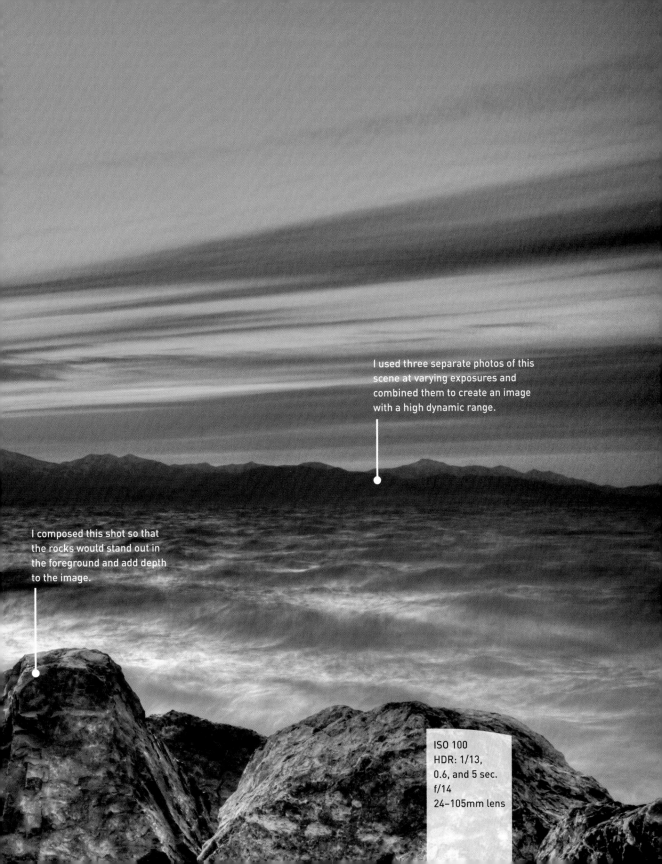

I used three separate photos of this scene at varying exposures and combined them to create an image with a high dynamic range.

I composed this shot so that the rocks would stand out in the foreground and add depth to the image.

ISO 100
HDR: 1/13,
0.6, and 5 sec.
f/14
24–105mm lens

PORING OVER THE PICTURE

This photograph of The Three Gossips in Arches National Park is one of my favorite shots from my time spent in the park. Each time I set up my camera to photograph a landscape it draws me in, and this was no exception. I find this location particularly intriguing and was spellbound by the different rock formations there.

I used the electronic level on my camera to make sure the horizon was even.

I created this HDR image from three different photographs and decided it would look best in black and white.

I photographed this with a wide focal length to add detail to the foreground of the image.

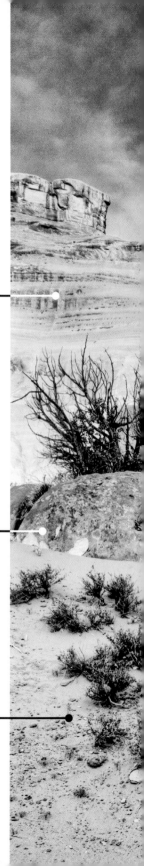

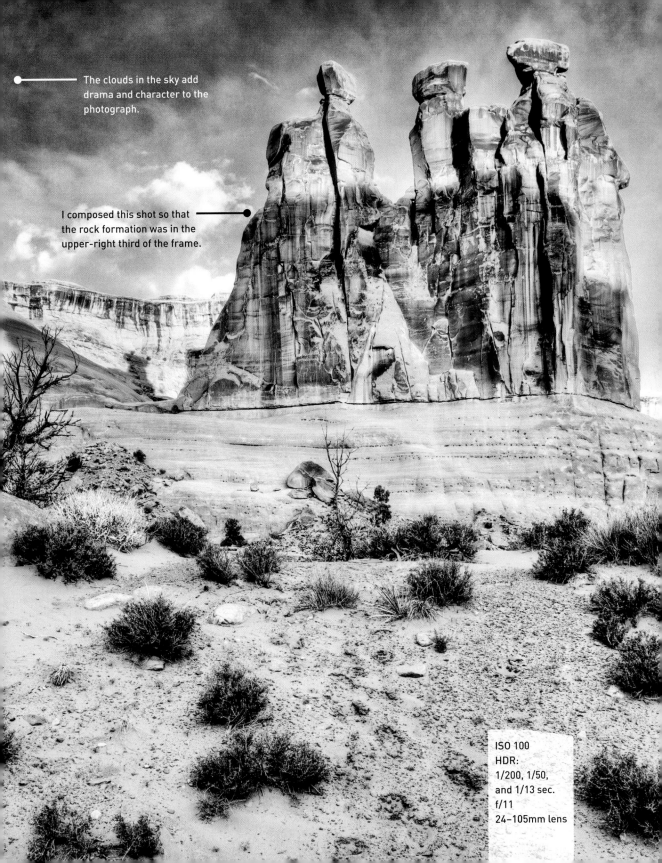

The clouds in the sky add drama and character to the photograph.

I composed this shot so that the rock formation was in the upper-right third of the frame.

ISO 100
HDR:
1/200, 1/50,
and 1/13 sec.
f/11
24–105mm lens

SHARP AND IN FOCUS: USING TRIPODS

Many features of the 7D will help you create amazing images, but you'll quickly discover that there is another piece of equipment that's crucial when photographing landscapes: the tripod. Tripods are critical to your landscape work for a couple of reasons. The first relates to the time of day you will be shooting. To get the best light in your images, you will be shooting at sunrise or sunset, when it's rather dark. When shooting in a dark environment, you need to increase the exposure time, which will result in a slow shutter speed—too slow for handheld photography.

The second reason is that when you are shooting landscapes, you usually want the entire field of view to be in focus (for greater depth of field). In order to achieve this, you will be shooting at very small apertures, which will require you to compensate with a longer, slower shutter speed.

Let's quickly review why using a tripod is so important when you have a slow shutter speed. As you already know, the physical shutter on your camera opens and closes to capture light coming through your lens. The longer this shutter stays open, the more camera shake and blur you could potentially add to your image if the camera or subject is moving. With landscapes, your subject is not moving (for the most part), so by keeping your camera still, you prevent adding blur to your image. Keeping your image sharp and in focus is one of the key ingredients in creating a beautiful landscape photo.

TRIPOD STABILITY

Most tripods have a center column that allows the user to extend the height of the camera above the point where the tripod legs join together. This might seem like a great idea, but the reality is that the more you raise that column, the less stable your tripod becomes. Think of a tall building that sways near the top. To get the most solid base for your camera, try to use it with the center column at its lowest point so that your camera is right at the apex of the tripod legs.

So, what type of tripod should you use? There are so many options that it can be difficult to find the right one if you're not sure what you're looking for. I suggest finding a tripod that is light, portable, and very sturdy. These features will add to the expense, but if you plan on photographing a lot of images using a tripod, it's worth the investment. Tripods last for a long time—they don't need upgrades or have hardware failures like other mechanical and electronic equipment. You are also much more likely to use something that is easy to take with you. I have three different tripods: a very large, sturdy tripod that usually stays in my studio because it's so heavy; a cheap, light, flimsy tripod that I don't take anywhere because it isn't sturdy enough for my camera; and one that's right in-between the two—a lightweight, portable, sturdy tripod. If you can afford one, get yourself a tripod made out of carbon fiber. It's an extremely lightweight and strong material, so you'll be more likely to strap it to your camera bag and take it with you.

You'll also need a tripod head so you can attach your camera to the tripod. It's best to get a head with a quick-release plate so you can easily put your camera on and take it off the tripod.

IS LENSES AND TRIPODS DON'T MIX

If you are using image stabilization (IS) lenses on your camera, remember to turn off this feature when you use a tripod (**Figure 5.1**). The reason is that, while trying to minimize camera movement, the image stabilization can actually *create* movement when the camera is already stable. To turn off the IS feature, just slide the Stabilizer selector switch on the side of the lens to the Off position.

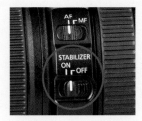

FIGURE 5.1
Be sure to turn off image stabilization when attaching your camera to a tripod.

CAMERA MODES AND EXPOSURE

When photographing traditional landscapes, you'll most likely want the entire scene to be in focus. To achieve this, you will need to use a small aperture to get great depth of field (**Figure 5.2**). You could always set your camera to Av mode (Aperture Priority) and set your aperture at around f/11 or f/16, but because the camera chooses the shutter speed it could vary, changing the look of your image. To prevent this, consider using Manual mode.

Just as with all other styles of photography, if you want to be in control of your images, you should select a shooting mode that allows you that control. Once you are set up and ready to shoot, the light in your scene probably won't change drastically in a short period of time, so your exposure will stay consistent as well. Shooting in Manual mode will ensure that you get the look you want, because you will have full control over both shutter speed and aperture.

FIGURE 5.2
This image was photographed at a very small aperture to ensure that the details in both the foreground and background were in focus.

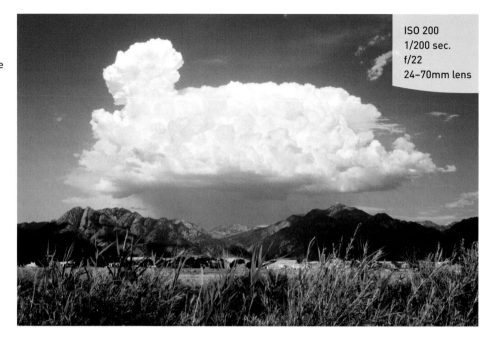

ISO 200
1/200 sec.
f/22
24–70mm lens

Now, just because most landscapes are photographed with great depth of field doesn't mean you *always* have to photograph your images the same way (**Figure 5.3**). There's no "right way" to do any one thing, so feel free to break the rules and try something new.

FIGURE 5.3
I used a wide aperture and focused on the flowers in the foreground to give the image shallow depth of field.

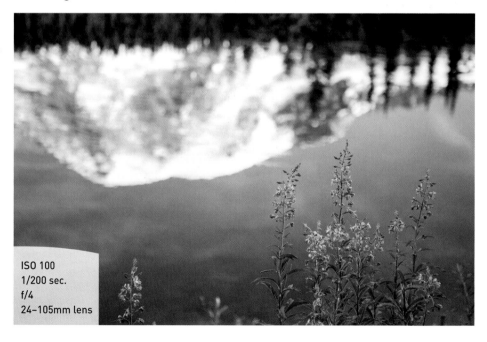

ISO 100
1/200 sec.
f/4
24–105mm lens

SELECTING THE PROPER ISO

We've already discussed setting your exposure and using a tripod; the next important factor to consider is the ISO. Since you're already shooting with a slow shutter speed, you are free to shoot with a very low ISO, such as 100. By using a low ISO you'll introduce very little digital noise into your images, thereby increasing the detail in your shots (**Figures 5.4** and **5.5**).

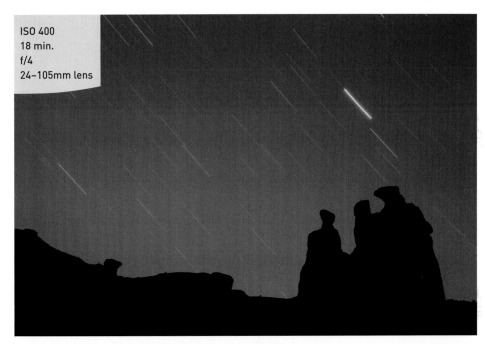

ISO 400
18 min.
f/4
24–105mm lens

FIGURE 5.4
I used a long exposure to photograph star trails, and there was enough ambient light to capture the image at a low ISO.

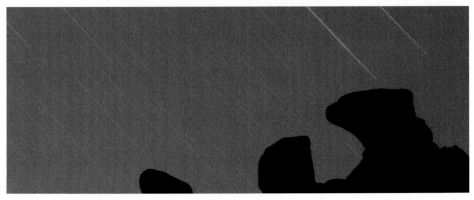

FIGURE 5.5
When zoomed in to 100%, there is some noticeable grain in this ISO 400 image, but it's still a small amount when compared with a much higher ISO.

A high ISO will not only add grain to the image; you'll also notice the colorful grain in the shadows. This is something you should generally try to avoid in order to get the highest-quality photographs you can (**Figures 5.6** and **5.7**).

FIGURE 5.6
I used a very high ISO in order to capture the stars at a fast exposure time and prevent creating star trails.

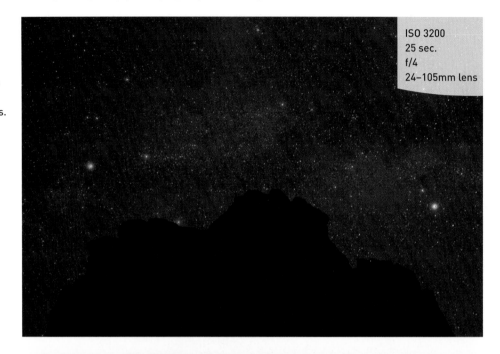

ISO 3200
25 sec.
f/4
24–105mm lens

FIGURE 5.7
The grain in this ISO 3200 image is very noticeable, detracting from the quality of the photograph.

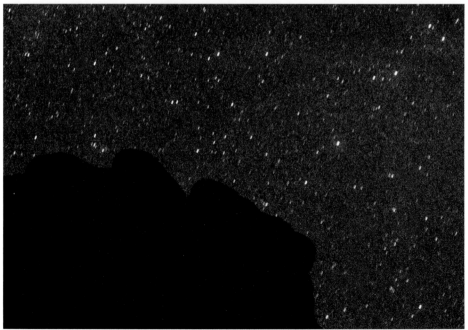

SELECTING A WHITE BALANCE AND PICTURE STYLE

You'll probably want to capture your image with a proper white balance, and with landscapes your options (such as the Daylight and Cloudy settings) are more straightforward than with some other types of photography. If you're shooting in RAW, you have some leeway when selecting the white balance in-camera, because it's easy to change it non-destructively after the fact. But my philosophy is that it's always best to get things right in-camera.

Just because there is a "correct" white balance for each scene doesn't necessarily mean that you need to stick with that setting. Try experimenting with different white balance settings to give your landscape images new looks. Changing the white balance in an image can even give the feel of photographing a landscape at different times of day (**Figures 5.8** and **5.9**).

WARM AND COOL COLOR TEMPERATURES

These two terms are used to describe the overall colorcast of an image. Reds and yellows are said to be *warm*, which is the look that you usually get from the late afternoon sun. Blue is usually the predominant color when talking about a *cool* cast.

I really like to use Live View to make changes to some of the settings, such as white balance. We discussed this feature in Chapter 1, but did you know that you can also use the same method to change your Picture Style settings? You may already realize that the likely picture style to use is Landscape, but maybe you want to try out some of the other styles or make detailed changes to their settings and see how it affects your image. Using Live View is an excellent way to preview those changes even before you take your first shot.

FIGURE 5.8
This image was photographed at sunset with the "proper" white balance—in this case, the Daylight setting.

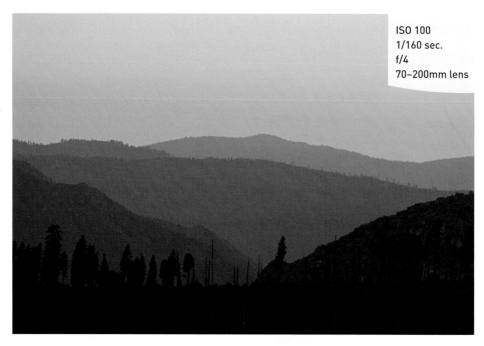

ISO 100
1/160 sec.
f/4
70–200mm lens

FIGURE 5.9
Switching the white balance to Fluorescent creates the impression that this image was taken in the early hours of the morning.

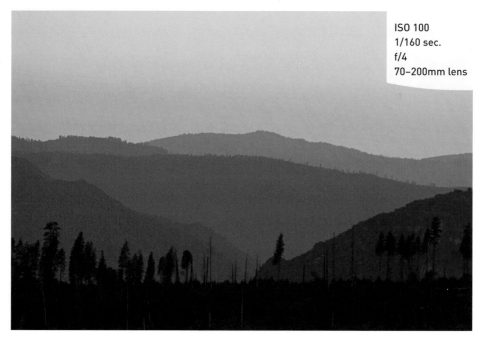

ISO 100
1/160 sec.
f/4
70–200mm lens

USING LIVE VIEW TO PREVIEW DIFFERENT PICTURE STYLE SETTINGS

1. Make sure the Live View shooting button is set to the white camera, and then press the START/STOP button.

2. With Live View activated, press the Picture Style Selection button to the left of the LCD Monitor.

3. Use the Main dial on the top of the camera to select among the different base picture style choices (**A**).

4. Once you've selected a picture style, you can change any of its four parameters by using the Quick Control dial to scroll among them (sharpness, contrast, saturation, and color tone). Once you've selected a parameter, use the Main dial to adjust its settings (**B**).

5. Press the Set button to lock in your changes.

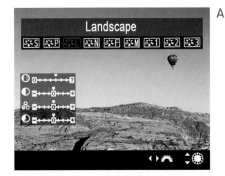

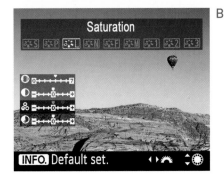

BALANCING YOUR IMAGE WITH THE ELECTRONIC LEVEL

Finding the horizon and making sure your camera is level is sometimes easier said than done. Photographing a flat landscape is one thing, but when you integrate mountains, rolling hills, and foliage into the image, you might not be able to see where the horizon line is, and you risk tilting your camera in one direction or the other.

Many tripods and tripod heads come with a bubble level, but there will be times that your tripod is propped at a weird angle and you won't be able to rely on it. The 7D has a really cool feature—called the electronic level—that can help you out with this. When the electronic level is activated, you can set the vertical and horizontal tilt and properly level your camera for landscape photography. You also have the option of viewing this feature either on the LCD Monitor or through the viewfinder (**Figures 5.10** and **5.11**). I usually prefer using the LCD Monitor, especially when my camera is on a tripod, but sometimes I don't want to take my eyes away from the viewfinder (which could slow down my shooting). In those situations, I use the viewfinder method.

FIGURE 5.10
You can view the electronic level in the LCD Monitor. This feature is available whether or not Live View is on (in this example, Live View is off).

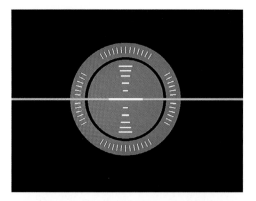

FIGURE 5.11
You can also view the electronic level through the viewfinder. In this example, the AF points that you see indicate that the camera is level horizontally and tilted upward vertically.

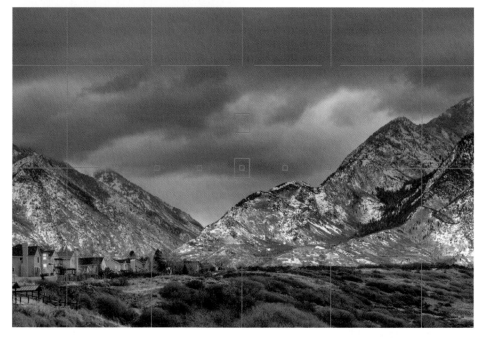

SETTING THE ELECTRONIC LEVEL IN THE LCD MONITOR

1. First be sure that you have the electronic level set up to display properly. To do so, press the Menu button and use the Main dial to select the third setup tab, then scroll down to INFO Button Display Options using the Quick Control dial (**A**). Press the Set button.

2. Make sure that there is a check mark next to the Electronic Level setting (**B**). If there isn't, use the Quick Control dial to scroll to it and then press the Set button (a check mark should appear). Use the Quick Control dial again to scroll down to OK, and then press Set.

3. Next, press the INFO button until the electronic level appears in the LCD Monitor. (To view the electronic level when using Live View, press the INFO button until it appears in the LCD Monitor.) You'll know the horizontal and vertical tilt are leveled when the red lines turn green (**C**).

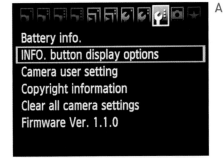

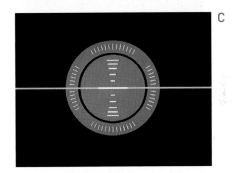

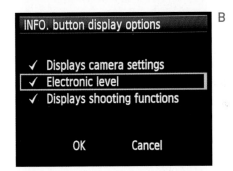

SETTING THE ELECTRONIC LEVEL IN THE VIEWFINDER

1. Press the Menu button and use the Main dial to scroll to the Custom Functions tab, and then use the Quick Control dial to highlight the C.Fn IV: Operation/Others item (**A**). Press the Set button.

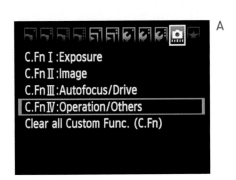

Continued on next page

2. Use the Quick Control dial to select C.Fn IV-1 (Custom Controls). Press the Set button and use the Main dial to highlight the M-Fn item (**B**). Press Set.

3. Scroll over to the VF Electronic Level item (**C**). Press Set to lock in your change.

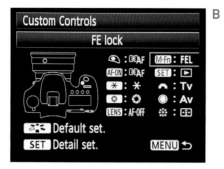 B

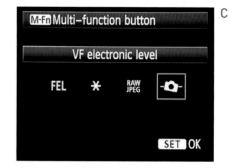 C

4. Now, look through the viewfinder as if you are going to take a photo. Press the M-Fn button (located next to the Shutter button). A grid will appear and you'll see black or red squares where your AF points usually appear. You'll know that the camera is level both vertically and horizontally when the only AF point visible is the one in the center (**D**). To exit from this mode, just press the Shutter button halfway.

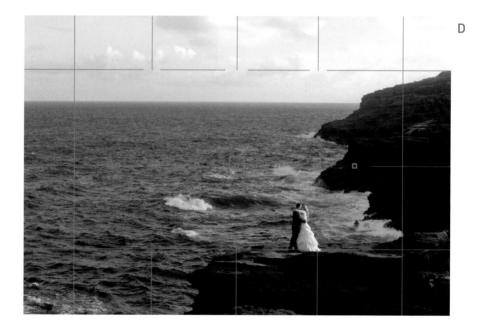 D

THE GOLDEN HOUR

In landscape photography, the quality of light is essential to making beautiful photos. Many photographers will tell you that their favorite time of day to take outdoor photographs is during the first and last hour of sunlight, also referred to as the "golden hour" or "magic hour" (**Figure 5.12**). This is because the light is coming from a very low angle to the landscape, creating shadows and providing depth and character. The light also adds color to the earth and the sky—and clouds in the image further add to that color.

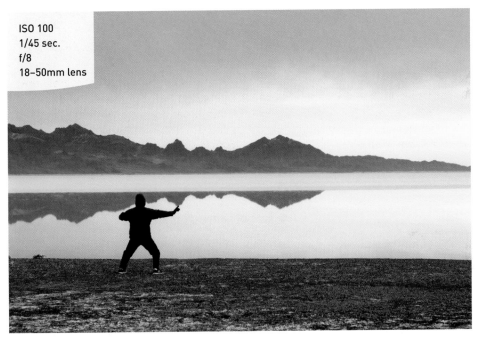

ISO 100
1/45 sec.
f/8
18–50mm lens

FIGURE 5.12
This image was photographed at sunrise, which added color to the sky and a beautiful reflection on the water.

If you ask me, the presence of clouds can always improve a landscape image, whether they're cute and fluffy or dark and stormy (**Figure 5.13**). During the golden hour, sunlight can reflect off the clouds, producing amazing color combinations that you would not see during the middle of the day. But be prepared—sometimes these color changes take place in a matter of minutes, so be ready to press that Shutter button!

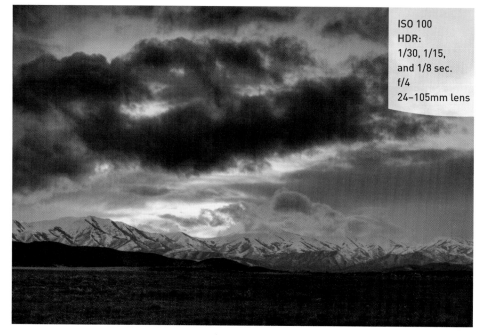

FIGURE 5.13
The presence of clouds, like those in this sunset photo, can transform an ordinary scene into an extraordinary one.

ISO 100
HDR:
1/30, 1/15, and 1/8 sec.
f/4
24–105mm lens

FOCUSING TIPS FOR LANDSCAPE PHOTOGRAPHY

We've already established that you will want to use a tripod to minimize camera shake and achieve sharper images, and that you should use a small aperture to get greater depth of field. But shooting at a small aperture doesn't necessarily mean that your entire scene will be in focus. Your goal is to find the spot within the scene that will help you get most of your image in focus.

Hyperfocal distance, also referred to as HFD, is the closest point of focus to the lens where the remaining distance (out to infinity) is acceptably in focus. Combining HFD with a small aperture will help you achieve a great depth of field, ideal for many landscape photographs. A simple way to achieve this is to focus on an object that is about one-third of the distance into your frame. This is the method used by most working pros and is the easiest to remember and apply while shooting.

When you view the image through the viewfinder, however, you don't always see the correct depth of field, and you might be tricked into thinking that you have more or less depth of field than you actually have. You can address this problem with your camera's Depth-of-Field Preview feature. This easy-to-use feature works when you look through the viewfinder and in Live View. When you have your focus set, just press the Depth-of-Field Preview button located on the front of the camera (**Figure 5.14**) and you'll see a visual representation of what the depth of field in the image will look like when you take the picture.

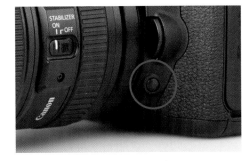

FIGURE 5.14
The Depth-of-Field Preview button will give you a preview of your image and shows how much of the scene will remain in focus.

MAKING WATER LOOK SILKY

Creating silky-looking images of streams, waterfalls, and even waves adds a beautiful touch to any landscape photo (**Figure 5.15**). Applying this effect to your images is simple—it's just a matter of using a very slow shutter speed to blur the water as it flows through your image. Of course, you'll need to place your camera on a tripod, and it's also a good idea to attach a cable release to prevent any potential camera shake when pressing the Shutter button. To achieve a great effect, use a shutter speed of at least 1/15 of a second or longer.

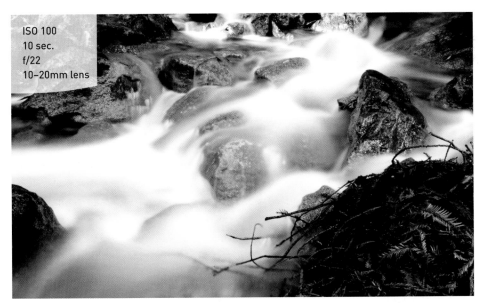

ISO 100
10 sec.
f/22
10–20mm lens

FIGURE 5.15
I used a neutral density filter to reduce the amount of light coming through the lens. This allowed for a longer exposure, which made the water in this stream look silky and fluid.

SETTING UP FOR A FLOWING WATER SHOT

1. Attach the camera to your tripod, and then compose and focus your shot.

2. Make sure the ISO is set to 100.

3. Using Av mode, set your aperture to the smallest opening (such as f/22 or f/36).

4. Press the Shutter button halfway so the camera takes a meter reading.

5. Check to see if the shutter speed is 1/15 or slower.

6. Take a photo and then check the image on the LCD Monitor.

When creating flowing water images, be sure to enable the Highlight Alert (see Chapter 1 for more information). Then check the water areas in the image on the LCD Monitor; if the water is blinking on the LCD, indicating that the scene is overexposed, you'll need to adjust the exposure compensation to underexpose the scene slightly and bring back the shadow details in the water.

It's possible that the light in the area in which you want to create this effect is too bright and won't allow you to use a slow enough shutter speed to effectively blur the water. In this case, you can use a filter—either a polarizing filter or a neutral density filter—to help reduce the amount of light that is coming through the lens. The polarizing filter redirects wavelengths of light to create more vibrant colors, reduce reflections, and darken blue skies. It's a handy filter for landscape work (**Figures 5.16** and **5.17**). The neutral density filter is typically just a dark piece of glass that serves to darken the scene by several stops. This allows you to use slower shutter speeds during bright conditions.

FIGURE 5.16
A polarizing filter helped to deepen the blue colors in this sky.

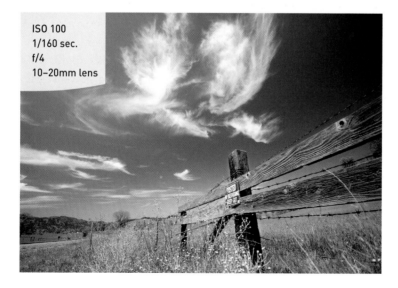

ISO 100
1/160 sec.
f/4
10–20mm lens

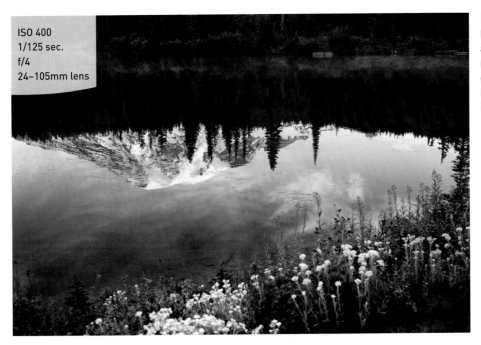

ISO 400
1/125 sec.
f/4
24–105mm lens

FIGURE 5.17
Polarizing filters
are also helpful in
reducing unwanted
glare and enhanc-
ing color saturation
in your images.

COMPOSING LANDSCAPE IMAGES

When we look at a photograph, our eyes tend to focus on certain parts of the image before we notice the rest. It's usually in those first few seconds of viewing a photograph that we decide if we like it or not. Test this out. Open a magazine and take a quick look at the first photo you see. Your eyes will most likely be drawn to the brightest part of the picture first. Next you'll probably notice the sharpest, most in-focus parts of the image, and then finally you'll start moving your eyes, looking for the most vibrant colors. The placement of these elements helps make up the photograph's overall composition, and your goal should be to keep the viewer's eyes interested and moving among all of the elements of your images.

RULE OF THIRDS

In Chapter 4, I discussed the importance of the rule of thirds, and you'll read even more about it in the chapters to come. It's one of the most basic rules of composition, and it works with nearly every type of image.

In landscape photography, you will often compose your image so that both the earth and the sky appear in the same shot. Pay attention to the placement of your horizon, as it's generally best to keep the horizon line away from the middle of the frame. Try to compose your shot so that the horizon falls on either the top or bottom third-line of the frame (**Figure 5.18**).

FIGURE 5.18
I photographed this sunset image so that the horizon fell directly on the top third-line and placed the sun so that it was on an intersecting point of the grid.

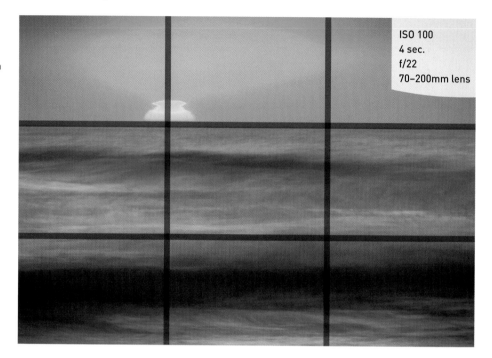

ISO 100
4 sec.
f/22
70–200mm lens

For a scene with a specific point of interest, such as a building or tree, compose that object on one of the intersecting third-lines within your frame. If you would like a little extra help, you can enable the grid display to show up in your viewfinder or on the LCD Monitor (for Live View); please turn to Chapter 4 for more information.

CREATING DEPTH

With landscape photography, finding a scene with a foreground, a middle ground, and a background can add depth to your image (**Figure 5.19**). Effectively using all three of these areas gives the image a three-dimensional feel and offers several distinct spaces for the viewer's eyes to travel.

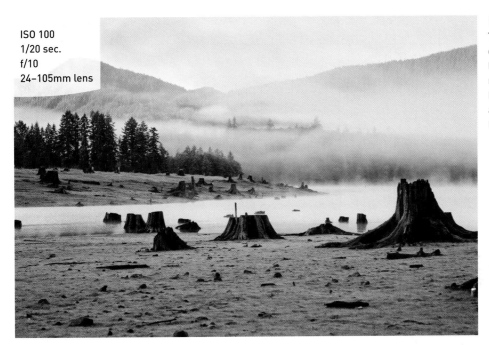

ISO 100
1/20 sec.
f/10
24–105mm lens

FIGURE 5.19
This image has a distinct foreground (tree stumps), middle ground (water/trees), and background (mountains/sky).

ADVANCED TECHNIQUES TO EXPLORE

The following two sections, covering panoramas and high dynamic range (HDR) images, require you to use image-processing software to complete the photograph. However, if you want to shoot for success, it's important that you know how to use these two popular techniques.

SHOOTING PANORAMAS

Sometimes you'll be in a location that is simply too big to cover within the typical camera frame. In these cases, you might consider photographing a panorama. You could always take a photo and crop off the top and bottom, making a "fake" panorama, but the purpose of a panorama image is to photograph an extended view of a scene, with minimal distortion, that can't typically be created with one shot.

If you want to make a true panorama, you either need a special camera that can move on its own to seamlessly photograph a scene, or you can use the following method to achieve similar results (**Figures 5.20** and **5.21**). You'll photograph a series of side-by-side images and stitch them together using editing software to produce one elongated panoramic shot.

FIGURE 5.20
This is the making of a panorama, with eight different shots overlapping about 30 percent of the frame.

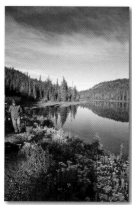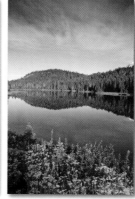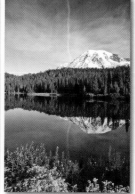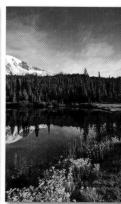

FIGURE 5.21
I used Adobe Photoshop to combine all of the exposures into one large panoramic image.

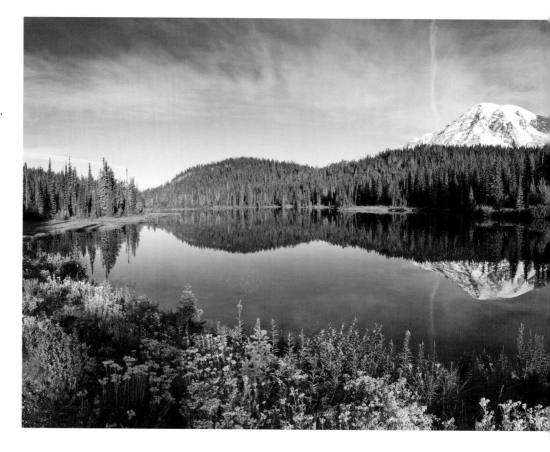

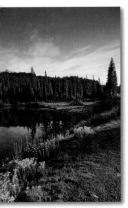
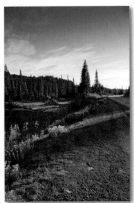
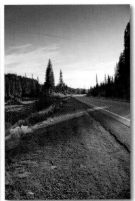
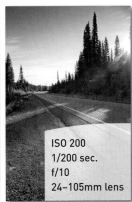

ISO 200
1/200 sec.
f/10
24–105mm lens

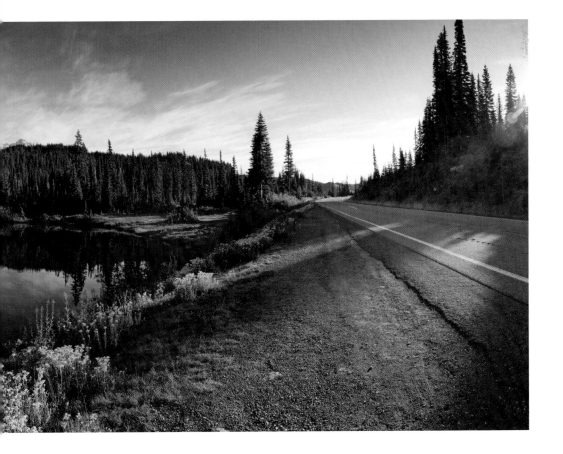

I won't get into details on how to edit the photographs, but if you have the proper software, such as Adobe Photoshop, the best thing you can do is learn how to photograph the images in a way that will make stitching them together a piece of cake.

SHOOTING FOR A MULTIPLE-IMAGE PANORAMA

1. Mount your camera on your tripod vertically and make sure it is level. (Shooting vertically will give your panorama more height and therefore more image detail.)

2. Choose a focal length for your lens that is between 35mm and 50mm.

3. In Av mode, use a very small aperture for the greatest depth of field. Take a meter reading of a bright part of the scene, and make note of it.

4. Now change your camera to Manual mode (M), and dial in the aperture and shutter speed that you obtained in the previous step.

5. Set your lens to manual focus, and then set your focus by finding a point one-third of the way into the scene. (If you use autofocus, you risk getting different points of focus from image to image, which will make the image stitching more difficult for the software.)

6. While carefully panning your camera, shoot your images to cover the entire area of the scene from one end to the other, leaving a 30 percent overlap from one frame to the next.

QUICK TIP: SORTING YOUR PANORAMIC IMAGES

Pulling panorama images into your editing software can sometimes be confusing because you're not sure where one series of images ends and another begins. Here's a quick tip for sorting your images.

When you're all set up and ready to start shooting your panorama, hold up one finger in front of the lens and take a quick shot. Then start your panorama shots. After you've photographed the last image, hold up two fingers in front of the lens and take another photo. This will help you find where each series begins and ends and should make it easier to sort and edit your panoramas.

SHOOTING HIGH DYNAMIC RANGE (HDR) IMAGES

A fun and popular way to create images is through a technique called high dynamic range (HDR). When you create an image that has a wide range of tones (shadows and highlights), such as a landscape image with a very bright sky, you need to decide what areas you want to emphasize and adjust your exposure to match. We can often find an exposure that is a balance between overexposing the sky and underexposing the ground. HDR photography allows you to photograph several different exposures of the same scene, capturing the shadows, midtones, and highlights, and then combine them to create a single image in editing software (**Figures 5.22, 5.23,** and **5.24**). For photographers who want to do some serious HDR shooting, I recommend using Adobe Photoshop or HDRsoft's Photomatix Pro. I'm not going to get into the details of how to edit your image, but I will walk you through the steps to set up your camera and create the photographs for HDR.

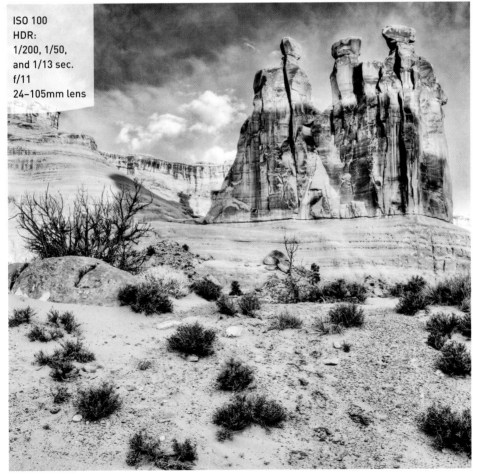

ISO 100
HDR:
1/200, 1/50,
and 1/13 sec.
f/11
24–105mm lens

FIGURE 5.22

I created this HDR image using the same method as in Figure 5.24, but notice how in HDR, recovering detail in the shadows and highlights is not limited only to color photographs. The images in this scene were more important to me than the colors, so I converted the shot to black and white, and the HDR processing brought out details in the well-lit and shaded areas.

FIGURE 5.23
To create an HDR image, I shot three consecutive photos at different exposures using AEB (Auto Exposure Bracket) mode.

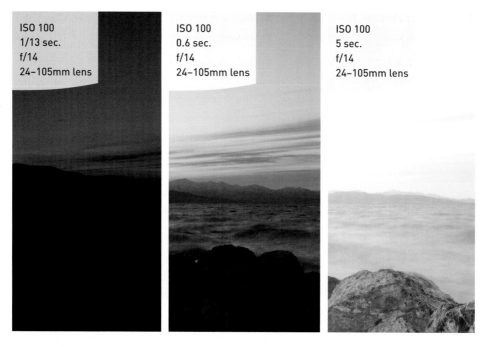

ISO 100
1/13 sec.
f/14
24–105mm lens

ISO 100
0.6 sec.
f/14
24–105mm lens

ISO 100
5 sec.
f/14
24–105mm lens

FIGURE 5.24
Using Photomatix Pro, I merged the three exposures in the previous image to create the final HDR photo.

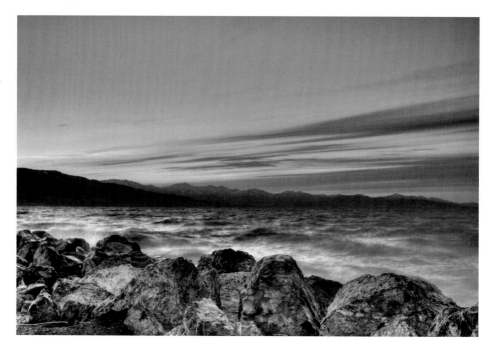

Note that it's absolutely necessary to use a tripod when using this technique because all the images must be aligned perfectly to combine them during the editing process.

The first step is to set your camera to automatically bracket your exposures. You will want one image that is underexposed, one that is overexposed, and one that is right in the middle. The 7D allows you to set this up so that it automatically photographs a series of three shots with each of those exposures.

SETTING UP AUTO EXPOSURE BRACKET (AEB) MODE FOR HDR

1. Press the Menu button and use the Main dial to get to the second shooting tab, and then use the Quick Control dial to highlight the Expo. Comp./AEB item (**A**). Press the Set button.

2. Scroll the Main dial to the right until the exposures are set to two stops between each shot (-2, 0, +2) (**B**). Then press the Set button. (Note that this setting will remain in place until you change it or turn off your camera. To set it back to normal, just scroll the Main dial to the left until only the center line is highlighted in red.)

3. Press the Menu button and then press the AF-DRIVE button on the top of your camera. Use the Quick Control dial to select High-speed continuous shooting mode. (This will allow you to

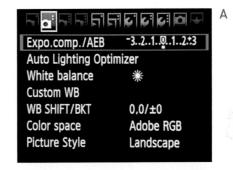

A

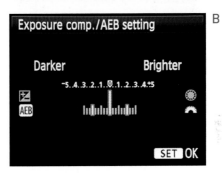

B

photograph your three bracketed images very quickly. This is important because some things in your image may be moving, such as clouds or leaves.)

Now that Auto Exposure Bracket mode is set up, let's go through the steps to create photographs for an HDR image.

SETTING UP FOR SHOOTING AN HDR IMAGE

1. Mount your camera on your tripod and then set your ISO to 100 to ensure clean, noise-free images.

2. Set your program mode to Av. During the shooting process, you will be taking three shots of the same scene, creating an overexposed image, an underexposed image, and a normal exposure. Since the camera is going to be adjusting the exposure, you want it to make changes to the shutter speed, not the aperture, so that your depth of field is consistent.

3. Set your camera file format to RAW. This is extremely important because the RAW format contains a much larger range of exposure values than a JPEG file, and the HDR software needs all of this information.

4. Focus the camera manually using the focus method discussed earlier in the chapter, compose your shot, secure the tripod, and hold down the Shutter button until the camera has fired three consecutive times.

5. Download the images to your computer and create the HDR image using specialized editing software.

BRACKETING YOUR EXPOSURES

In HDR, *bracketing* is the process of capturing a series of exposures at different stop intervals. You can bracket your exposures even if you aren't going to be using HDR. Sometimes this is helpful when you have a tricky lighting situation and you want to ensure that you have just the right exposure to capture the look you're after. In HDR, you bracket to the plus and minus side of a "normal" exposure, but you can also bracket all of your exposures to the over or under side of normal. It all depends on what you are trying to do. If you aren't sure whether you are getting enough shadow detail, you can bracket a little toward the overexposed side. If you aren't sure you're getting enough detail in your highlights, bracket a little toward the underexposed side. You can bracket in increments as small as a third of a stop. This means that you can capture several images with very subtle exposure variances and then decide later which one is best.

Chapter 5 Challenges

We've covered a lot of ground in this chapter, so it's definitely time to put this knowledge to work in order to get familiar with these new camera settings and techniques.

Experiment with white balance and picture styles

Set your camera up and use the Daylight white balance and Landscape picture style settings. Then turn on the Live View setting and change the white balance to the other modes, previewing each change in the LCD Monitor. Next, do the same with the picture styles and see how many different looks you can create with the same scene.

Level the horizon

Set your camera up on a tripod and do your best to eyeball the horizon and get it level in your scene. Then turn on the electronic level, either in the viewfinder or on the LCD Monitor, and see how close you were to getting your scene level. If you were off, then go ahead and adjust your camera until it's balanced and leveled both vertically and horizontally. Don't forget to preview your composition before you take the shot—just because the camera thinks it looks good doesn't necessarily mean it will turn out that way.

Applying hyperfocal distance to your landscapes

Pick a scene that contains objects positioned near the camera, as well as something that is clearly defined in the background. Try using a wide to medium-wide focal length (18–35mm). Use a small aperture and focus on the object in the foreground, then recompose and take a shot.

Without moving the camera position, use the object in the background as your point of focus and take another shot.

Finally, find a point that is one-third of the way into the frame from near to far and use that as the focus point.

Compare all of the images to see which method delivered the greatest range of depth of field from near to infinity.

Placing your horizons

Find a location with a distinct horizon and, using the grid on the viewfinder or using Live View on the LCD Monitor, take three shots: one with the horizon in the top third of the frame, one with it in the middle of the frame, and one along the bottom third of the frame. Compare each shot to see which one is most visually striking.

Share your results with the book's Flickr group!

Join the group here: flickr.com/groups/canon7dfromsnapshotstogreatshots

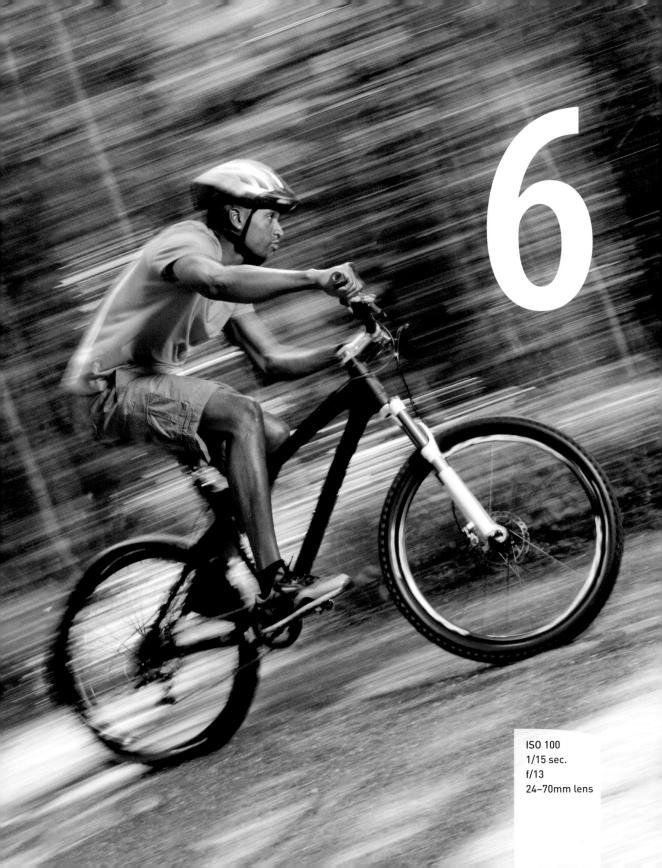

6

ISO 100
1/15 sec.
f/13
24–70mm lens

Moving Target

THE TRICKS TO SHOOTING SPORTS AND MORE

Photographing moving subjects is exciting, especially when you catch something you weren't expecting. When I was a kid photographing on the sidelines of my high school's football games, I used to dream of becoming a professional sports photographer—there's just something surreal about capturing a moment in time that only you could see with your camera. Whether you're photographing sports or your child running around the backyard, this chapter will give you the tools you need to get some great action shots.

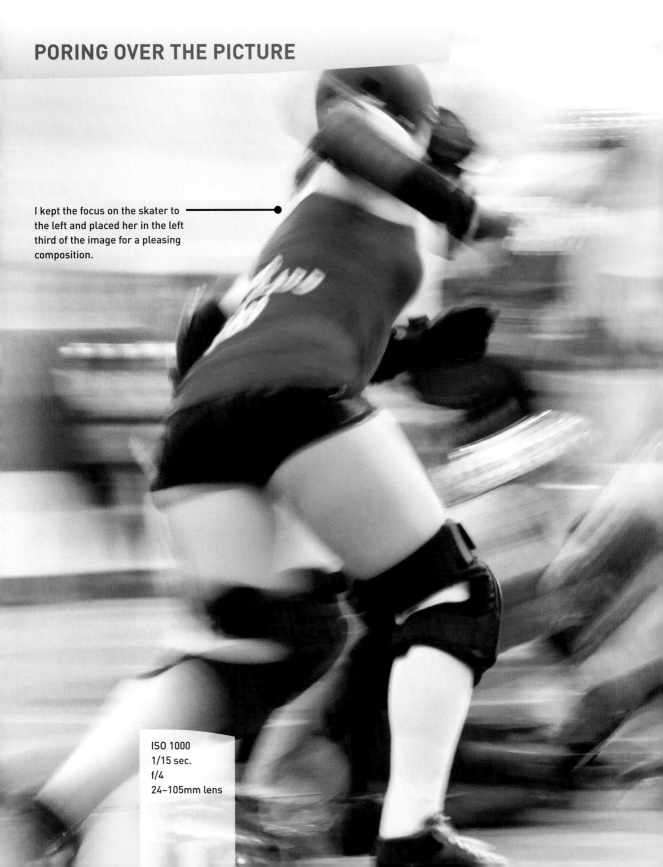

PORING OVER THE PICTURE

I kept the focus on the skater to the left and placed her in the left third of the image for a pleasing composition.

ISO 1000
1/15 sec.
f/4
24–105mm lens

Sometimes you'll photograph an event where you're guaranteed to get some pretty good shots. I attended a roller derby scrimmage one evening and found it to be a prime location for some fun, expressive, and unique action photographs. This shot is one of my favorites of the night because it highlights the players' brightly colored jerseys and shows the intensity of the moment with the blur and motion of the players falling in the background.

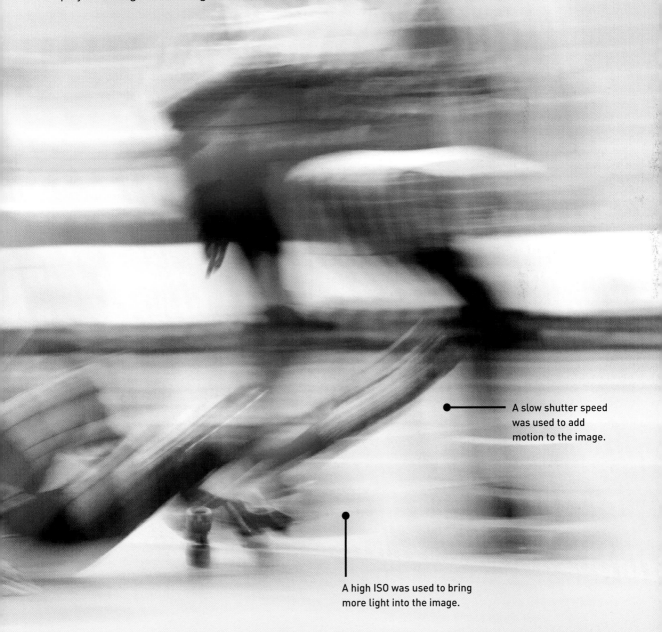

A slow shutter speed was used to add motion to the image.

A high ISO was used to bring more light into the image.

PORING OVER THE PICTURE

Action photography does not equate only to sports—capturing fast-moving subjects and quick-changing facial expressions are good examples of other types of action shots. When I created this photograph, I was trying my best to catch the girl mid-air, in a specific position, and with a happy expression on her face. I used a fast shutter speed and some strobe lights to freeze the action while she was jumping.

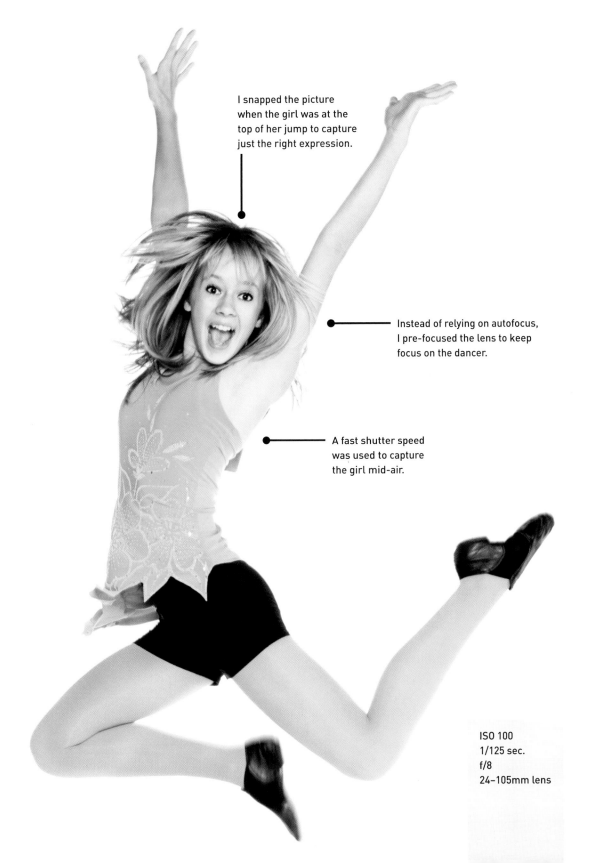

I snapped the picture when the girl was at the top of her jump to capture just the right expression.

Instead of relying on autofocus, I pre-focused the lens to keep focus on the dancer.

A fast shutter speed was used to capture the girl mid-air.

ISO 100
1/125 sec.
f/8
24–105mm lens

STOP RIGHT THERE!

When you are photographing a fast-moving subject, the most important setting to be aware of is your shutter speed. If the shutter speed is fast enough to freeze your subject, then you should see little or no motion blur. If your shutter speed is too slow, your subject will end up being a colorful streak across the frame.

Shutter speed is measured in fractions of a second, so when you are reading the numbers on the top LCD Panel or in the viewfinder, look for a very high number for a fast shutter speed—even though you are shooting in fractions, the camera won't actually show shutter speeds that way but instead will display whole numbers. There's no single setting you can stick with to be sure you will freeze the action—the shutter speed you use will depend on the subject you are photographing and how fast they are moving. Also keep in mind what direction the subject is traveling and how far away you are from them. Let's take a brief look at each of these factors to see how they might affect your shooting.

DIRECTION OF TRAVEL

When determining exposure for action photography, the first thing you might think about is how fast the subject is moving, but in reality your first consideration should be the direction in which it is traveling. The speed of something moving from left to right is perceived differently from that of something moving toward you. With the subject moving left to right, you'll need to set your camera to a faster shutter speed to freeze them in place, since using too slow of a shutter speed could blur your subject. With a subject moving toward the camera, you can get away with a slower shutter speed since they appear more stationary (**Figure 6.1**). A subject that is moving in a diagonal direction—both across the frame and toward or away from you—requires a shutter speed in between the two.

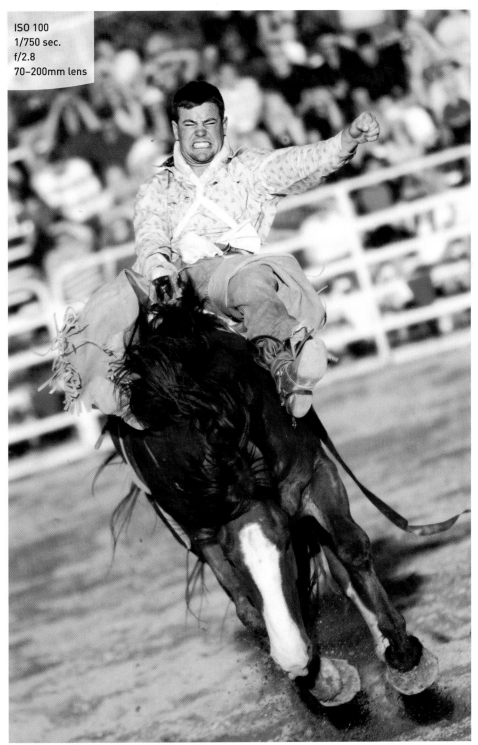

ISO 100
1/750 sec.
f/2.8
70–200mm lens

FIGURE 6.1
The subject in this photograph was moving toward me, so I was able to use a slower shutter speed than if he were traveling from left to right.

SUBJECT SPEED

Once you've determined the direction your subject is heading, you will need to assess the speed at which it is moving. The faster your subject is moving, the faster your shutter speed needs to be in order to "freeze" the action (**Figure 6.2**). A person walking on a sidewalk is moving quite slowly, so you will be able to use a slower shutter speed, such as 1/60 of a second, in order to photograph him with little or no motion blur. Using the same shutter speed to photograph a speeding car would result in the car being blurred across your image, so to compensate, you would need to use a much faster shutter speed.

SUBJECT-TO-CAMERA DISTANCE

One final factor to keep in mind when photographing moving subjects is their distance from you and your camera. Imagine that you are standing on top of a tall building looking down at the street below. You can watch the cars moving with little effort—in other words, your eyes don't have to move very far to see cars travel from one block to another, and you don't have to turn your head much to follow them. Now put yourself on the sidewalk directly next to the street and try to follow those cars traveling the same speed—you need to move your head from left to right to keep your eyes on one car. Standing on the street requires a lot more movement on your part to keep up with the moving traffic.

Now imagine you are holding your camera and trying to photograph the cars in both of the above scenarios. Although the subject is traveling at the same speed in both instances, the movement of your camera will affect the shutter speed you'll need to use in order to freeze the action. Photographing a fast-moving subject that is farther from you requires a slower shutter speed than if you were standing a few feet away from it, because the perceived speed is much slower.

This same principle can also be applied to the lens you use. If you are using a wide-angle lens, you can probably get away with a slower shutter speed, whereas using a telephoto lens brings you in closer to the subject and will require a faster shutter speed to compensate for the movement of the lens following your subject (**Figure 6.3**).

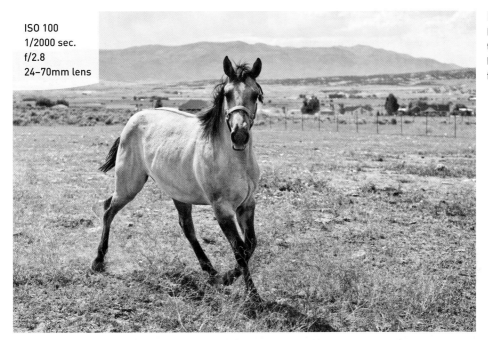

ISO 100
1/2000 sec.
f/2.8
24–70mm lens

FIGURE 6.2
I was able to freeze the action of this horse by using a fast shutter speed.

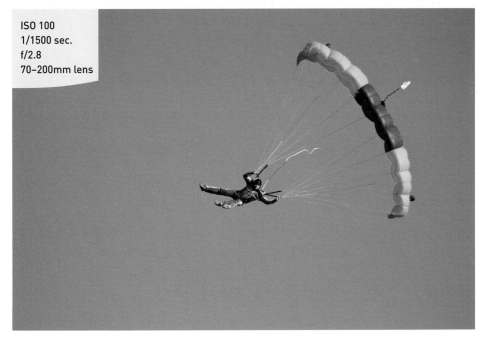

ISO 100
1/1500 sec.
f/2.8
70–200mm lens

FIGURE 6.3
For this image I used a telephoto zoom, which required a much faster shutter speed to compensate for the movement of the lens.

USING SHUTTER PRIORITY (TV) MODE TO STOP MOTION

In Chapter 3 you learned about the different shooting modes. Tv mode gives you full control over the shutter speed—you pick the shutter speed and the camera determines the aperture. In many instances of sports and action photography, you will be working with very fast shutter speeds, and using the Tv mode will give you the control you need to capture high-speed images (**Figure 6.4**).

In order to use a fast shutter speed, you need to be in an environment with sufficient light available for the speed you want to use. You might decide to set your aperture at a wide f-stop in order to bring more light into the sensor to balance the fast shutter speed. However, there may be times when your environment is just too dark for what you want to shoot—you'll know this because the aperture value will flash on the top LCD Panel and also on the viewfinder info screen. When the light is insufficient for the shutter speed and aperture combination you want to use, you'll need to change your ISO settings.

FIGURE 6.4
I used a fast shutter speed to capture the expression of this little girl as she was jumping.

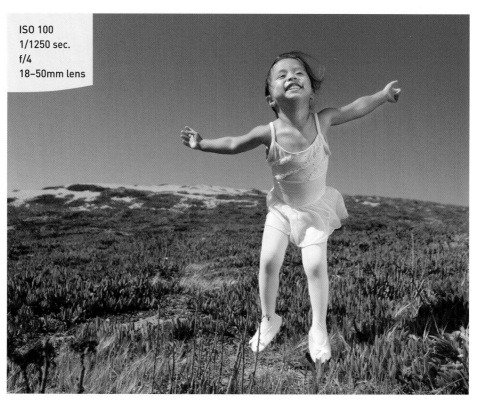

ISO 100
1/1250 sec.
f/4
18–50mm lens

What's great about digital cameras is that they allow the user to change the ISO as often as needed. With film, each individual roll of film had a specific ISO number and couldn't be changed from frame to frame, as can be done with digital cameras today. It can be difficult for new photographers to decide what ISO to use at first, but once you understand how the process works, it's much easier to make that decision.

When I'm on a photo shoot, I like to keep my ISO very low and usually shoot at its lowest setting (ISO 100). I do this because at low ISO numbers, the digital noise is insignificant and hardly visible. When you start cranking that number up, the camera's sensor becomes more sensitive to light and you can increase your shutter speeds; however, the noise level will be much greater. For my line of work, I tend to keep my images as noise-free as possible, but in a photo where the subject and activity being photographed are more important than the technical quality of the pixels, having the ability to change the ISO is a big advantage. It's a good option to have when you're in an environment that you can't control, and depending on the final output (web, print, and so on), it may or may not make much difference in the overall quality of the image. With the 7D you can quickly adjust the ISO number as needed with just a few simple steps.

ADJUSTING YOUR ISO ON THE FLY

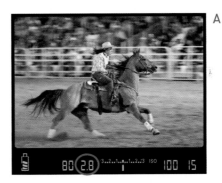

A

1. Check for the blinking aperture read-out in the bottom portion of your viewfinder (**A**).

2. A blinking aperture is an indication that your image will be underexposed. In this case the aperture is at its lowest setting, so your only option is to increase the ISO. To do so move your index finger back from the Shutter button and press the ISO button (**B**).

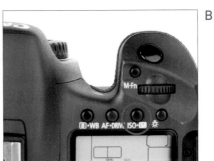

B

3. Now move your finger forward to the Main dial and raise the ISO to the next highest level by rotating it right.

4. Lightly press the Shutter button and check to see if the aperture is still blinking.

5. If it's not blinking, shoot away. If it is, repeat steps 2–4 until it is set correctly.

GET CREATIVE

When photographing sports and action images, try to find new and creative ways to capture your subject. In this image (**Figure** 6.5), I knew that I would need a fast shutter speed to catch the basketball player mid-air, so I positioned myself facing the sun and silhouetted him as he was jumping up to take a shot. The bright light from the sun not only allowed me to use a fast enough shutter speed to catch the action but also added a unique quality to the scene.

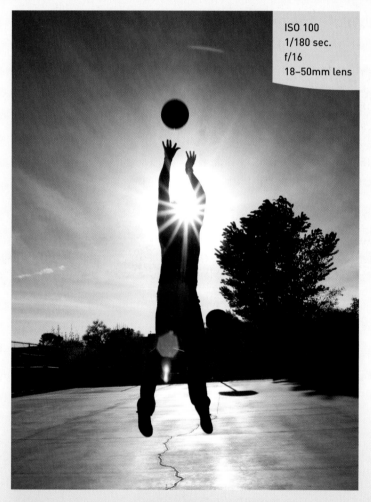

ISO 100
1/180 sec.
f/16
18–50mm lens

FIGURE 6.5
By photographing directly into the sun, I was able to silhouette the
basketball player and freeze him in place with a fast shutter speed.

USING APERTURE PRIORITY (AV) MODE TO ISOLATE YOUR SUBJECT

When you are shooting in Tv mode, your camera will often be set at its widest aperture to bring in as much light as possible through the lens. Using a very large aperture allows you to use a faster shutter speed and narrows your depth of field (**Figure 6.6**).

As you learned in Chapter 3, using a wide aperture will help to reduce the sharpness of the photo's background. This is quite effective with sports and action photography, because by isolating the subject, you move the viewer's attention to the focal point of the image.

So when will you want to use the Av mode for action and sports? You already know that using the Tv mode allows you to choose your shutter speed, so if you need a specific and fast shutter speed, Tv mode is a good choice. But if you want to isolate your subject and blur the background by using a large aperture, then you will probably want to set your camera to Av. One benefit to using the Av mode with the aperture at its widest setting is that the camera will always use the fastest possible shutter speed depending on the available light in your environment.

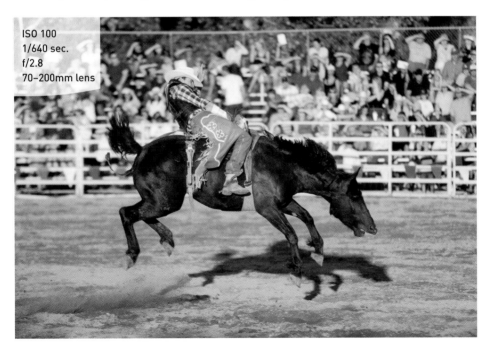

ISO 100
1/640 sec.
f/2.8
70–200mm lens

FIGURE 6.6

Using a wide-open aperture in this image allowed me to blur the crowd in the background.

You can also change the ISO quickly when shooting in the Av mode, just as you learned in the previous section. Just remember to keep an eye on the shutter speed—if it's too slow, boost the ISO number to increase the sensitivity of the sensor and allow the use of faster shutter speeds.

One challenge you'll face when using a wide-open aperture in action photography is that you need to be sure you maintain proper focus on your subject because you have less wiggle room with a larger aperture than with a smaller one. You also want to be able to take several continuous photos of your subject to make sure you get the shot ("machine gun" style). With portrait and landscape photography, you can easily get away with One Shot Single-Point AF (autofocus) and the Single shooting drive mode. But when you are trying to focus on something that is constantly moving, it's much easier to use a focusing system that can track your subject. In the next section, I will discuss the 7D's drive modes, AI Servo AF, and the different AF areas you can use when photographing fast-moving subjects.

SETTING UP YOUR CAMERA FOR CONTINUOUS SHOOTING AND AUTOFOCUS

In order to photograph fast-moving subjects, get several shots at a time, and stay focused on the subject through the entire process, you'll need to make a few changes to your camera settings. The 7D makes the process simple, but it can be a bit confusing when you first start to work with it. Here, I briefly explain each of the three areas that are addressed in this section: drive modes, AF (autofocus) modes, and AF areas.

DRIVE MODES

The 7D's drive mode determines how quickly each photo is taken and how many photos it will take continuously. The drive modes available on your camera include the following:

- **Single shooting:** With this setting you will take only one photo each time you press and hold the Shutter button.

- **High-speed continuous shooting:** When you press and hold the Shutter button, your camera will continuously take photos very quickly until you release the Shutter button, up to 8 frames per second.

- **Low-speed continuous shooting:** When you press and hold the Shutter button, your camera will continuously take photos at a slower pace until you release the Shutter button, up to 3 frames per second. You can also easily take just one shot by quickly pressing and releasing the shutter.

- **10-sec self-timer:** Self-timer mode: the camera waits 10 seconds to take a photo once the Shutter button is pressed.

- **2-sec self-timer:** Self-timer mode: the camera waits 2 seconds to take a photo once the Shutter button is pressed.

For action and sports photography, the best option is High-speed continuous shooting. In this mode you will take several consecutive photos very quickly and are more likely to capture a good image of your fast-moving subject. Keep in mind that taking this many images at a time will fill up your memory card much more quickly than taking just one image at a time. The speed of your CF (Compact Flash) card also limits how many images you can take in a row.

Within your camera is a *buffer,* a feature that processes the image data before it can be written to the CF card. When you take a photo, you'll see a red light on the back of your camera (the Card Busy indicator)—you usually won't notice anything is happening because the buffer is big enough to hold data from several photos at a time. When you take a lot of photos in a row with the High-speed continuous drive mode, the buffer fills up more quickly—if it completely fills up while you are shooting, your camera will "freeze" momentarily while the images are written to the card. If you have a fast memory card, such as a UDMA (Ultra Direct Memory Access), you can often avoid this problem.

One way to stay on top of this while you are shooting is to look inside the viewfinder—in the lower-right corner you'll see a number. This number tells you how many photos you can take before the buffer is full (**Figure 6.7**). In general, it's a good idea to do short bursts of photos instead of holding the Shutter button down for several seconds. This will help keep the buffer cleared, and the card won't fill up as quickly.

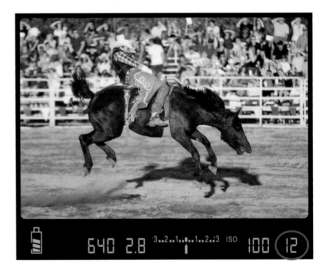

FIGURE 6.7
The number on the far-right side of the viewfinder shows you how many shots you have left (max bursts) before the buffer is full.

USE THE CONTINUOUS MODE TO CAPTURE EXPRESSIONS

Using a fast shutter speed is not just for fast-moving subjects, but also for catching the ever-changing expressions of people, especially small children. This image (**Figure 6.8**) shows how an expression can go from happy to sad in a matter of seconds. Taking several consecutive shots allowed me to capture each moment as it happened without missing a thing.

FIGURE 6.8

This baby changed her expression from a smile to a frown in less than 10 seconds—I was able to capture this change by taking several consecutive photographs.

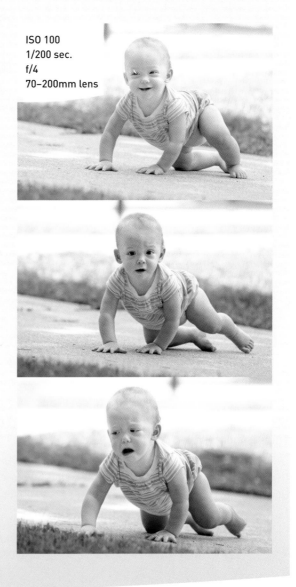

ISO 100
1/200 sec.
f/4
70–200mm lens

SELECTING AND SHOOTING IN HIGH-SPEED CONTINUOUS DRIVE MODE

1. Press the AF • DRIVE button on the top of the camera.

2. Use your thumb to rotate the Quick Control dial until you see the drive setting that shows an "H."

3. Locate and focus on your subject in the viewfinder, and then press and hold the Shutter button to take several continuous images.

Manual Callout

The number of frames that you can capture varies depending on the image format that you are using (JPEG, RAW, or RAW+JPEG). To find out the frame rates, as well as the maximum number of frames that you can take in one continuous burst, check out page 59 of your user's manual.

FOCUS MODES

Now that your drive setting is ready to go, let's move on to focusing. The 7D allows you to shoot in three different modes: One Shot, AI Focus, and AI Servo (AI stands for Artificial Intelligence). The One Shot mode is designed for photographing stationary objects, or subjects that don't move around very much—this setting is typically not very useful with action photography. You will be photographing subjects that move often and quickly, so you'll need a focus mode that can keep up with them. The AI Servo mode will probably be your best bet. This setting will continue to find focus when you have your Shutter button pressed halfway, allowing you to keep the focus on your moving target.

SELECTING AND SHOOTING IN AI SERVO FOCUS MODE

1. Press the AF • DRIVE button on the top of the camera.

2. Use your index finger to rotate the Main dial until AI SERVO appears in the top LCD Panel.

3. Locate your subject in the viewfinder, then press and hold the Shutter button halfway to activate the focus mechanism. You'll notice that with this mode you won't hear a beep when the camera finds focus.

4. The camera will maintain focus on your subject as long as the subject remains within one of the focus points in the viewfinder, or until you take a picture.

The AI Focus mode is another setting that can be useful when you have a subject that is stationary at first but then starts to move—it's the "best of both worlds" when it comes to focusing on your subject. Imagine that you are photographing a runner about to sprint in a race—you want to focus on the person's eyes as they take the "ready" position and don't want your camera to change focus. But just as the runner starts running down the track, the camera will kick into AI Servo mode to track and focus on the runner as they are moving.

You should note that holding down the Shutter button for long periods of time will quickly drain your battery because the camera is constantly focusing on the subject. You can also activate the focus by pressing the AF-ON button on the back of the camera (**Figure 6.9**). This is a great way to get used to the focusing system without worrying about taking unwanted pictures.

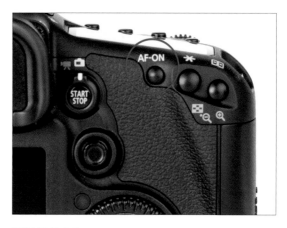

FIGURE 6.9

The AF-ON button will activate the autofocusing system in your 7D without your having to use the Shutter button. Note that this button will not work when shooting in one of the fully-automatic modes.

FOCUS AREAS

The third setting that is extremely important in action photography is the area of focus within the frame. As I discussed in Chapter 1, there are three different focusing areas to choose from:

- **Single-Point AF:** You choose from one of the 19 focus points within the viewfinder.

- **Zone AF:** You pick a general area within the viewfinder where you want the camera to maintain its focus.

- **Auto Select:** With this option, the camera selects one of the 19 focus points for you.

My advice is to use Zone AF when photographing action shots. You will want to follow along with your moving subject, but you won't always have a specific focus point like you would with the Single-Point AF and a non-moving subject. For example, if you know that you will be following a person riding a motocross bike and they will always be centered in the frame, set the focus point somewhere in the middle (**Figure 6.10**). As long as you keep the subject centered, the camera will use that area to find the best point of focus. There are five areas that you can use: left, right, top, bottom, and middle. The one you use will depend on the subject you are photographing and the composition you are trying to achieve.

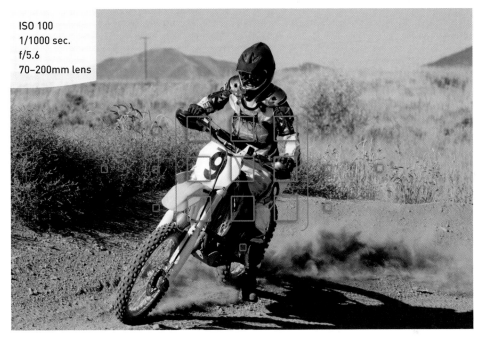

ISO 100
1/1000 sec.
f/5.6
70–200mm lens

FIGURE 6.10

When you set your focus to the center area in Zone AF, your camera will look for areas within the nine center AF points to focus on.

SETTING THE FOCUS MODE TO ZONE AF

1. Press the AF Point Selection button on the back of the camera.

2. Press the Multi-function button (M-Fn) on the top of the camera next to the Shutter button until you reach the Zone AF setting (you will see a cluster of focus points grouped in one area of the viewfinder).

3. Rotate either the Main dial or the Quick Control dial to change the focus area (you can also use the Multi-Controller on the back of the camera to toggle from one area to the next).

4. Now point your camera at your subject and press the Shutter button halfway to set focus. You'll see the camera finding the focus point(s) somewhere within the area you just chose in the above steps.

Another option is to use the Auto Select focus mode. I tend to stay away from settings in which the camera decides everything, and in this case the camera has full control over where the focus is set, but sometimes this mode can be useful (**Figure 6.11**). Just try to use this mode sparingly and only in situations when it's very unlikely that the camera will find the wrong area of focus.

FIGURE 6.11
For this image, the guitar player was jumping up from a trampoline and I wasn't able to anticipate where the focus would be, so using the Auto Select focus mode was a good choice.

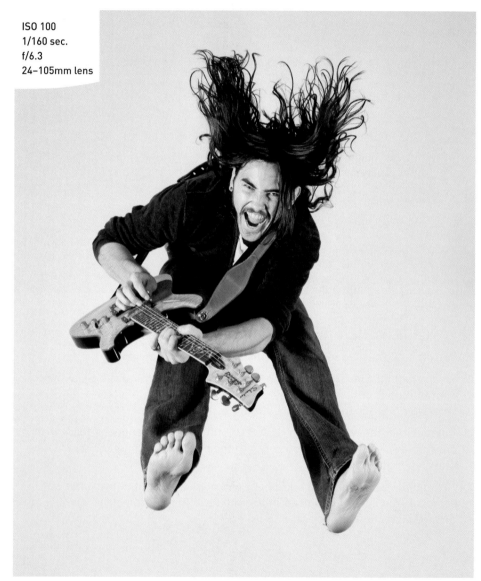

ISO 100
1/160 sec.
f/6.3
24–105mm lens

MANUAL FOCUS FOR ANTICIPATED ACTION

I tend to stick with autofocus for the majority of my work; however, sometimes when photographing fast-moving subjects, focusing manually can actually make it easier to get the shot. In **Figure 6.12** I knew that the young girl was going to be jumping straight up, and if I were to rely on autofocus it might try to focus on the wrong part of her body. My goal was to capture her eyes as sharply as possible, so I pre-focused my lens before she jumped. Then when she made her move, I was ready to go and didn't have to worry about my camera finding a new, incorrect focus area.

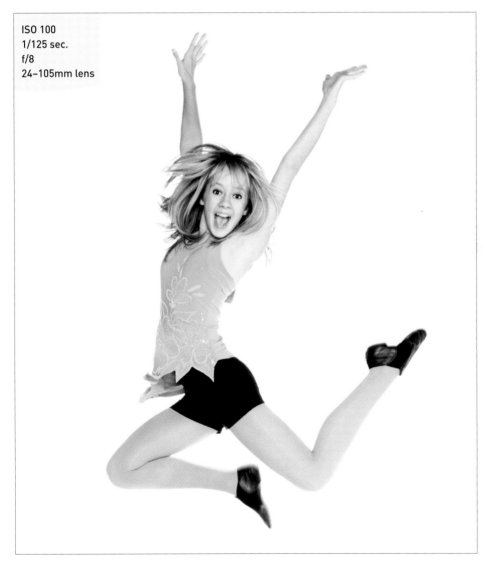

ISO 100
1/125 sec.
f/8
24–105mm lens

FIGURE 6.12
I knew where the dancer would be jumping, so I manually focused my lens to be sure that the focus area was accurate.

Another example in which manual focus is effective is with panning shots. Because your subject is moving very quickly, you will want to be sure the focus is set on them since you might otherwise miss the shot as they whiz past you. If you know where they are heading, as I did with the motorcycle shot in **Figure 6.13**, then you can pre-focus your lens rather than rely on the camera to find focus. (I'll discuss panning photography more in the next section.)

FIGURE 6.13
Using manual focus is a good choice when photographing panning images.

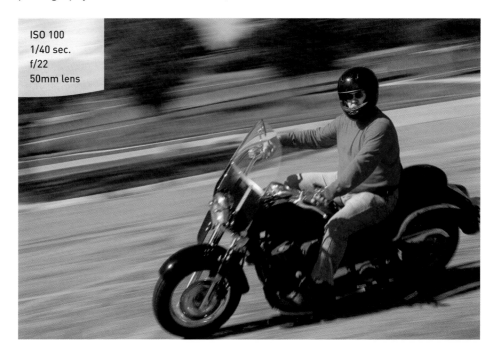

ISO 100
1/40 sec.
f/22
50mm lens

A SENSE OF MOTION

When photographing a moving subject you might not always want to freeze everything in its tracks—sometimes you'll want to convey to the viewer the sense of movement in the image. Two techniques you can use to achieve this effect are panning and motion blur.

PANNING

One of the most common ways to portray motion in an image is by panning. Panning is the process of using a slower-than-usual shutter speed while following your subject across the frame, moving your camera along with it. This technique adds motion blur to the background. The key here is a slow shutter speed, but the exact shutter speed you use depends on the speed of the subject. Choose a shutter speed that is slow enough to capture motion in the background but fast enough to allow you to capture your subject with little or no blur. You also want to follow through with your camera until you are sure that your shutter is closed and you've completed the shot. You can further maintain the sharpness of the subject by using a flash source (such as the built-in flash on your 7D) to freeze the subject (**Figure 6.14**).

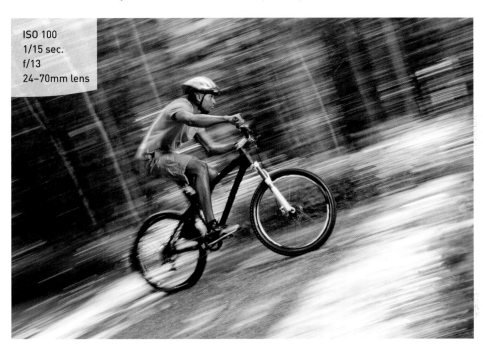

ISO 100
1/15 sec.
f/13
24–70mm lens

FIGURE 6.14
Using a separate light source can help to prevent blurring your panning subject—in this photo I used an off-camera strobe to keep the biker tack-sharp.

Panning photography often involves a lot of trial and error until you get the perfect combination of shutter speed and camera movement. The beauty of digital photography is that we get instant feedback and can keep tweaking our settings until we have them set just right for the image we want to create.

MOTION BLUR

Another way to let the viewer in on the feel of the action is to include some blur in the image. This blur is less refined than it is in a panning shot and there's no specific or correct composition, colors, or way to move your camera to get a desirable effect. Sometimes you might even achieve this effect by mistake. In **Figure 6.15**, I was attempting to create some panning shots while photographing a scrimmage of local roller derby players. During the shot a few of the players fell down, which added a lot of blur within the photo that I wasn't expecting. The shot I ended up with was very colorful and creative and turned out to be my favorite image of the day.

FIGURE 6.15
Adding blur to your images can be a fun and creative way to imply a sense of motion in the scene.

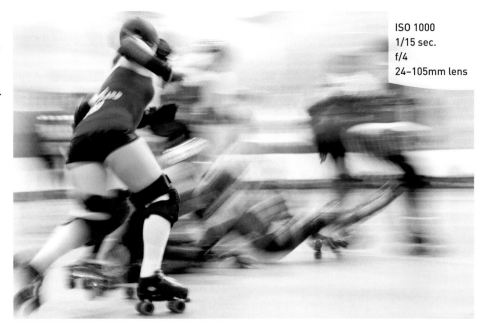

ISO 1000
1/15 sec.
f/4
24–105mm lens

ZOOM IN TO BE SURE

When reviewing your shots on the LCD Monitor, don't be fooled by the display. The smaller your image is, the sharper it will look. To ensure that you are getting sharp, blur-free images, make sure that you zoom in on your LCD Monitor.

To zoom in on your images, press the Playback button located below the rear LCD Monitor and then press the Magnify button to zoom (**Figure 6.16**). Continue pressing the Magnify button to increase the zoom ratio.

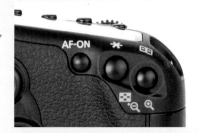

FIGURE 6.16
The Magnify button is a useful tool to check for proper focus while reviewing your images.

You can also use the Multi-Controller to check focus and scroll around to different areas of the frame while zoomed in.

To zoom back out, simply press the Reduce button (the magnifying glass with the minus sign on it) or press the Playback button again.

As with a panning shot, there is no set shutter speed and aperture combo that you can use every time for this effect. It may take a lot of trial and error to get the outcome you want, but in my opinion, that challenge makes it all the more fun and is a great reason to give it a try.

TIPS FOR SHOOTING ACTION

GIVE THEM SOMEWHERE TO GO

It can be easy to get wrapped up in the moment when photographing fast-moving subjects, but it's important that you remember some basic rules of composition and framing. One of my goals is to keep the elements of the photo within the frame so that the viewer's eyes focus on what I want them to see. With action photography the subject is most likely moving, so you need to make sure that there is room for the subject in the direction they are heading. Do your best to keep from cropping the image too tightly or pushing the subject too close to the left or right edges of the frame (**Figure 6.17**).

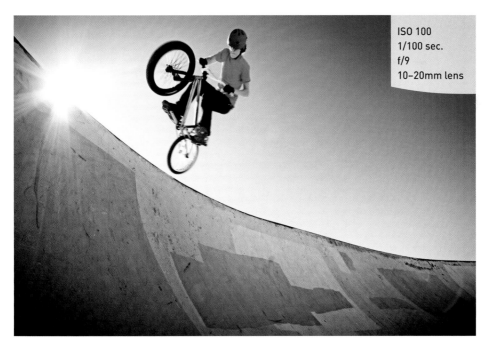

ISO 100
1/100 sec.
f/9
10–20mm lens

FIGURE 6.17
I composed this image so that the biker would appear in the upper-left third of the frame and on his way down from the jump.

GET IN FRONT OF THE ACTION

Another technique to keep in mind is to try to photograph the action coming toward you (**Figure 6.18**). When you are photographing people or animals, it's always best to show their faces and expressions, which can convey a sense of urgency and the emotion of the moment.

FIGURE 6.18
Always try to capture your subject moving toward you. For this photo, I placed myself so that the rider and her horse would be facing me as they made the turn around the barrel.

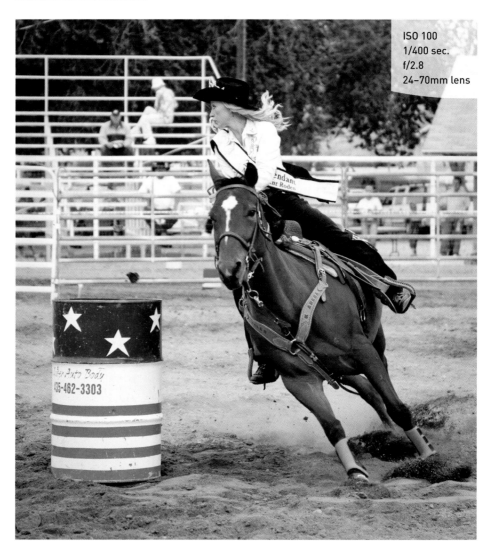

ISO 100
1/400 sec.
f/2.8
24–70mm lens

PUT YOUR CAMERA IN A DIFFERENT PLACE

Finding new perspectives and ways to photograph your subject can be a fun way to add interest to an image. Sometimes you are limited in the location you shoot from, but there are still ways to add depth and uniqueness to your images just by finding a different spot to place your camera.

When photographing this motocross driver, I wanted to add some dimension to the image by blurring the foreground elements (**Figure 6.19**). I was in an open field with few other elements in the area, so I ducked down behind some tall grass and shot through it to add it to the foreground. I was still able to capture the driver and his bike exactly how I wanted while adding depth to the image with shallow depth of field.

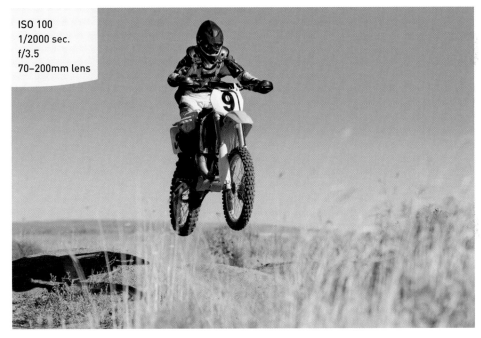

ISO 100
1/2000 sec.
f/3.5
70–200mm lens

FIGURE 6.19
I got down behind some tall grass to shoot this moto-cross driver as he made the jump—the foreground elements add depth to the photograph.

Chapter 6 Challenges

The mechanics of motion

Find a fast-moving subject, such as cars on a busy street, set your camera to Tv (Shutter Priority mode), and take some photos using different shutter speeds. Be sure to keep your camera still while you are taking the photos. Start with a slower speed, such as 1/30 of a second, and then gradually increase the speed until you find one that freezes the action of your subject.

Wide vs. telephoto

Just as with the first assignment, photograph a subject moving in different directions, but this time use a wide-angle lens and then a telephoto. Check out how the telephoto setting on the zoom lens will require faster shutter speeds than the lens at its wide-angle setting.

Getting a feel for focus modes

Set your camera to AI Servo and the Zone AF mode. Find a moving subject and follow it around with your lens while looking through the viewfinder and pressing the Shutter button halfway. Watch how the camera looks for the focus point in the area you have selected.

Now switch the focusing mode over to Auto Select. Follow the same subject with your camera and notice the differences in where the camera wants to find focus. Switching between these two different modes will help you determine which mode works best for your shooting situation.

Anticipating the spot using manual focus

For this assignment, you will need to find a subject that you know will cross a specific line that you can pre-focus on, such as a street with moderate traffic or a person jogging along a path. Set your lens to manual focus and focus on a spot that the subject will travel across. It's also a good idea to set your camera to the High-speed continuous shooting mode for this to work well. Now, when your subject approaches the spot, start shooting. Try shooting in three- or four-frame bursts.

Following the action

Panning is a great way to show motion. To begin, find a subject that will move across your path at a steady speed and practice following it in your viewfinder from side to side. Now, with the camera in Tv mode, set your shutter speed to 1/30 of a second (try to pre-focus on the spot where you think they will be traveling, as you did in the previous challenge). Now pan along with the subject, and shoot as it moves across your view. Experiment with different shutter speeds and focal lengths. Panning is a skill that takes some time to get a feel for, so try it with different types of subjects moving at different speeds.

Share your results with the book's Flickr group!

Join the group here: flickr.com/groups/canon7dfromsnapshotstogreatshots

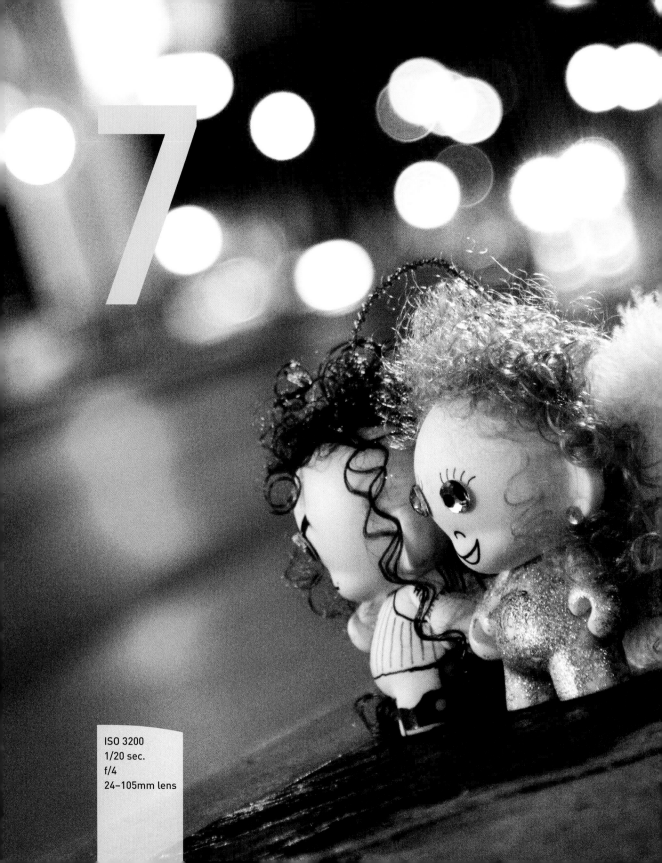

7

ISO 3200
1/20 sec.
f/4
24–105mm lens

Mood Lighting

SHOOTING WHEN THE LIGHTS GET LOW

The advances in digital camera technology have made it possible to capture images in some of the most challenging lighting situations, and the 7D allows you to keep on shooting even after the sun goes down. In this chapter we'll explore ways to use your camera with available light and with the 7D's built-in flash, but let's start with the obvious solution to shooting when the light is low—raising the ISO.

There was very little available light in the room, so I raised the ISO to capture this shot.

I measured the exposure by metering off the candlelight reflected on the girl's face.

On Christmas Eve, my church held a candlelight vigil during the service, and I saw it as a prime opportunity to get some beautiful low-light images. The overhead lights were dimmed and the only light source I was able to use in this image was candlelight. The girl's somber expression helps to convey the emotion of the room and to tell the story of the moment we

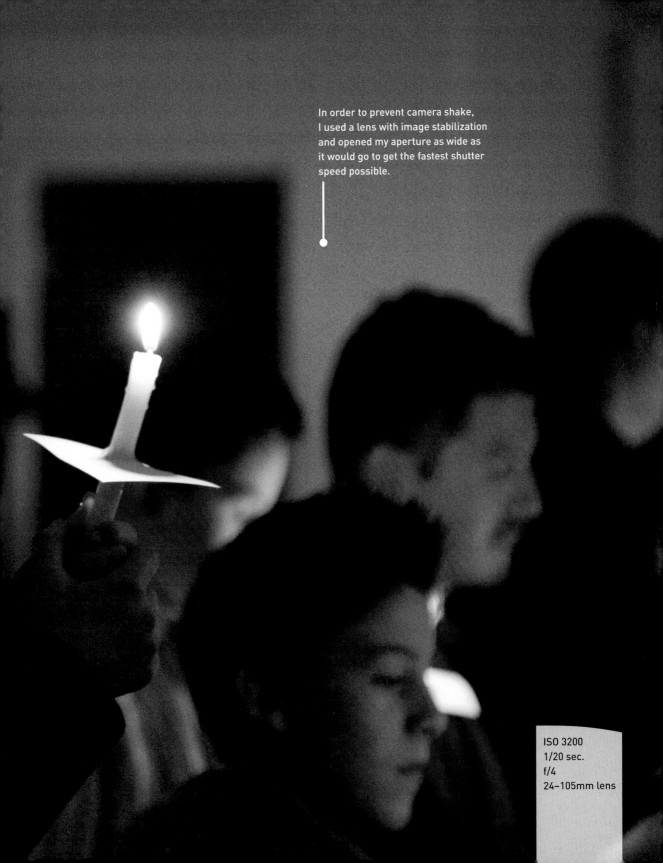

In order to prevent camera shake,
I used a lens with image stabilization
and opened my aperture as wide as
it would go to get the fastest shutter
speed possible.

ISO 3200
1/20 sec.
f/4
24–105mm lens

PORING OVER THE PICTURE

A musician friend of mine was in town to perform for a small group of friends, and I was there with my camera to get some shots of him in action. Because the room was so dark, I needed to push the ISO extremely high, and I really like the grain that the high ISO created.

I changed this image to black and white to eliminate the distraction of color and focus attention on the musician and his expression.

A very high ISO added grain and noise to this photo, providing greater texture and character.

The light coming from behind the musician rimmed the microphone and his face, helping separate him from the background.

ISO 6400
1/80 sec.
f/4
70–200mm lens

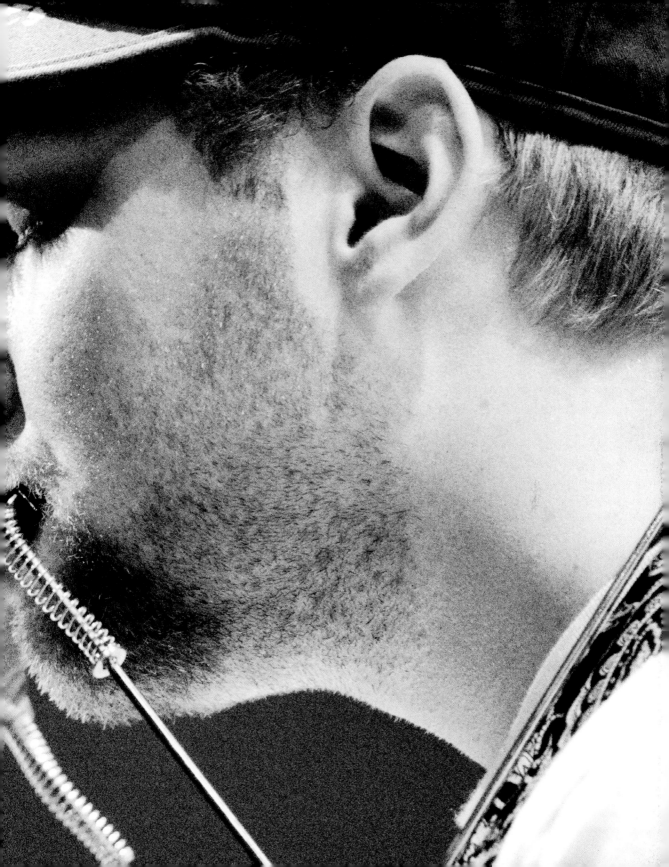

RAISING THE ISO: THE SIMPLE SOLUTION

Capturing moments in low-light situations is easy with digital cameras—just raise the ISO. Adjusting the ISO on the fly is easy; simply press the ISO button on the top of the camera and change the ISO number by using the Main dial (see Chapter 1 for more information). In most lighting situations, you will probably be working with an ISO range of 100–800. But as your available light gets lower, pushing the ISO to extremely high numbers will increase the amount of noise in the image (**Figure 7.1**).

FIGURE 7.1
There was very little available light in the room, so I needed to increase the ISO in order to take photos without using a flash.

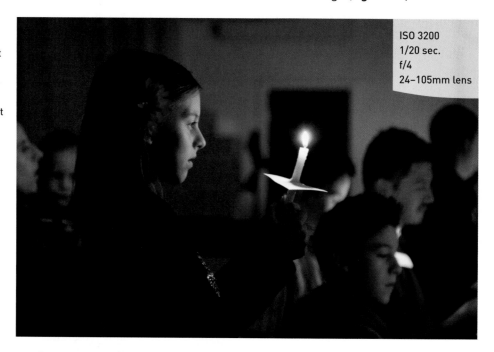

ISO 3200
1/20 sec.
f/4
24–105mm lens

Another option is to use the flash when working in locations with low light, but if your subject is too far away, the flash won't reach them. There may also be situations in which flash photography is prohibited or not appropriate.

Using a tripod with a slow shutter speed and low ISO setting is another option when the lights are low, but if your subject is moving too fast, you won't be able to freeze them in place. Tripods also tend to attract a lot of attention, and they are not allowed in some

Manual Callout

The light produced from the built-in flash on your 7D can only reach certain distances, but this distance is dependent on your aperture and ISO speed combination. For a detailed chart that lists the effective range of your built-in flash, please turn to page 112 in your user's manual.

areas. I find that hauling a tripod around can be cumbersome—if I know that I need one for a specific image, it's not a big deal, but if I'm not sure what I'll be shooting, I prefer other methods that don't require as much gear.

So if you find that raising your ISO level above 800 is your only option, you can reduce the amount of noise in the image by turning on the High ISO Speed Noise Reduction feature in the Custom Function Settings menu on your 7D. Keep in mind that you may not always notice noise when viewing your images on the back of your camera, since what you're seeing is a scaled-down version of the original. Using the zoom features on the back of your camera to preview your shots at 100% will give you a better idea of the amount of noise that higher ISO levels introduce into your images.

TURNING ON HIGH ISO SPEED NOISE REDUCTION

1. Press the Menu button and locate the Custom Function screen.

2. The ISO Expansion setting is located in the C.Fn II: Image section. Highlight it and press Set (**A**).

3. Use the Quick Control dial to locate the High ISO Speed Noise Reduction section (it's the second menu item), and then press the Set button.

4. Use the Quick Control dial to select the level of noise reduction you would like applied to your images (**B**). Then press the Set button.

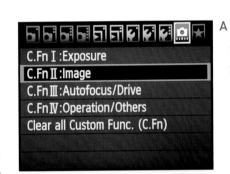

A

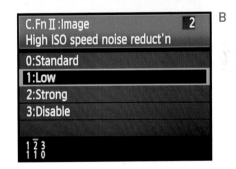

B

Press the Menu button twice to exit. This noise reduction will be applied to all ISO speeds but will be much more noticeable at higher ISO levels.

USING VERY HIGH ISOS

If you're finding that ISO 6400 just isn't high enough for you, you have the option of increasing it to the next level, ISO 12800. This setting won't appear as a number, but as an "H" on your top LCD Panel and within the viewfinder. Once again we'll tap into the 7D's custom settings to allow you to raise your ISO and shoot at this setting.

SETTING UP THE ISO EXPANSION FEATURE

1. Press the Menu button and locate the Custom Function screen.

2. The ISO Expansion setting is located in the C.Fn I: Exposure section. Highlight it and press Set (**A**).

3. Use the Quick Control dial to locate the ISO Expansion section (it's the third menu item), and then press the Set button.

4. Using the Quick Control dial, change the setting to On and then press the Set button (**B**).

5. Press the Menu button twice to exit, then press the ISO button and set it to the H setting with the Main dial.

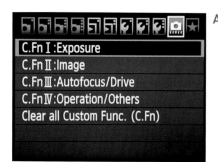

A

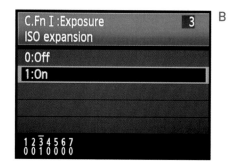

B

While you are able to capture images in extremely low light situations, the noise from this setting is highly visible (**Figure 7.2**). My recommendation is to use the H setting sparingly and only as a last resort.

Manual Callout

For a table that lists all of the programmable custom functions, including the ISO Expansion feature, turn to page 204 in your user's manual.

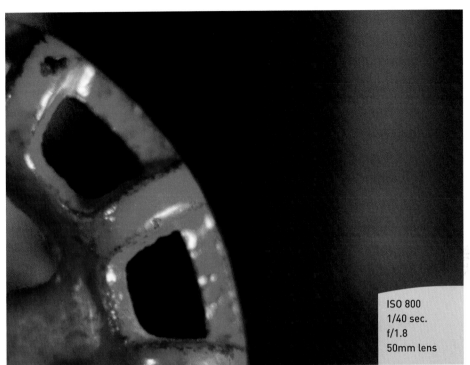

ISO 800
1/40 sec.
f/1.8
50mm lens

FIGURE 7.2

It's not difficult to see the difference in quality that the extremely high ISO levels can produce. This is a cropped portion of an image photographed at two different ISO settings. The top half shows the photo taken at ISO 800 and has a very tolerable amount of noise, while the bottom half was photographed at ISO 12800 (the H setting) and produces an enormous amount of noise and grain.

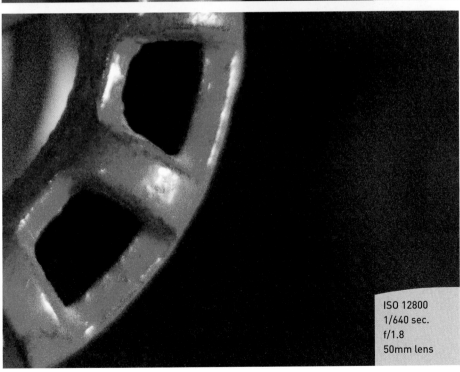

ISO 12800
1/640 sec.
f/1.8
50mm lens

STABILIZING THE SITUATION

Many of today's Canon lenses come with a feature called image stabilization (IS). If you happen to have one of these lenses, you have a little extra help keeping your lens stable while doing any type of handheld photography. This is extremely useful in situations where the light is low and, to prevent camera shake, you need to set your shutter speed slower than you normally would when shooting without a tripod (**Figure 7.3**). Most people can hold their camera steady at 1/60 of a second or faster. The longer your focal length, the faster your shutter speed needs to be in order to keep your images sharp and free of camera shake.

FIGURE 7.3
I used an image stabilization (IS) lens to photograph this image with a shutter speed that would have normally been too slow to shoot hand-held with the focal length I was using.

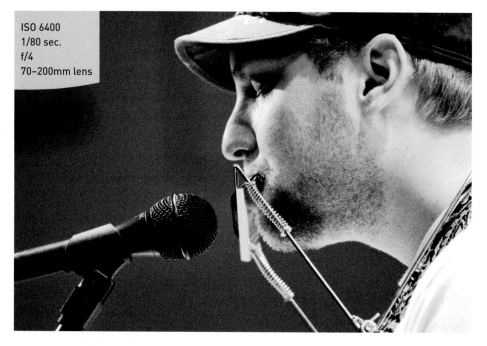

ISO 6400
1/80 sec.
f/4
70–200mm lens

The Canon IS lenses contain small gyro sensors and servo-actuated optical elements that correct for camera shake and stabilize the image. The IS function is so good that it is possible to improve your handheld photography by two or three stops, meaning that if you are pretty solid at a shutter speed of 1/60, the IS feature lets you shoot at 1/15, and possibly even 1/8 of a second (**Figures 7.4** and **7.5**).

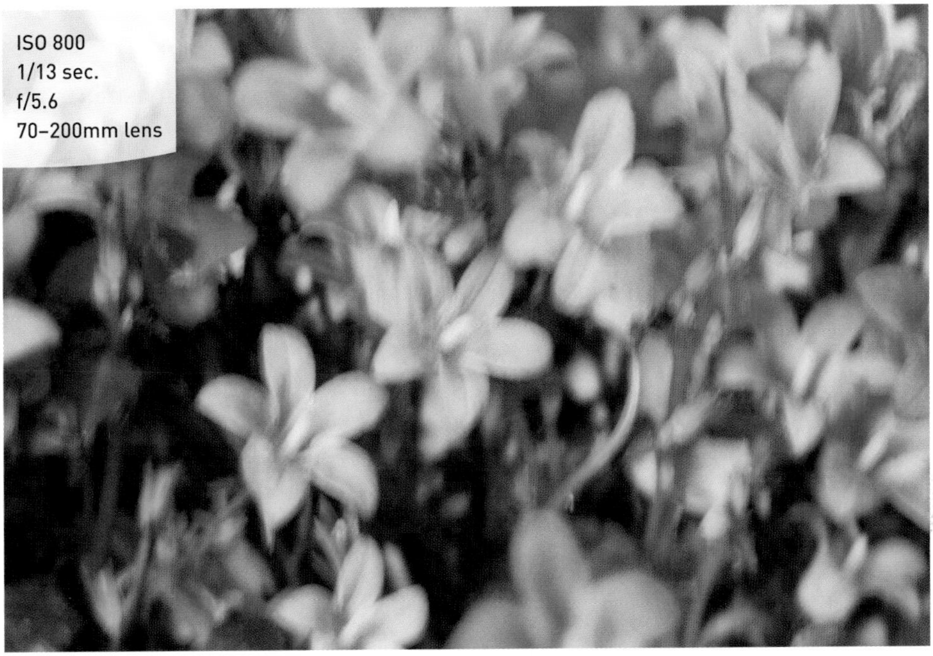

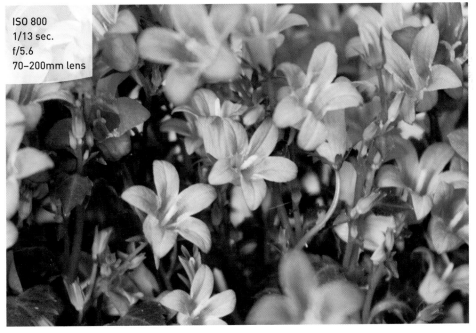

ISO 800
1/13 sec.
f/5.6
70–200mm lens

FIGURE 7.4
This image was photographed without the use of image stabilization.

ISO 800
1/13 sec.
f/5.6
70–200mm lens

FIGURE 7.5
I took the same shot as Figure 7.4, but this time I turned on the image stabilization to help steady my shot and prevent motion blur.

FOCUSING IN LOW LIGHT

When you are taking photos in low-light situations, you will find that the camera's autofocus doesn't always work. But before you can properly and consistently find focus in these instances, you need to understand how your camera's focusing system operates.

First, you should know that when you are trying to focus on your subject, the camera utilizes contrast in the viewfinder in order to establish a focus point. If you were to point your camera at a clean, blank wall and try to focus it right in the center, the lens would hunt around and probably not find focus (**Figure 7.6**). By moving the focus point to an area where there is contrast, the camera will be able to set focus much more quickly (**Figure 7.7**).

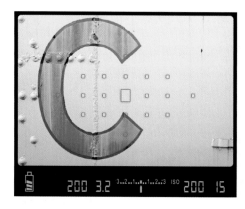 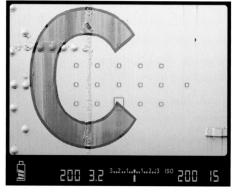

FIGURE 7.6
The camera wasn't able to autofocus on this image because the focus point was set to the center, where there wasn't enough contrast for it to work properly.

FIGURE 7.7
By changing the focus point to an area where there was contrast, I was able to properly focus this shot.

If your subject doesn't have enough contrast for the camera to read, you can always use the "focus and recompose" method of shooting if you find an area of contrast that is at the same distance as your subject. To do this, press the Shutter button halfway to set focus, and then—with the button still pressed halfway—recompose your shot in the viewfinder. When you have it composed how you like it, press the Shutter button fully. The focus should stay where you originally set it.

Another option is to use the manual focusing system. If you are photographing something that is difficult to focus on, like fireworks, you should set your camera's focusing manually. If you point the camera into the dark sky, the autofocusing system will just keep searching for—and not finding—a focus point (**Figure 7.8**). To set your focus manually, just flip the switch on the lens from AF to MF and rotate the front of the lens until your focus is set.

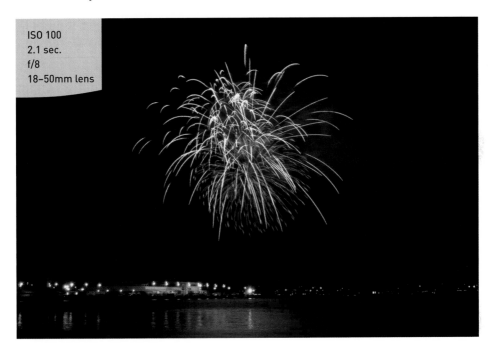

ISO 100
2.1 sec.
f/8
18–50mm lens

FIGURE 7.8
In order to focus properly for this fireworks photograph, I manually focused my lens.

FOCUS ASSIST

Another way to ensure good focus is to enable the 7D's Focus Assist mode. This setting uses the flash to send out short bursts of light on your subject to help the camera in locating detail. If you don't want to use the flash, you can disable it while you take your photos—the flash would only be used temporarily to help find focus but wouldn't actually appear in your shot. If you are using the Full Auto or Creative Auto modes, this feature is automatically enabled.

TURNING ON THE FOCUS ASSIST FEATURE

1. Press the Menu button and then use the Main dial to get to the Custom Function menu tab.

2. Rotate the Quick Control dial to highlight the C.Fn III: Autofocus/Drive setting and press the Set button (**A**).

3. Use the Quick Control dial to get to the eleventh item, the AF-Assist Beam Firing section.

4. Press the Set button and select Enable, and then press Set to lock in your choice (**B**).

5. Press the Menu button twice to exit, and then press the Flash button located on the front of your camera. Now with the flash in the "up" position, press the Shutter button to focus and activate Focus Assist.

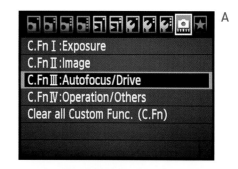

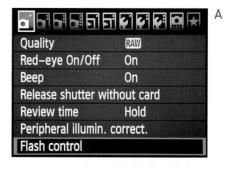

If you don't want the flash to fire during the actual exposure, you must first disable the flash.

DISABLING THE FLASH

1. Press the Menu button and then scroll the Main dial to highlight the first camera setup tab.

2. Scroll down to Flash Control and press the Set button (**A**).

3. Set the Flash Firing option to Disable (**B**).

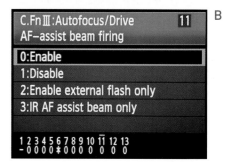

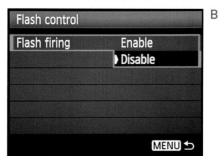

SHOOTING LONG EXPOSURES

Sometimes you'll want to shoot in low light and use a long exposure, such as when photographing fireworks, star trails, or streaks of light coming from cars on the street. The first thing you'll need in order to capture quality images with long shutter speeds is a sturdy tripod. It's also a good idea to use a cable release (see Chapter 3) or the self-timer to prevent any type of movement in your image when pressing the Shutter button.

Because your camera is stabilized on a tripod, you don't need a high ISO. In fact, it's actually better to keep the ISO low (usually between 100 and 400) to reduce the amount of noise in an image. Often with long exposures you'll introduce a different type of noise in your image because of the amount of time the shutter is open—this noise is referred to as "pattern noise" or "hot pixels," and the 7D has a setting that helps to reduce this noise.

SELF-TIME YOUR WAY TO SHARPER IMAGES

Whether you are shooting with a tripod or resting your camera on a counter, you can increase the sharpness of your pictures by taking your hands out of the equation. Whenever you use your finger to depress the Shutter button, you are increasing the chance that there will be a little bit of shake in your image. If you don't have a cable release to trigger the Shutter button, try setting your camera up to use the self-timer. To turn on the self-timer, just press the AF · Drive button and rotate the Quick Control dial until the self-timer icon appears in the top LCD Panel. (You

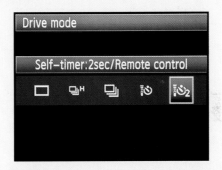

FIGURE 7.9

The Drive mode has two options for self-timer: 10 seconds and 2 seconds.

can also adjust the Drive mode by using the Quick Control button located on the back of the camera as in **Figure 7.9**.) There are two self-timer modes to choose from: 2 seconds and 10 seconds. I generally use the 2-second mode to cut down on time between exposures.

TURNING ON LONG EXPOSURE NOISE REDUCTION

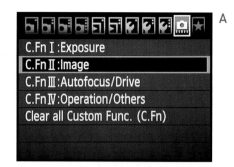

1. Press the Menu button and locate the Custom Function screen.

2. The Long Exposure Noise Reduction setting is located in the C.Fn II: Image section. Highlight it and press Set (**A**).

3. Use the Quick Control dial to locate the Long Exposure Noise Reduction section (it's the first menu item), and then press the Set button.

4. Use the Quick Control dial to select Auto, and then press the Set button (**B**).

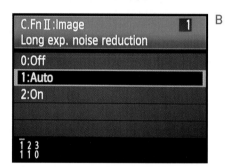

5. Press the Menu button twice to exit. This noise reduction will be applied to all images with exposures that are 1 second or longer.

6. When using the Long Exposure Noise Reduction setting, you'll notice some lag-time after taking each photograph. This is because the camera is working and reducing the noise in the most recent shot. You won't be able to take another photo until this process is complete.

Now that the noise is under control, you need to determine the camera mode to use when photographing long exposures. When I photograph long exposures, I will use either the Av or Manual modes. Sometimes I start in Av so I can choose the aperture and then see what the camera thinks is the best shutter speed. After I take a few test shots to get an idea of what range works well, I switch into Manual mode and continue from there. You will probably find that using manual focus is the best choice as well, since it will usually be too dark for your camera to find focus on its own.

USING THE BUILT-IN FLASH

There are going to be times when you have to turn to your camera's built-in flash to get the shot. The pop-up flash on the 7D is not extremely powerful, but with the camera's advanced metering system, it does a pretty good job of lighting up the night… or just filling in the shadows.

The built-in flash will automatically pop up in the Full Auto and Creative Auto modes if the camera senses that there isn't sufficient light for your scene. In all other modes (P, Av, Tv, and so on) you'll need to push the Flash button, located on the front of your camera, to activate it.

SHUTTER SPEEDS

The standard flash synchronization speed for your camera is between 1/60 and 1/250 of a second. If you set the shutter speed faster than 1/250 of a second, it will be too fast to catch all the light produced from the flash. In fact, you'll find that your camera won't let you go beyond 1/250 of a second when the pop-up flash is activated.

The key to great flash photography is controlling the shutter speed. The longer your shutter is open, the more ambient light you can let into your image. If you are photographing a person during a sunset and drop your shutter speed low enough to capture the light behind them, you can add beautiful colors to the background. Using different shutter speeds with a flash makes it possible to create some fun and creative shots as well (see Chapter 10). Let's take a look at how each of the camera modes affects the shutter speed when using your flash.

- **Program (P):** The shutter speed is automatically set between 1/60 and 1/250 of a second. The only adjustment you can make in this mode is to your exposure compensation by using the Quick Control dial to change the f-stop.

- **Shutter Priority (Tv):** You can adjust the shutter speed to as fast as 1/250 of a second all the way down to 30 seconds. The lens aperture will adjust accordingly, but typically at long exposures the lens will be set to its largest aperture.

- **Aperture Priority (Av):** This mode has three custom settings for adjusting the shutter speed when using the flash, depending on your needs. The default setting is Auto, which will set your shutter speed and is the recommended setting to start off with.

METERING MODES

The built-in flash uses a technology called E-TTL II (Evaluative Through The Lens) metering to determine the appropriate amount of flash power to output for a good exposure. When you press the Shutter button halfway, the camera quickly adjusts focus while gathering information from the entire scene to measure the amount of ambient light. As you press the Shutter button down completely, a pre-flash occurs to meter the light off the subject from the flash, and a determination is made as to how much power is needed to balance the subject with the ambient light. This applies to the P, Tv, and Av camera modes.

The default setting for the flash meter mode is Evaluative. You can set the meter to Average mode, but that should probably be avoided. Your best results will come from the E-TTL mode.

However, if you have special metering needs, such as a background that is very light or dark, you might consider using the Flash Exposure (FE) Lock to meter off your subject and then recompose your image in the viewfinder.

This feature works much like the Automatic Exposure (AE) Lock function that was discussed in Chapter 4.

USING THE FE LOCK FEATURE

1. Press the Flash button on the front of your camera to turn on the built-in flash. Then point the camera at the area that you want to base the flash exposure on (this is normally your subject).

2. Press the Multi-function button (M-Fn), located next to the Shutter button. You will see "FEL" (Flash Exposure Lock) appear on the bottom of the viewfinder momentarily, and the flash will fire a pre-flash to measure exposure. The AE/FE lock symbol (an asterisk) will also appear in the viewfinder.

3. Recompose the scene as you like, focus, and press the Shutter button completely.

The FE Lock will cancel after each exposure, so you have to repeat these steps each time you need to lock the flash exposure.

Using the Average metering mode might also require that you tweak the flash output by using Flash Exposure Compensation. This is because the camera will be metering the entire scene to set the exposure, so you might have to add or subtract flash power to balance out the scene.

COMPENSATING FOR THE FLASH EXPOSURE

Sometimes your flash will be too bright or too dark for your subject. While the E-TTL system is highly advanced and will get the flash's output close to where it should be, it doesn't always know what you want the image to look like. What's great about your flash is that it has its own exposure compensation that you can adjust as easily as the aperture and shutter speed exposure compensation that you learned about in Chapter 3.

CHANGING SETTINGS USING THE QUICK CONTROL DIAL

You can change the Flash Exposure Compensation, along with several other settings, by using the Quick Control button on the back of your camera. Just press the Q and use the Multi-Controller to scroll to the setting you want to change, in this case the Flash Exposure Compensation (**A**). You can adjust your settings directly from the main screen using either the Quick Control dial or the Main dial, or you can press Set to see a detailed view of each item and adjust your settings from there (**B**).

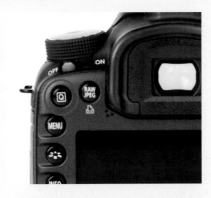

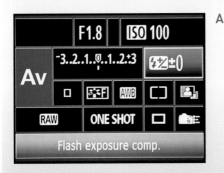

A

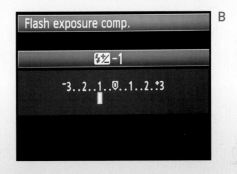

B

Like exposure compensation, flash compensation allows you to dial in a change in the flash output in increments of 1/3 of a stop. You will probably use this most often to tone down the effects of your flash, especially when you are using the flash as a subtle fill light.

USING THE FLASH EXPOSURE COMPENSATION FEATURE TO CHANGE THE FLASH OUTPUT

1. Press the ISO/Flash Exposure Compensation button to get to the compensation setup mode.

2. Look at the top LCD Panel (or in the viewfinder) and spin the Quick Control dial to change the output of the flash. Turning clockwise towards the plus-sign side of the scale adds exposure (more flash power), and turning counterclockwise toward the minus sign reduces exposure (less flash power). Note that turning the Main dial will result in a change of ISO, so be sure to use the Quick Control dial.

3. Press the Shutter button halfway to return to shooting mode, and then take the picture.

4. Review your image to see if more or less flash compensation is required, and repeat these steps as necessary.

5. The Flash Exposure Compensation feature does not reset itself when the camera is turned off, so whatever compensation you have set will remain in effect until you change it. Your only clue to knowing that the flash output is changed will be the presence of the Flash Exposure Compensation symbol in the viewfinder. It will disappear when there is zero compensation set.

REDUCING RED-EYE

When photographing people with an on-camera flash, one thing that we've all seen and would like to avoid is red-eye. This effect is the result of the light from the flash entering the pupil and then reflecting back as an eerie red glow. This is especially true when it is dark and the subject's eyes are dilated. It occurs most often when you're using an on-axis flash (a flash that's aligned with the lens of your camera), since most people will be looking at the camera's lens, and thus very near the flash, when their photo is taken.

There are two ways to avoid this problem. The first is to move the flash away from the lens, but if you're using the built-in flash that's not an option. The second is to turn on the 7D's Red-Eye Reduction feature. This is a simple feature that shines a light from the camera at the subject, causing their pupils to shrink, thus eliminating or reducing the effects of red-eye.

The feature is set to Off by default and needs to be turned on in the shooting menu.

TURN ON THE LIGHTS!

When shooting indoors, another way to reduce red-eye—or just to shorten the length of time that the reduction lamp needs to be shining into your subject's eyes—is to turn on a lot of lights. The brighter the ambient light levels, the smaller the subject's pupils will be. This will reduce the time necessary for the red-eye reduction lamp to shine, and it will allow you to take more candid pictures because your subjects won't be required to stare at the red-eye lamp while waiting for their pupils to reduce.

TURNING ON THE RED-EYE REDUCTION FEATURE

1. Press the Menu button and then turn the Main dial to get to the first shooting menu tab.

2. Use the Quick Control dial to scroll down to Red-eye On/Off (**A**).

3. Press the Set button and then, using the Quick Control dial, select On and press the Set button (**B**).

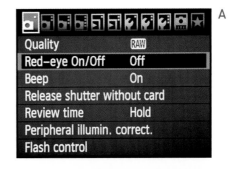

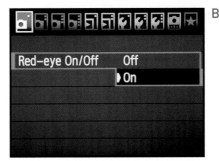

Press the Menu button or the Shutter button to return to shooting mode.

To get the full benefit from the Red-Eye Reduction feature, you should hold down the Shutter button halfway, which causes the reduction light to shine into your subject's eyes. A small scale will appear in the viewfinder that shows how long to hold the Shutter button before pressing completely. Once the countdown scale has reduced down to nothing, press the Shutter button completely to take the picture.

2ND CURTAIN SYNC

The 7D has two flash synchronization modes: first curtain and second curtain. The term *curtain* relates to the opening and closing of the shutter—the first curtain refers to when the shutter is being opened, and the second curtain describes the point just before the shutter is closed (try to visualize a curtain on a stage opening and closing; the amount of time it's opened is how long your shutter speed is).

The built-in flash on your camera can be synchronized to fire during the first curtain or the second curtain. This only applies to shutter speeds of 1/30 of a second or slower, since a faster shutter speed moves so quickly that the mode wouldn't really matter. But for longer exposures, I find that using the second curtain flash is usually the best option.

FLASH SYNC

The basic idea behind the term *flash synchronization* (*flash sync* for short) is that when you take a photograph using the flash, the camera needs to ensure that the shutter is fully open at the time that the flash goes off. This is not an issue if you are using a long shutter speed such as 1/15 of a second, but it becomes more critical for fast shutter speeds. To ensure that the flash and shutter are synchronized so that the flash is going off while the shutter is open, the 7D implements a top sync speed of 1/250 of a second. This means that when you are using the flash, your shutter speed cannot be any faster than 1/250. If you used a faster shutter speed, the shutter would actually start closing before the flash fired, causing a black area to appear in the frame where the light from the flash was blocked.

For example, imagine you are photographing a person running (let's say from left to right) in a race. It's somewhat dark outside, maybe at sunset, so you can get away with a slower shutter speed of 1/15 of a second, but you also want to use your flash to freeze the subject in place. If you take their photo in 1st Curtain Sync mode, the flash will fire right away and the person will run across the frame during the rest of the exposure. Because you used a slower shutter speed, you will see blur in front of the runner, as the flash froze them in place at the beginning of the exposure. If you change your flash setting to 2nd Curtain Sync and take the same photograph, you'll see some blur across the frame after you press the Shutter button, but the flash will fire at the end of the exposure, making the blur appear behind the runner.

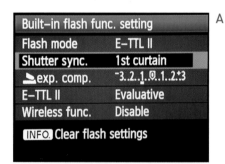

SETTING 2ND CURTAIN SYNC

1. Press the Menu button and use the Main dial to navigate to the first camera setup menu tab, select Flash Control, and press Set.

2. Use the Quick Control dial to select the Built-in Flash Function setting, and then press the Set button (**A**).

3. Use the Quick Control dial to select Shutter Sync, press Set, and select 2nd curtain (**B**).

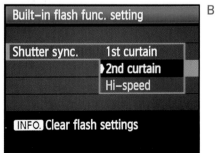

Now, when you are using a slow shutter speed (slower than 1/30 of a second), once you press the shutter you'll notice a quick burst of light from the flash to measure exposure, then the full burst at the end of the exposure to light your subject.

A FEW WORDS ABOUT EXTERNAL FLASH

The built-in pop-up flash on the 7D is a nice addition to the camera and, as you've learned in this chapter, it can be useful, but as far as quality of light goes, it's average. I don't use this flash very frequently in my photography since I find that there are other, more flattering ways to light my subjects.

Many professional photographers use an external flash, or Speedlite, in their photography when they need an additional and portable light source (**Figure 7.10**). Speedlites are extremely sophisticated for their size and can produce an amazing quality of light with customizable settings. You can place them almost anywhere in the scene to light a subject.

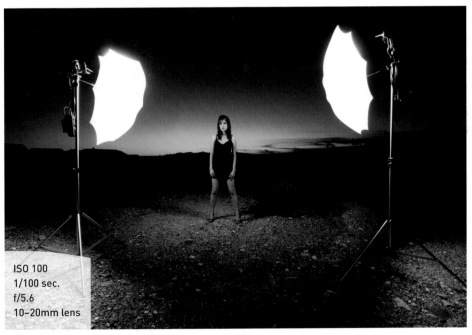

ISO 100
1/100 sec.
f/5.6
10–20mm lens

FIGURE 7.10
This image was photographed using two off-camera radio-triggered Speedlites.

One new feature on the Canon 7D is its ability to wirelessly fire any of the Canon Speedlites by using the pop-up flash as a trigger. This powerful feature opens up a lot of photographic opportunities when it comes to using off-camera flash. I won't go into the details of how to use this feature (or any other off-camera flash photography methods) in this book, but many resources are available if you're interested in trying it out. Your manual is a good place to start, but a Web site like Strobist™ (http://strobist.blogspot.com) will offer more advanced information about creating great images using small flashes.

Manual Callout

There are a lot of different ways to set up and use the wireless flash settings on your Canon 7D. If you are interested in learning more about this feature, I recommend reading pages 119–128 of your user's manual. Don't forget to take a look at your Speedlite owner's manual as well.

Chapter 7 Challenges

Now that we have looked at the possibilities of shooting after dark, it's time to put it all to the test. These assignments cover the full range of shooting possibilities, both with flash and without. Let's get started.

Steadying your shots with IS

It's important to understand just how powerful your IS lens can be in steadying your shots. Using your IS lens, find a subject and set your camera to Tv mode. With the IS button turned to On, take a few photos at 1/30, 1/15, and 1/8 of a second. Then turn the IS feature to Off and take the same shots with the same settings. Compare your images to see how much more camera shake you are creating in each shot.

Pushing your ISO to the extreme

Turn on the Extended ISO feature. Now find a place to shoot where the ambient light level is low. This could be at night or indoors in a darkened room. Using the mode of your choice, start increasing the ISO from 100 until you get to 12800. Make sure you evaluate the level of noise in your image, especially in the shadow areas. Only you can decide how much noise is acceptable in your pictures.

Getting rid of the noise

Turn on the High ISO Speed Noise Reduction feature and repeat the previous assignment. Find your acceptable limits with the noise reduction turned on. Also pay attention to how much detail is lost in your shadows with this function enabled.

Long exposures in the dark

If you don't have a tripod, find a stable place to set your camera outside and try some long exposures. Set your camera to Av mode and then use the self-timer to activate the camera (this will keep you from shaking the camera while pressing the Shutter button). Or, use a cable release if you have one.

Shoot in an area that has some level of ambient light, be it a streetlight or traffic lights, or even a full moon. The idea is to get some late-night low-light exposures. For best results, perform this assignment and the next assignment in the same shooting session using the same subject.

Reducing the noise in your long exposures

Now repeat the last assignment with Long Exposure Noise Reduction set to On. Look at the difference in the images that were taken before and after the noise reduction was enabled.

Testing the limits of the pop-up flash

Wait for the lights to get low and then press the pop-up flash button to start using the built-in flash. Try using the different shooting modes to see how they affect your exposures. Use the Flash Exposure Compensation feature to take a series of pictures while adjusting from –2 stops all the way to +2 stops so that you become familiar with how much latitude you will get from this feature.

Getting the red out

Find a friend with some patience and a tolerance for bright lights. Have them sit in a darkened room or outside at night and then take their picture with the flash. Now turn on Red-Eye Reduction to see if you get better results. Don't forget to wait for the red-eye timer to completely extinguish before taking the picture.

Getting creative with 2nd Curtain Sync

Now it's time for a little creative fun. Set your camera up for 2nd Curtain Sync and start shooting. Moving targets are best. Experiment with Tv and Av modes to lower the shutter speeds and exaggerate the effect. Try using a low ISO so the camera is forced to use longer shutter speeds. Be creative and have some fun!

Share your results with the book's Flickr group!

Join the group here: flickr.com/groups/canon7dfromsnapshotstogreatshots

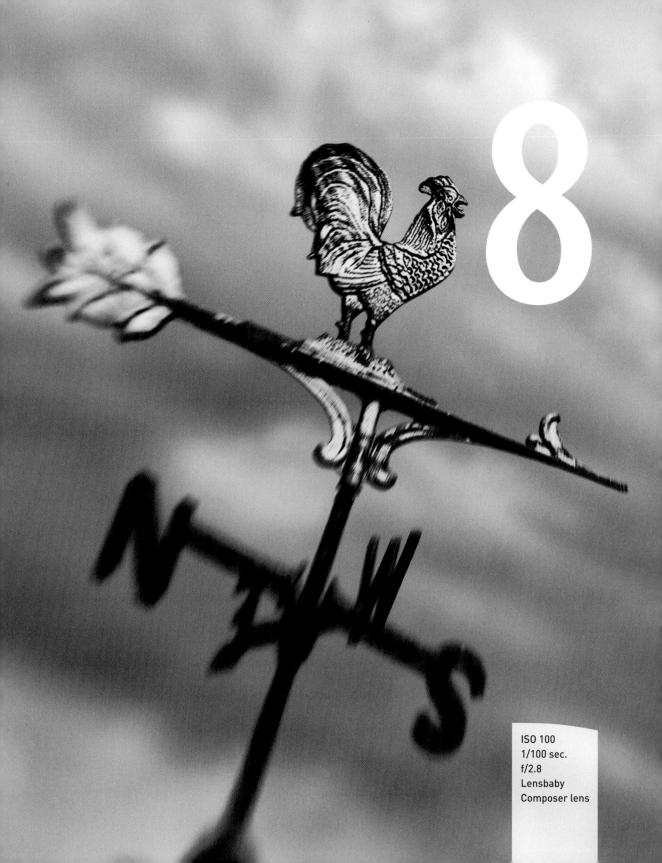

8

ISO 100
1/100 sec.
f/2.8
Lensbaby
Composer lens

Creative Compositions

IMPROVE YOUR PICTURES WITH SOUND COMPOSITIONAL ELEMENTS

To make a beautiful photograph you need more than just knowledge about your camera and its settings—you should also have a good understanding of how to compose your images. Being able to create beautiful compositions is an extremely useful skill and is sometimes more important than the nitty-gritty technical aspects of photography. Just knowing one or two tricks isn't enough, but learning several methods and piecing them together will help you to create great images. In this chapter, we will examine how you can add interest to your photos by utilizing common compositional techniques.

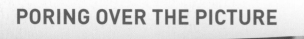

The Lensbaby lens was angled toward the bottom of the frame to give the image a slanted look. ●———————

One of my favorite lenses to use on the 7D is the Lensbaby. It's a specialty lens that allows you to give your images a unique blur, and while photographing on the streets of Las Vegas, I decided to play around with it. Instead of actually focusing on something, I used it at its widest aperture and found that the completely out–of–focus lights on the street were beautiful, colorful, and ever changing. I waited until some cars passed by and snapped a few pictures. Even though this image doesn't have a distinct subject, I'm really pleased with the colorful circles that the Lensbaby helped to create.

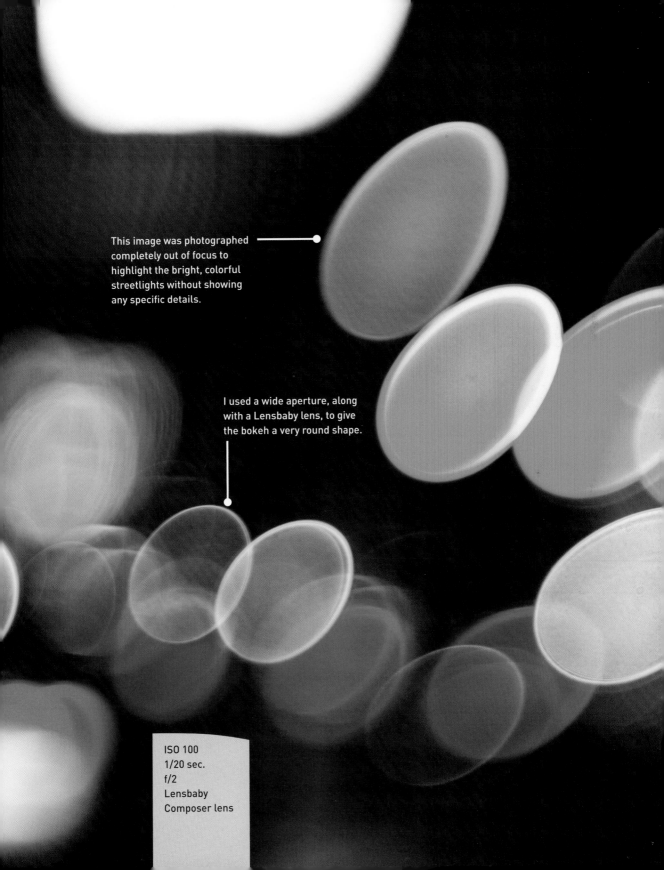

This image was photographed completely out of focus to highlight the bright, colorful streetlights without showing any specific details.

I used a wide aperture, along with a Lensbaby lens, to give the bokeh a very round shape.

ISO 100
1/20 sec.
f/2
Lensbaby
Composer lens

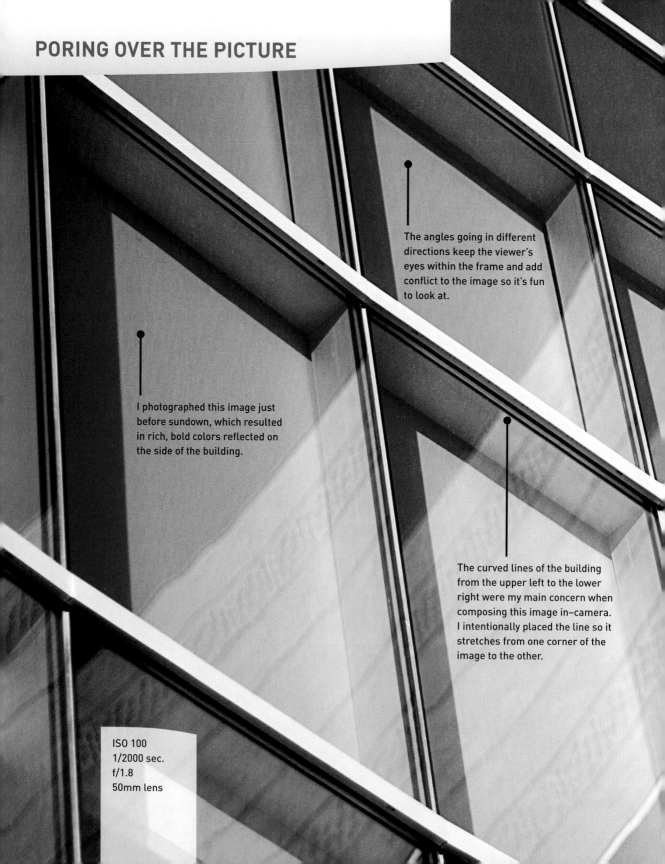

The angles going in different directions keep the viewer's eyes within the frame and add conflict to the image so it's fun to look at.

I photographed this image just before sundown, which resulted in rich, bold colors reflected on the side of the building.

The curved lines of the building from the upper left to the lower right were my main concern when composing this image in-camera. I intentionally placed the line so it stretches from one corner of the image to the other.

ISO 100
1/2000 sec.
f/1.8
50mm lens

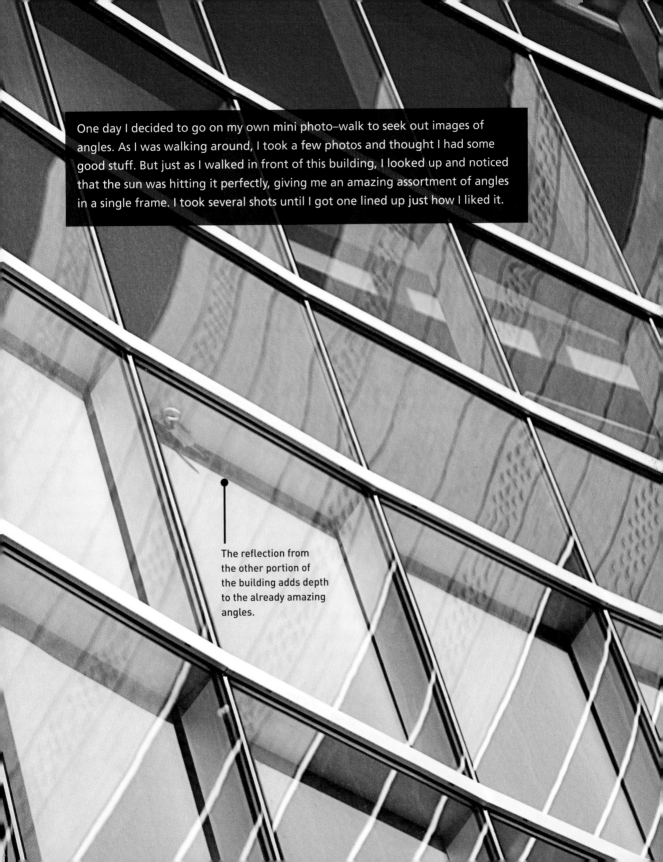

One day I decided to go on my own mini photo–walk to seek out images of angles. As I was walking around, I took a few photos and thought I had some good stuff. But just as I walked in front of this building, I looked up and noticed that the sun was hitting it perfectly, giving me an amazing assortment of angles in a single frame. I took several shots until I got one lined up just how I liked it.

The reflection from the other portion of the building adds depth to the already amazing angles.

DEPTH OF FIELD

Selective focusing with a wide aperture can add a lot of creativity to your images. You are telling the viewer where you want the focus of the image to be, and the meaning and story changes depending on what is in focus. Using a telephoto lens can compress your background even more, decreasing the depth of field and making the background or foreground even blurrier. But take into consideration that just because your background or foreground is blurry, it doesn't mean you can't show detail in those areas (**Figure 8.1**).

FIGURE 8.1
A very wide aperture was used in this image to create a blurred background; the man in the background is still fully visible even though the focus is on the woman.

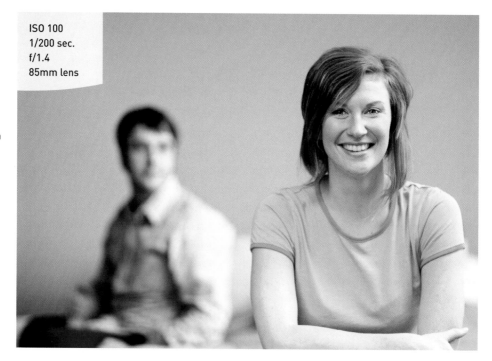

ISO 100
1/200 sec.
f/1.4
85mm lens

If you want the entire image to be in focus, you would use a smaller aperture. Images with great depth of field, such as a landscape or an image with a lot of detail, direct the viewer to look at the entire scene (**Figure 8.2**).

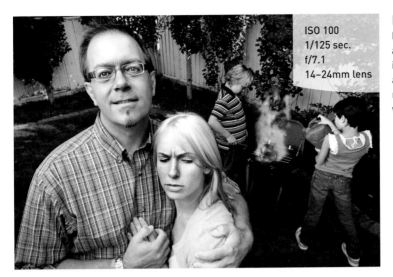

ISO 100
1/125 sec.
f/7.1
14–24mm lens

FIGURE 8.2
In order to capture all the details in this image, I used a small aperture so that the majority of the scene was in focus.

BACKGROUNDS

When taking pictures we usually pay close attention to our subject. This, of course, is a wise thing to do when using your camera, but it's also very important (and sometimes even more important) to pay attention to the background or backdrop *behind* your subject (**Figure 8.3**). The background can make or break your photograph. You should be careful of anything behind your subjects that could appear to be sticking out of their heads (trees are a common culprit) or of busy backgrounds that could compete with whatever or whoever you are photographing.

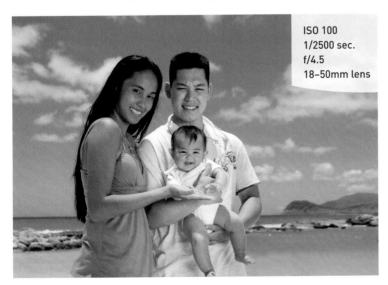

ISO 100
1/2500 sec.
f/4.5
18–50mm lens

FIGURE 8.3
This family was framed so that there were no distracting elements behind them.

ANGLES

Strong angles in an image can add a lot to the composition, especially when the angles and lines are going in different directions (**Figure 8.4**). This can create a tension that is different from the standard horizontal and vertical lines that we are so accustomed to seeing in photos.

You can accentuate the angles in your images by tilting the camera, thus adding an unfamiliar angle to the subject, which draws the viewer's attention (**Figure 8.5**).

FIGURE 8.4
The assortment of angles and lines reflected on this building added visual interest to the image.

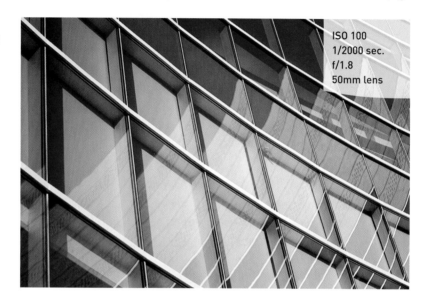

ISO 100
1/2000 sec.
f/1.8
50mm lens

FIGURE 8.5
I tilted the camera when photograph-ing this plate of food—a technique referred to as "Dutch angle."

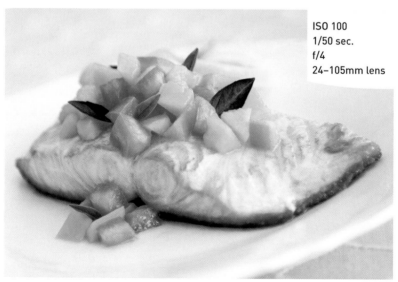

ISO 100
1/50 sec.
f/4
24–105mm lens

CREATIVE AND SPECIALTY LENSES

You can create shallow and great depth of field effects with any lens you own, but some specialty lenses create unusual and unique *bokeh* (the area that is out of focus in your image) and also offer an enormous range of creative photographic possibilities.

Tilt-Shift Lens

The tilt-shift lens was created to correct lens distortion in images. It's a popular lens for architectural photography because it keeps the lines of structures straight, not curved like you would see with wide-angle lens distortion. One side benefit of using this lens is that it creates unique bokeh and can make things look miniature if photographed from high up (**Figure 8.6**).

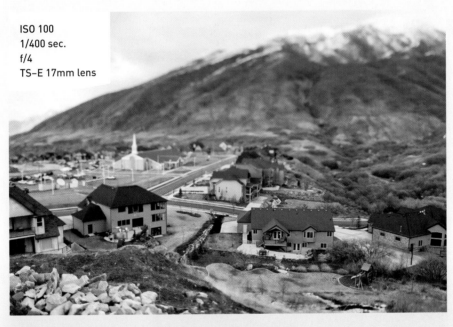

ISO 100
1/400 sec.
f/4
TS–E 17mm lens

FIGURE 8.6
The unique bokeh effect of the tilt–shift lens makes the houses in this image look like a miniature model.

Continued ➤

Lensbaby

The Lensbaby (**Figure 8.7**) creates a similar bokeh effect to the tilt-shift lens, but instead of a focus area that is straight across, it has a "sweet spot" within the frame that can be moved around to give the image a different look, depending on the subject (**Figure 8.8**). The moveable lens comes with an array of accessories that can change the look of the image. One of my favorites is the Creative Aperture kit. It allows you to change the shape of the aperture, which will affect the shape of the bokeh. The bokeh shapes of apertures in traditional lenses and the normal Lensbaby are usually circular or octagonal (**Figure 8.9**), but with the Creative Aperture kit you can change the shape to hearts, stars—virtually anything you can imagine (**Figure 8.10**).

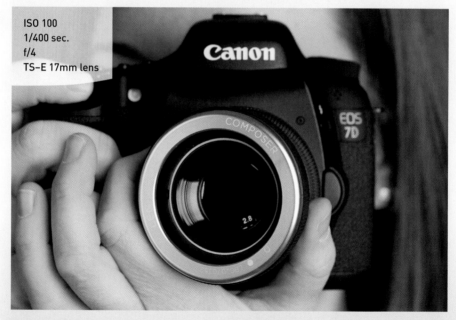

ISO 100
1/400 sec.
f/4
TS–E 17mm lens

FIGURE 8.7
Lensbaby Composer lens on the Canon 7D. (Photo by Rich Legg)

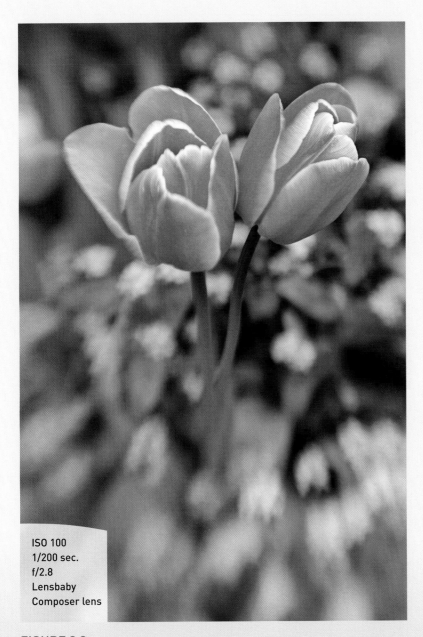

ISO 100
1/200 sec.
f/2.8
Lensbaby
Composer lens

FIGURE 8.8

In this photo, the petals on the tulip are in focus and the rest of the image is blurred.
The area that is in focus is sometimes referred to as the "sweet spot."

Continued ➤

FIGURE 8.9
I photographed this image with the Lensbaby Composer lens at its widest aperture and with nothing in focus.

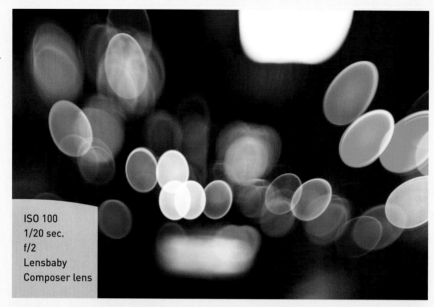

ISO 100
1/20 sec.
f/2
Lensbaby
Composer lens

FIGURE 8.10
The Lensbaby allows you to change the bokeh shape by using "shaped" apertures. I used a heart–shaped aperture in this photo to change the shape of the lights in the background.

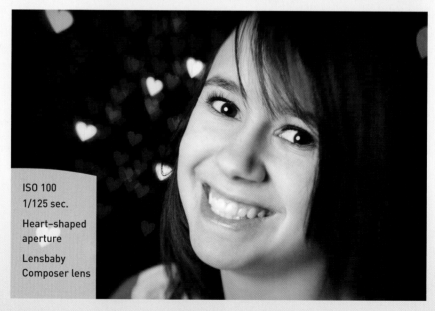

ISO 100
1/125 sec.

Heart–shaped aperture

Lensbaby
Composer lens

POINT OF VIEW

One thing I love about photography is that I get to show the world what I see, and it's always fun to try photographing a subject from a different point of view to see what I can create. You don't have to change your perspective drastically to get results—sometimes you can capture a great image simply by moving yourself up or down a few feet (**Figures 8.11** and **8.12**). Not only will you be looking at the subject from a different perspective, but your background will also change, sometimes for the better. Try moving up and down when taking photos to see what kind of results you can get.

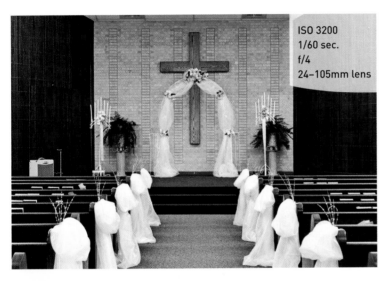

ISO 3200
1/60 sec.
f/4
24–105mm lens

FIGURE 8.11

This image of the inside of a church before a wedding was taken from a standing position.

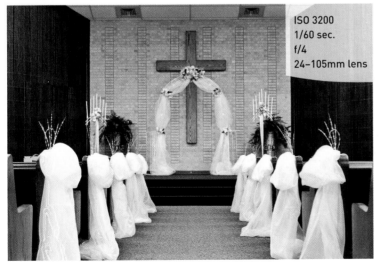

ISO 3200
1/60 sec.
f/4
24–105mm lens

FIGURE 8.12

Moving down a few feet and photographing the same scene from my knees changed the look of the entire bottom half of the image and is an improvement from the first photo. Notice that the back wall in the image doesn't change from Figure 8.11 to this one.

Giving your images a different perspective can also change the dynamics of the image (**Figure 8.13**). By getting in close, you bring the viewer into the scene so they feel as if they are experiencing the moment along with you.

FIGURE 8.13
I got in close to photograph this staged riot to make my viewers feel as if they were a part of it.

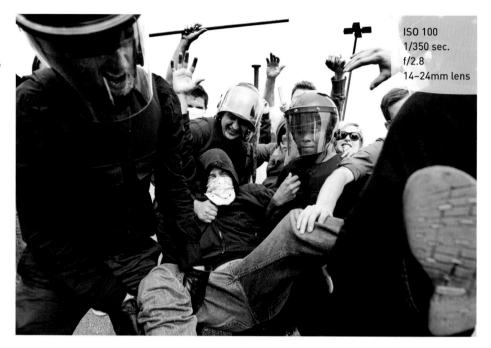

ISO 100
1/350 sec.
f/2.8
14–24mm lens

PATTERNS AND SHAPES

Geometric patterns are visually appealing and can be found almost anywhere you look (**Figure 8.14**). You see patterns not only in fabricated objects but also in nature, where some of the most beautiful and balanced patterns appear.

You can also use patterns, shapes, and even textures as a contrast to the main subject of your image (**Figure 8.15**). This is a very popular technique in portrait and bridal photography, where beautiful people are often photographed against harsh, textured surfaces or in urban environments.

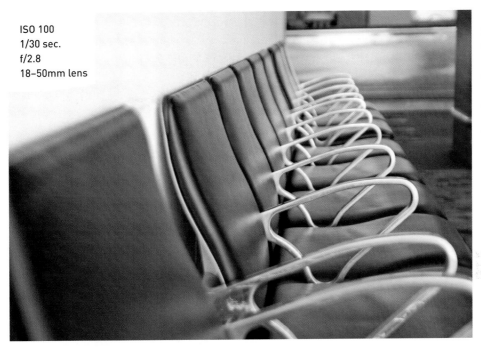

ISO 100
1/30 sec.
f/2.8
18–50mm lens

FIGURE 8.14
Sometimes you can find unusual patterns and shapes amidst ordinary objects, such as these chairs in an airport terminal.

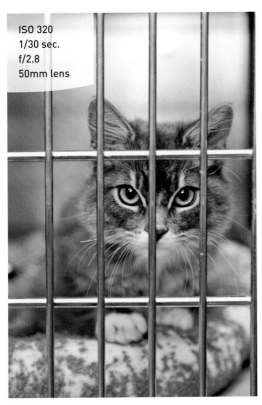

ISO 320
1/30 sec.
f/2.8
50mm lens

FIGURE 8.15
The harsh lines in the bars of this cage contrast with the soft features of the kitten.

COLOR

Color can play an extremely important part in composition, and understanding how color works will only help your images. In color theory, every color has an "opposite" color that is complementary. The primary colors are red, green, and blue, and their complementary colors are cyan, magenta, and yellow. Using these colors correctly can add balance and symmetry to your images (**Figure 8.16**).

You can use color as a theme in your photographs (**Figure 8.17**). It's always a bonus when a person I'm photographing has bright-colored eyes. I try to match the background with their eye color—this highlights the color in their eyes and can really make them "pop" (**Figure 8.18**).

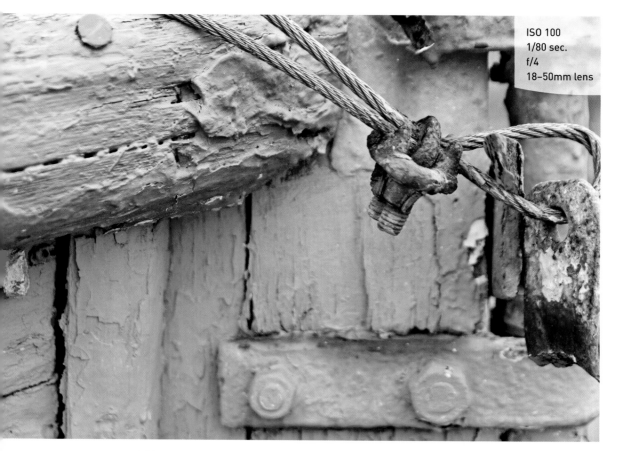

ISO 100
1/80 sec.
f/4
18–50mm lens

FIGURE 8.16
The pink and turquoise colors in this image are complementary and help to balance the composition of the shot.

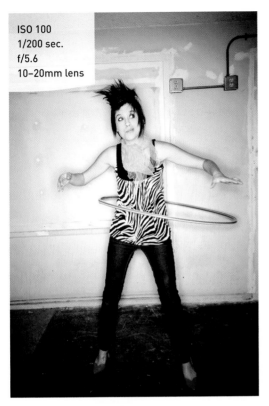

ISO 100
1/200 sec.
f/5.6
10–20mm lens

FIGURE 8.17
Try to find color themes in your photos—in this image the yellow in the woman's scarf matches the yellow paint on the wall directly behind her.

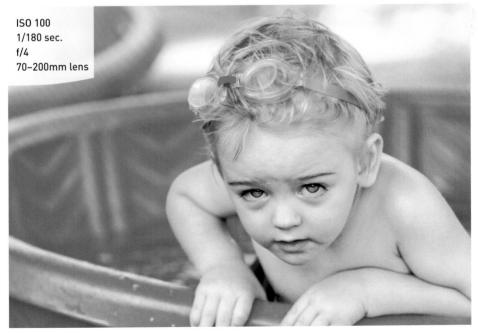

ISO 100
1/180 sec.
f/4
70–200mm lens

FIGURE 8.18
Matching the background with your subject's eye color can make their eyes really stand out.

LEADING LINES

Finding ways to draw your viewer's eyes toward the subject of your photo is important in photographic composition, and one way to do this is to incorporate leading lines in the image (**Figure 8.19**). You can also use this technique to create a vanishing point when the subject you are photographing is creating the lines—for example, a winding road twirling toward the corner of your frame or a row of trees going off into nowhere (**Figure 8.20**).

FIGURE 8.19
The leading lines of the windows draw the viewer's eyes to the main subjects.

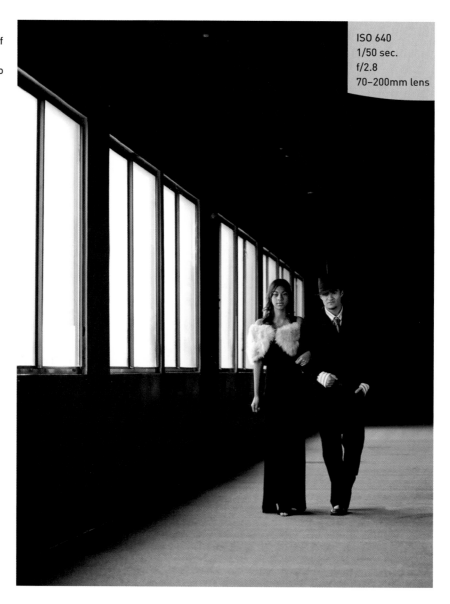

ISO 640
1/50 sec.
f/2.8
70–200mm lens

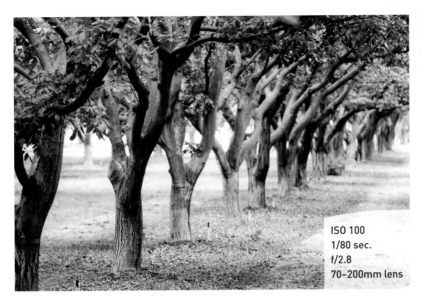

ISO 100
1/80 sec.
f/2.8
70–200mm lens

SPLITTING THE FRAME

As mentioned in previous chapters, it's usually a good idea to avoid placing your subject directly in the center of the frame. Sticking to the rule of thirds principle—placing the subject or horizon line one-third of the way from the edge of the frame—typically results in a pleasing composition (**Figure 8.21**).

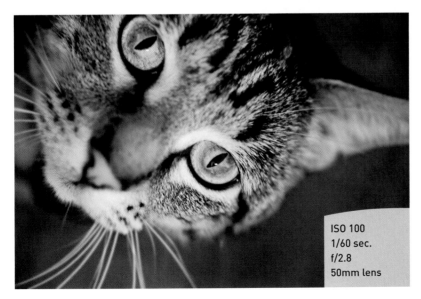

FIGURE 8.21
Even though the focus is centered in the middle of the frame on the cat's eye, the eyes and nose create a triangle that is in the left third of the frame.

ISO 100
1/60 sec.
f/2.8
50mm lens

FRAMES WITHIN FRAMES

The image you are photographing is already framed inside the confines of the viewfinder, but placing your subject within another frame can be a good way to draw the viewer's eyes toward the part of the image you would like to emphasize (**Figure 8.22**). You can also give the image a feeling of depth and help tell a story by being creative with the depth of field (**Figure 8.23**).

FIGURE 8.22
The vacant house in the background is framed by the broken window in the foreground.

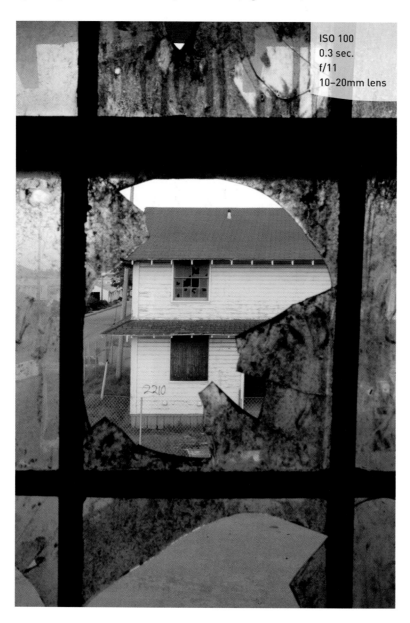

ISO 100
0.3 sec.
f/11
10–20mm lens

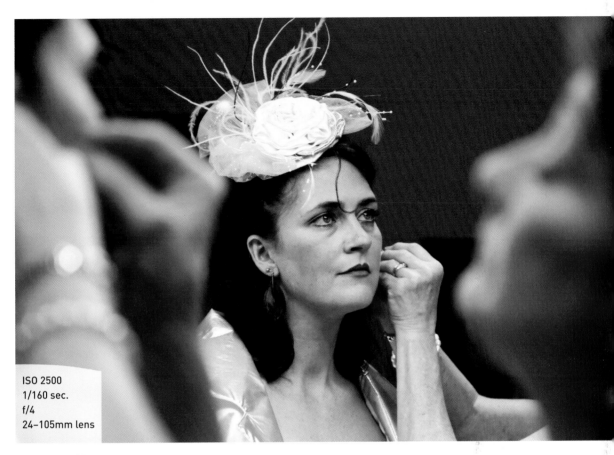

ISO 2500
1/160 sec.
f/4
24–105mm lens

FIGURE 8.23
The bride in the mirror is framed by her mother in the foreground. I used a wide aperture to give the image depth.

Chapter 8 Challenges

Apply the shooting techniques and tools that you've learned in the previous chapters to these assignments, and you'll improve your ability to incorporate good composition into your photos. Make sure you experiment with all the different elements of composition and see how you can combine them to add interest to your images.

Learning to see lines and patterns

Take your camera for a walk around your neighborhood and look for patterns and angles. Don't worry as much about getting great shots as about developing an eye for details.

Photographing a theme

Go on a photo-walk and give yourself a theme to photograph, such as a specific color or shape. Try to stick to this theme, and only take photos and look for images that contain that theme. Doing this will help you open your eyes to your environment in a new way and perhaps discover things you wouldn't have seen at first.

Changing your perspective

Take a photo from standing position, then move down lower to the ground and photograph the same thing. Try to get up higher by using a stepladder or just by inching up on your toes. Compare your images and see how different your subject looks from each point of view.

Using the aperture to focus attention

Depth of field plays an important role in defining your images and establishing depth and dimension. Practice shooting wide open, using your largest aperture, for the narrowest depth of field. Then find a scene that would benefit from extended depth of field, using very small apertures to give sharpness throughout the scene.

Leading viewers into a frame

Look for scenes where you can use elements as leading lines and then look for framing elements that you can use to isolate your subject and add both depth and dimension to your images.

Share your results with the book's Flickr group!

Join the group here: flickr.com/groups/canon7dfromsnapshotstogreatshots

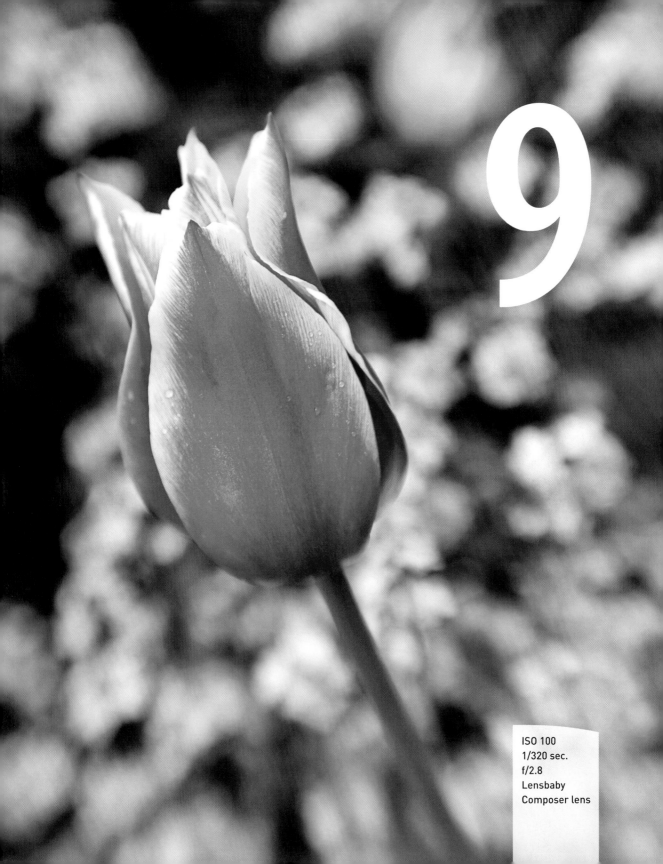

9

ISO 100
1/320 sec.
f/2.8
Lensbaby
Composer lens

Lights, Camera, Action!

MAKING MOVIES WITH THE CANON 7D

The ability to shoot still images and movies side by side is a huge advantage with today's digital SLR cameras. It opens up a world of creative possibilities, and the video feature on the 7D is one of the main reasons I decided to purchase this camera. Many still photographers are reinventing themselves and finding new ways to express their creativity and art through making videos, and your camera opens up those doors to make it possible for you, too.

CAMERA BACK

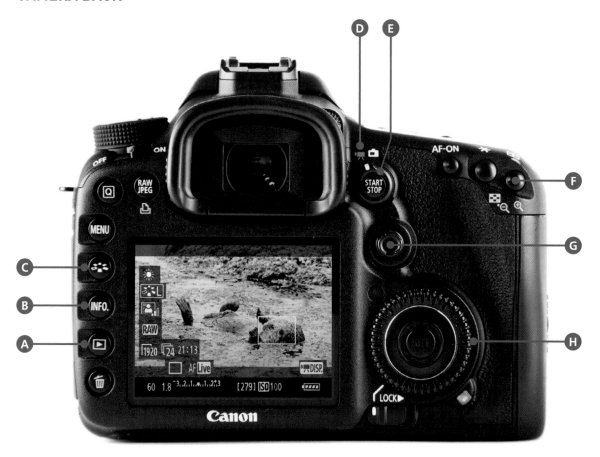

A   Playback Button
B   Info Button/Electronic Level
C   Picture Style Selection Button
D   Movie Shooting Switch
E   Start/Stop Button
F   Magnify Button
G   Multi-Controller
H   Quick Control Dial

LCD MONITOR

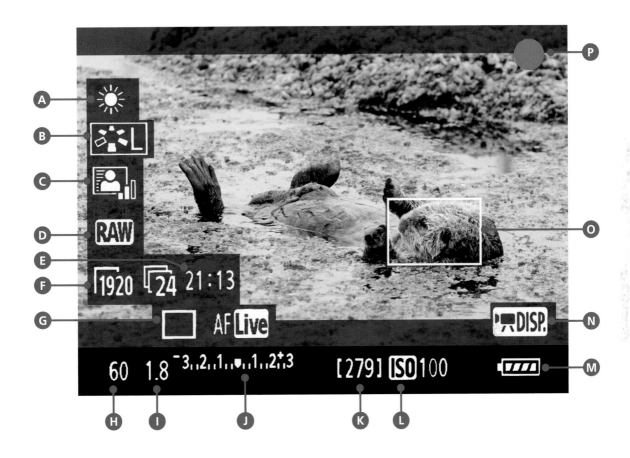

A   White Balance
B   Picture Style
C   Auto Lighting Optimizer
D   Image-Recording Quality
E   Movie-Shooting Remaining/Elapsed Time
F   Movie-Recording Size
G   Drive Mode
H   Shutter Speed

I   Aperture
J   Exposure Compensation Amount
K   Shots Remaining
L   ISO Speed
M   Battery Check
N   Exposure Simulation
O   AF Point
P   Recording Movie Indicator

GETTING STARTED

Before you jump into making movies of your own, let's go over some of the basic settings you'll use in order to ensure that you're getting the quality you want.

VIDEO QUALITY

The first setting that's important to understand is resolution. You'll need to know what movie-recording size you want to use, along with the frame rate, or frames per second (fps). The files are recorded as .mov files, and the quality and the resolution (size) of each file is measured in pixels. The fps rate is defined as how many frames (images) the camera records in a 1-second timeframe.

The 7D has three different sizes you can choose from:

- **1920 x 1080:** This is the full High Definition (HD) setting (16:9 aspect ratio). You have the option to record in 30, 25, or 24 fps. Using this setting at 24 fps is the standard for recording motion pictures. This setting is often referred to as "1080p."

- **1280 x 720:** This is another HD setting with an aspect ratio of 16:9, but in a smaller resolution. It records movies at 50 or 60 fps and is often referred to as "720p." This is good for shooting Web-sized videos or if you want to create a high-quality slow-motion effect with your movies using editing software. Using this setting will take up the same amount of space on your CF card as the 1080p setting since it records twice as many fps.

- **640 x 480:** This setting is for Standard Definition (SD) recording and records at a 4:3 aspect ratio.

FRAME RATES

The frame rate numbers listed on your camera are an approximate number of what the camera actually records. The true frame rates are as follows: **24:** 23.976, **25:** 25.00, **30:** 29.97, **50:** 50.00, and **60:** 59.94.

SLOW MOTION

If you want to slow down your videos and create high-quality slow-motion videos, then you'll want to start by shooting in 720p. This setting records the video at 60 fps so that when you bring it into an editing program you can set it to play back at 50 percent speed, or 30 fps. Your video will now play back half as fast as you originally recorded it without sacrificing image quality.

NTSC AND PAL

You can set your 7D to record video in one of two formats: NTSC (National Television Standards Committee) or PAL (Phase Alternate Line) (**Figure 9.1**). NTSC is the standard format for broadcasting in North America, South America, and Asia; and PAL is the standard format for most European countries and other parts of the world. The main difference between the two when shooting with the 7D is their frame rates (25/50 fps for PAL and 30/60 fps for NTSC). It's recommended that you set your video format to the broadcasting standard for whatever country you're located in.

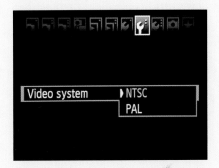

FIGURE 9.1
The 7D can record video in one of two formats: NTSC or PAL.

SETTING THE MOVIE-RECORDING SIZE

1. Set the camera to video mode using the Movie shooting switch (**A**).

2. Press the Menu button and use the Main dial to get to the fourth camera tab (**B**) (you'll notice a new icon at the top of this menu—this is because you are in video mode).

3. Scroll down to Movie Rec. Size using the Quick Control dial, and press the Set button (**C**).

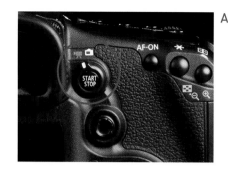

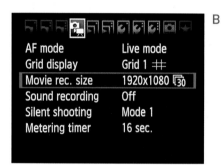

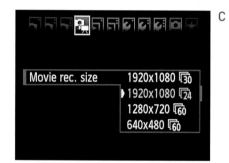

4. Use the Quick Control dial to select your preferred movie-shooting mode, and press the Set button to lock in your changes.

5. Press the Menu button to go back into Movie shooting mode.

The 7D is also limited in regard to the length of each individual movie file. The longest movie file you can record at a time is roughly 12 minutes for HD and 24 minutes for SD (a 4 GB file size). This typically should not be much of an issue since most videos are recorded in small segments and pieced together during the editing process, but it is good information to know since there may be times when you'll want to have a movie file that is longer than usual.

Manual Callout

Your manual gives a detailed description of each file size/fps and how much recording time you can shoot with a 4 GB or 16 GB card. To view this information, please turn to page 157 in your user's manual.

The next thing you'll need to consider is the type of compact flash card you are using. Because the camera will be writing the movie quickly and needs to process the information as fast as possible, I recommend using a card that has a very fast write speed (anything greater than 8 MB a second). In Chapter 6, I discussed using UDMA (Ultra Direct Memory Access) CF cards with high-speed photography, and shooting video with your 7D is another good example of when they are useful. It's also a good idea to use a card that is *at least* 4 GB in size—the amount of video you can record with a card smaller than 4 GB will be extremely limited.

IMAGE QUALITY—WHY DOES IT MATTER?

You might have noticed that an image quality setting (RAW/JPEG) displays when your camera is in the video mode (**Figure 9.2**). Whatever your image quality is usually set to, you'll see that this setting stays the same on the Info screen in between recordings—if you typically shoot in the RAW format, that setting will appear on your screen before you start recording movies. Just to clarify, the camera does not have the capability to shoot each frame of the video in the RAW format, but this setting does have a purpose...trust me!

Let's say you're in the middle of doing a video recording and you want to take a quick still photo but you don't want to stop the recording, go back to still shooting mode, change your camera mode and exposure settings, and so on. Instead of going through all of that trouble

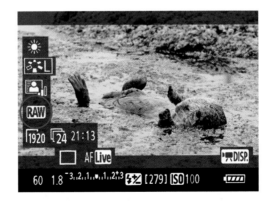

FIGURE 9.2
You can shoot still images while recording a movie—the image quality setting will appear on the rear LCD Monitor along with your video settings.

just to get one image, all you need to do is press the Shutter button down, even if you are still recording your movie. You'll notice a pause in the recording, but after the camera takes the photo it will automatically return to recording your video. The drawback to this feature is that it creates 1 second of a still image in your movie, but it's a nice feature to have if you need to jump to temporarily taking still photos.

SHOOTING AND PLAYBACK

So now that we've gone over some of the basics of getting started with video record-ing, I'm going to show you how to record your video and review it in the Playback mode. There are still a few other things to discuss in order to ensure that your videos are top-notch quality, but before we get to that, let's put everything to the test—and the only way to do that is to actually shoot some video.

RECORDING A MOVIE

1. Locate the Movie shooting switch on the back of the camera and turn it to the red video camera setting (**A**). The rear LCD Monitor will immediately go into Live View mode.

2. Compose and focus your scene and press the START/STOP button to begin your recording. You'll notice a red dot appears in the upper-right corner of the LCD Monitor (**B**). This indicates that video recording is in progress.

3. When you are finished recording, press the START/STOP button. The red dot will disappear, indicating that you are no longer recording video.

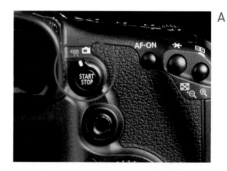

A

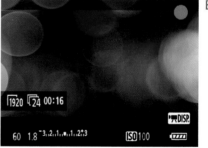

B

PLAYING MOVIES

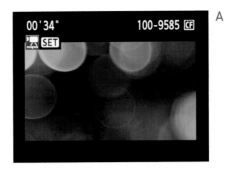

A

1. Press the Playback button located on the back of the camera.

2. Turn the Quick Control dial until you reach one of your videos. You'll know it's a movie when you see the video camera icon in the upper-left portion of the LCD Monitor (**A**). Then press the Set button.

3. To begin playback, press the Set button (the Play option on the bottom of the LCD Monitor will be highlighted by default) (**B**).

4. To stop or pause playback, press the Set button once again.

5. To exit from the playback screen, use the Quick Control dial to select the Exit option and then press Set (**C**).

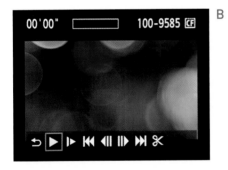

B

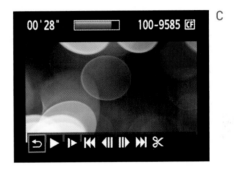

C

The 7D gives you several other options while in the playback screen. **Figure 9.3** shows all of the options you have when playing movies on your camera.

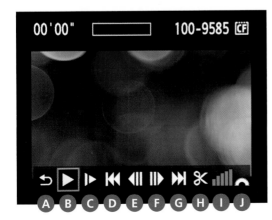

FIGURE 9.3

Use the Quick Control dial to select the other options in the Playback mode. If you recorded sound with your movie, you can also use the Main dial to adjust the sound volume during playback.

A	Exit	F	Next Frame
B	Play	G	Last Frame
C	Slow Motion	H	Edit
D	First Frame	I	Sound Volume
E	Previous Frame	J	Main Dial

Viewing movies on your computer that were recorded with your 7D is simple. Just download the .mov files to your computer from the memory card (you can also connect the camera to your computer using a USB cable). If you have a Mac, they will automatically play in QuickTime when you open the files (PC users can download this software online for free). The Canon Utility software that was included with your camera also has a program, ImageBrowser, that allows you to view still photos and play .mov files on your computer.

EXPOSURE SETTINGS FOR VIDEO

Setting the exposure for video is similar to setting exposure for still photographs, but you will notice a few differences that will only apply when recording movies.

One obvious difference is that you can only view your scene in Live View, and the LCD Monitor will display a simulated exposure for what your video will look like during the recording process. You'll know it's working properly when you see the exposure simulation icon displayed in white on the Information Display (**Figure 9.4**). There are also some limitations on shutter speed and exposure—keep on reading to learn more about them.

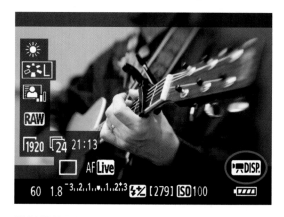

FIGURE 9.4
In video mode you will see a simulated exposure that is similar to what you will actually record.

AUTOEXPOSURE VS. MANUAL EXPOSURE

As with other types of photography, we have the option to shoot in auto or Manual mode (M), but with video the settings are a bit different. When using a shooting mode other than M (such as P, Tv, Av, and the Full Auto modes) the camera determines its exposure settings by using autoexposure. You have no control over the aperture, shutter speed, and ISO. This is a simple setting to use if you want to get a quick video and don't have the time to change the settings manually. However, with autoexposure you have limited control, and if you want to take full advantage of your DSLR and lenses when shooting video, you'll probably want to give the Manual mode a try.

The Manual mode for video functions in the same way as it does for still photography: You pick the aperture, shutter speed, and ISO. You can even change your settings while you are recording (although the microphone might pick up camera noises—read more about audio later in this chapter). I prefer to use the Manual mode when shooting video because I like to be in control over all of my settings, and I also like to use the largest aperture possible to decrease the depth of field in the scene.

One important thing to note when shooting video is that you have some shutter speed limitations, depending on your frames-per-second setting. The slowest shutter speed when shooting with a frame rate of 50 or 60 fps is 1/60 of a second, and for 24, 25, or 30 fps you can go down to 1/30 of a second. You can't go any faster than 1/4000 of a second, but it's recommended that you keep your shutter speed between 1/30 and 1/125 of a second, especially when photographing a moving subject. The slower your shutter speed is, the smoother and less choppy the movement in your video will be.

WHITE BALANCE AND PICTURE STYLES

When shooting video, you want to be sure to get the white balance right. Remember the difference between RAW and JPEG that you learned about in Chapter 2? Well, think of a video file as a JPEG—if you were to edit the video file on your computer, it would be difficult to change the white balance without damaging the pixels, and if the white balance is completely off, you might not even be able to salvage the video's original colors.

What's neat about shooting video is that you can see what the video quality will be like before you start recording. This means that you can set the white balance and see it changing right in front of you (this works in the same way as changing your white balance in Live View mode, just like we did in Chapter 1).

Picture styles are also a very useful tool when shooting video. They work the same way as with still photography (see Chapter 1 for more information), and you can preview your scene with the changes while in the video Live View mode. Just remember that once you record in one of these settings, you can't change this quality of the video. For example, when using the Monochrome (black and white) Picture Style, once you've recorded a movie, there is no way to go back and retrieve the color information.

COMPOSITION

When creating movies, most of the same rules of composition you use with still photography apply (see Chapter 8). The rule of thirds is one important rule to keep in mind when shooting video. The 7D's grid overlay feature places a grid over the LCD Monitor to help you frame your shot properly. Changes to this menu item will apply to both Live View and video recording modes (**Figure 9.5**).

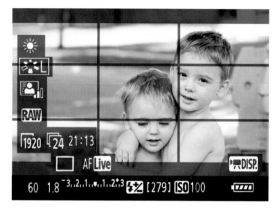

FIGURE 9.5

You can set your camera to display a grid overlay on the LCD Monitor in video mode and Live View.

SETTING THE GRID DISPLAY FOR VIDEO RECORDING

1. Set the camera to video mode using the Movie shooting switch.

2. Press the Menu button and use the Main dial to get to the fourth camera tab. Use the Quick Control dial to scroll down to Grid Display and press Set (**A**).

3. Using the Quick Control dial, once again select the grid of your choice (**B**). Press the Set button to lock in your change.

4. Press the Menu button to go back into Movie shooting mode. You will now see a semi-transparent grid over the LCD Monitor on the back of your camera.

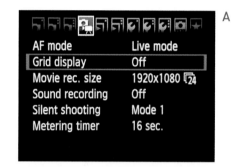

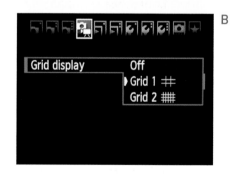

When you are in video mode, you will notice a semi-transparent mask covering parts of the LCD Monitor (**Figures 9.6** and **9.7**). The space within the mask is the area that will be recorded; the semi-transparent mask on either the top and bottom (HD) or left and right (SD) will not be recorded. This is extremely helpful when composing images for movies, because you will know where the edges of the frame will be.

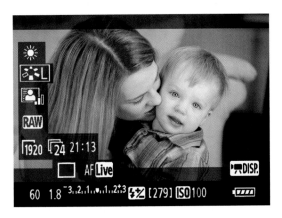

FIGURE 9.6
In HD resolutions, your camera will display a semi-transparent mask over the top and bottom portions of your LCD Monitor.

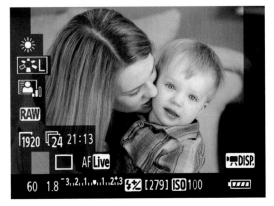

FIGURE 9.7
In SD resolution, your camera will display a semi-transparent mask over the left and right portions of your LCD Monitor.

If you place your camera on a tripod to record your movies, one very useful feature is the electronic level, which you learned about in Chapter 5 (**Figure 9.8**). It can some-times be difficult to see the horizon line in your scene, and the electronic level will help you keep your camera leveled both vertically and horizontally. With still photography you can always go in and straighten the photo in editing software, but with video you don't have as much wiggle room, so it's always best to get it correct in-camera. Note that if you set the autofocus mode to "Face detection Live mode," the electronic level won't appear. Be sure to set it to either "Live mode" or "Quick mode" for it to show (please read the next section for more information on focus settings for video recording).

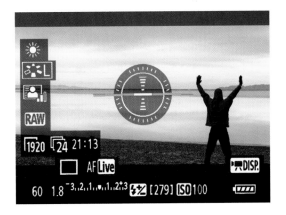

FIGURE 9.8
The electronic level is a helpful feature to use when placing your camera on a tripod.

USING A TRIPOD

To get the best possible quality when recording video with your camera, it's a good idea to have a sturdy tripod and a fluid video head. I use a Manfrotto 501HDV video head with my Canon 7D when I use it on a tripod (**Figure 9.9**). There are also other options for stabilizing your camera, including handheld rigs and additional equipment.

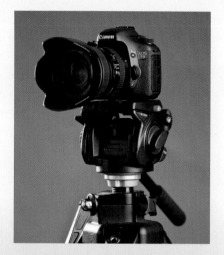

FIGURE 9.9

A sturdy tripod and a fluid video head are good tools to have when shooting video with your 7D.

FOCUSING

Focusing for video is a little bit different than still-image focusing since you can't look through the viewfinder to set focus, and all of it is done on the Live View screen. However, some things are the same—just like with still photography, you can either manually focus or autofocus your lens. The 7D makes it easy to autofocus and gives you three different settings to choose from (**Figure 9.10**):

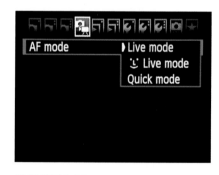

FIGURE 9.10

The 7D offers three autofocus modes for video recording.

- **Live mode:** With Live mode, the image sensor is used to focus. This method can take longer than focusing through the viewfinder (which uses the dedicated AF sensor).

- **Face detection Live mode:** This is the same as Live mode focusing, but it detects and focuses human faces.

- **Quick mode:** With this setting, the dedicated AF sensor is used to set the focus; however, the Live View image is momentarily interrupted for this to take place. This is the fastest method of focusing when in Live View or video mode.

To use these focusing modes, just point the camera at your subject, use the Multi-Controller to select your focus point, and press the shutter down halfway. The focus point will flash green and you'll hear a beep when the camera finds the focus.

Using autofocus is easy, but if you ask me, the best way to set focus in Live View or video mode is to manually focus the lens. I actually find it to be much quicker and more accurate than relying on the camera's autofocus. The great thing about setting focus using the LCD Monitor on the back of the camera is the ability to zoom in to your subject. This feature allows you to compose your shot and use the same buttons you would use to preview your images at 100 percent in Playback mode (See Chapter 6), but in Live View you are viewing the subject that you are about to photograph or record.

MANUALLY FOCUSING YOUR VIDEOS

1. Set the camera to video mode using the Movie shooting switch.

2. Use the Multi-Controller to select the area you want to focus on (**A**). When you have it set, press the Magnify button once to zoom in (**B**). Pressing it once will magnify your image by a factor of 5 (5x) and pressing it twice will magnify it by a factor of 10 (10x).

3. Set the focusing switch on your lens to MF, and then turn the front part of the lens until your image is in focus.

4. Press the Magnify button until the image on the LCD Monitor is back to Normal view.

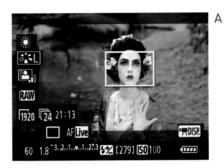

A

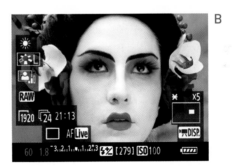

B

LIVE VIEW

As you may have already guessed, many of the techniques used in this chapter to set focus and exposure for recording videos can also be applied to shooting still images in Live View mode. Chapter 10 lists some techniques for using Live View, and for even more information please turn to page 131 in your user's manual.

AUDIO

The Canon 7D records audio by utilizing the microphone located on the front of the camera (**Figure 9.11**). It records monaural sound, meaning the sound is recorded on a single channel. This audio basically gets the job done. It's not top-notch, but if you are making quick, simple movies and don't need high-quality sound, then this microphone will work quite well for you.

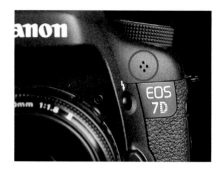

FIGURE 9.11
The built-in microphone is located on the front of your camera.

One huge drawback to using the built-in microphone is that it will pick up operational noises made by your camera. Changing the ISO or manually refocusing your lens during the recording process might not sound loud to your ears, but when you play back the video you'll hear every click, bump, and swish your camera made during those changes.

If you're serious about shooting videos and want to ensure that you have the best audio possible to go along with your movies, your best option is to invest in additional audio gear instead of using the built-in microphone (**Figure 9.12**). You can plug in this equipment by using the external microphone IN terminal located on the side of your camera, beneath the Terminal cover. The advantages to using an external microphone and other equipment are that you can record your sound in stereo and you can regain control over the sound recording level.

It's possible, however, that you don't need to record any audio with your videos. With the 7D you have the option of turning sound recording off so that you are only recording the video. Be sure that you turn the Sound Recording setting back to On when you are finished so you don't unintentionally record silent movies!

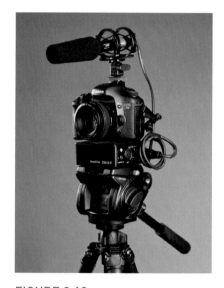

FIGURE 9.12
The 7D can easily be equipped with external audio gear; here is a simple setup with a BeachTek DXA-SLR active DSLR adapter and Audio-Technica AT875 shotgun microphone.

TURNING OFF THE SOUND RECORDING

1. Set the camera to video mode using the Movie shooting switch. This feature is only changeable when in video mode.

2. Press the Menu button and use the Main dial to get to the fourth camera tab. Use the Quick Control dial to scroll down to Sound Recording, and press Set (**A**).

3. Using the Quick Control dial once again, select Off (**B**). Press the Set button to lock in your change.

4. Press the Menu button to go back into Movie shooting mode.

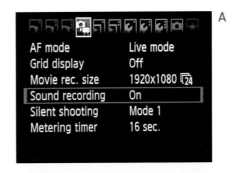

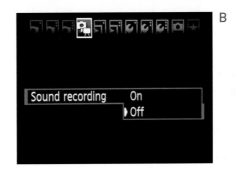

TIPS FOR SHOOTING VIDEO

Transitioning from being a still photographer to making movies might seem like a piece of cake, but you'll find that there are still a few things to keep in mind to make those videos shine.

SEE DIFFERENTLY

When I first started creating videos with my DSLR, I really started to pay attention to the cinematography of TV and movies. I noticed that the camera was usually still while the world around it moved. Subjects moved into the frame and out of the frame, and the camera didn't always try to follow them. It can be tempting to move the camera to follow your subject, but sometimes keeping still can add more impact and drama to your scene (plus a lot of movement might make your viewers dizzy!). So let your subjects move in and out of the frame while you take a deep breath, relax, and keep your camera pointed in the same, unchanging direction.

DON'T RUSH

As still photographers, we tend to see things "in the moment." When recording videos those moments last longer, and they need to flow through from one scene to the next. A common mistake that new video photographers tend to make is that they cut their videos short, meaning they stop the recordings too soon. It's important that you have extra time before and after each scene not only to allow for smooth transitions in and out of the video, but also for editing purposes. It's always good to have more than you need when piecing video clips together in postproduction.

So, when you think you are done with your video clip and you want to turn it off… don't! Count to three, or four or five, and then stop your recording. It will feel odd at first, but don't worry; you'll get the hang of it. Those extra couple of seconds can make a world of difference.

VIDEO EDITING

Once you have recorded your movies, you might want to do a little bit more with them, such as assemble several video clips into one movie, or add sound or additional graphics and text. If so you'll probably want to learn a thing or two about how to edit your videos using video editing software. Many different software programs are available for you to choose from. With some of the free or inexpensive programs, like iMovie (for Macs) or QuickTime Pro, you can do basic editing on your video clips. Other programs, such as Final Cut Pro or Adobe Premier Pro, will allow you to do even more advanced editing and to add creative effects to your movies. Using editing software is not required to play back and share movies created with your 7D, but it is a fun way to take your movies to the next level.

Chapter 9 Challenges

Now that we've covered most of the basics behind shooting video with your 7D, take some time to familiarize yourself with all of the features listed in this chapter. Here are a few exercises to get you started.

Movie recording sizes

Take some time to discover the different movie recording sizes on your 7D. Set the camera to one of the HD settings (1920 × 1080 or 1280 × 720), then change the setting to SD (480 × 640). Note the different aspect ratios (16:9 vs. 4:3) and areas that are covered with the semi-transparent mask. Shoot a few short videos in each recording size and then play them back on your computer.

White balance and picture styles

Set your camera on a tripod and set it to Movie shooting mode. Set the exposure so you can see your scene properly, then change the white balance, scrolling through all the different options, and watch the screen as you try each setting. Do the same with the picture styles and pay attention to the colors in your scene as you make the changes.

Set your focus

Familiarize yourself with the different autofocus modes by going into the menu and trying each of them out. Once you've got the hang of it, set the lens to MF (Manual Focus) and zoom in using the Magnify button on the back of your camera to focus on a specific area of your scene.

Understanding the built-in microphone's limitations

Make sure the Sound Recording feature is set to On and the Shooting mode is set to Manual, and then start to record a short video clip. During the recording process, change the shutter speed by turning the Main dial to the right or left. Then, while still recording, set the lens to MF and set your focus manually by turning the front part of the lens. Stop the recording, and then go into Playback mode. Pay attention to the noises you hear while you were making changes to the exposure and focus—it's a lot louder than it seemed, right?

Share your results with the book's Flickr group!

Join the group here: flickr.com/groups/canon7dfromsnapshotstogreatshots

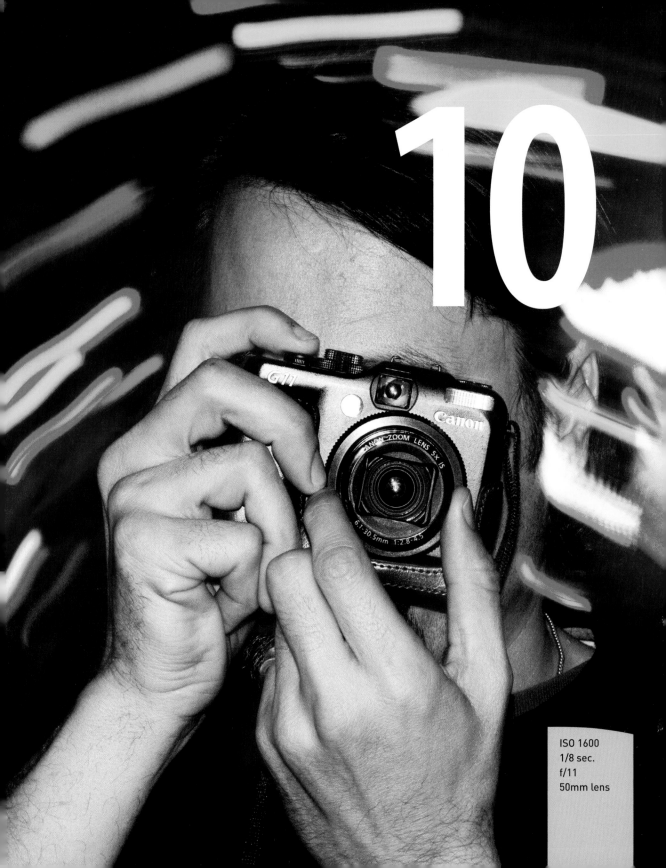

10

ISO 1600
1/8 sec.
f/11
50mm lens

Advanced Techniques

CUSTOMIZING YOUR CAMERA AND YOUR CREATIVITY

We've covered a lot of topics in the previous chapters, including the functions of many of the menu items and how to change the internal settings on your camera. But there are even more ways you can customize these settings to your liking. Here are a few additional photo techniques that I really enjoy playing around with—and I think you might too!

I was out one evening with a friend to do some night photography, and we found a great location to create light painting images. Light painting is a technique in which you use handheld light sources to add streaks of light to the image or illuminate an object within the frame by "painting" with the light source in front of the camera. For this photo I used a powerful flashlight to paint the ground, and my friend scribbled the haystacks with a laser pointer. This photo stands out as one of my favorites because of the stars in the night sky. This type of photography is always an adventure, and I find that I have a ton of fun when I'm making the images because I never know how they're going to turn out.

This image was photographed well after sundown, but the distant city lights were bright enough to reflect onto the clouds.

ISO 800
10 sec.
f/4
24–105mm lens

Blue and green gels attached to the end of my flashlight added color to the ground where I "painted" the light.

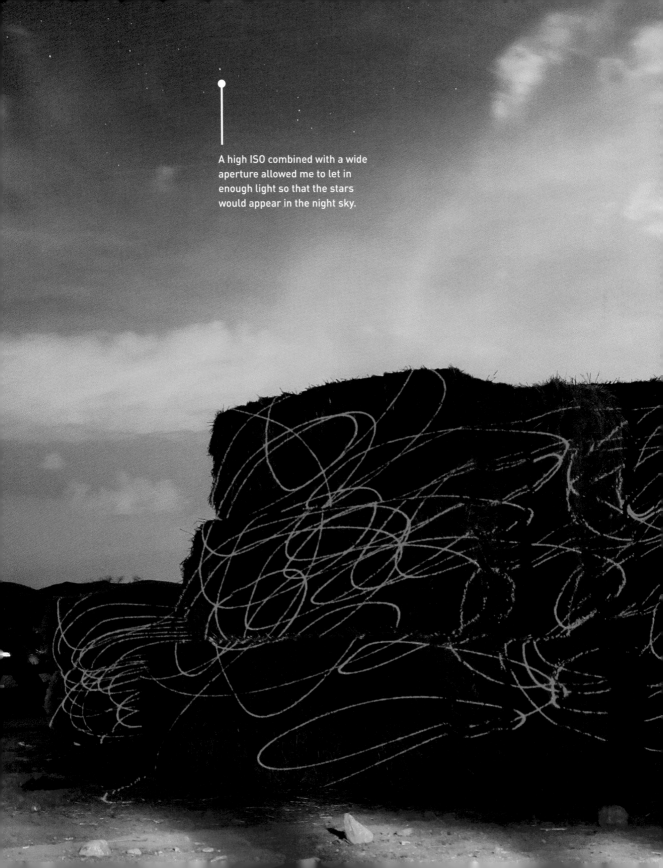

A high ISO combined with a wide aperture allowed me to let in enough light so that the stars would appear in the night sky.

PORING OVER THE PICTURE

I photographed this image of the Salt Lake City Public Library on a bright, sunny day. I've always found this building fascinating and lively, and the dramatic light shining through to the interior made this a perfect opportunity for high dynamic range (HDR).

I used a wide lens and shot vertically to show as much of the room as possible.

I created an HDR out of three different images so that I could capture details in both the highlights and shadow areas of the scene.

This image was photographed in the middle of the day, which allowed a lot of sun to shine through the windows and create an interesting pattern along the entire interior of the building.

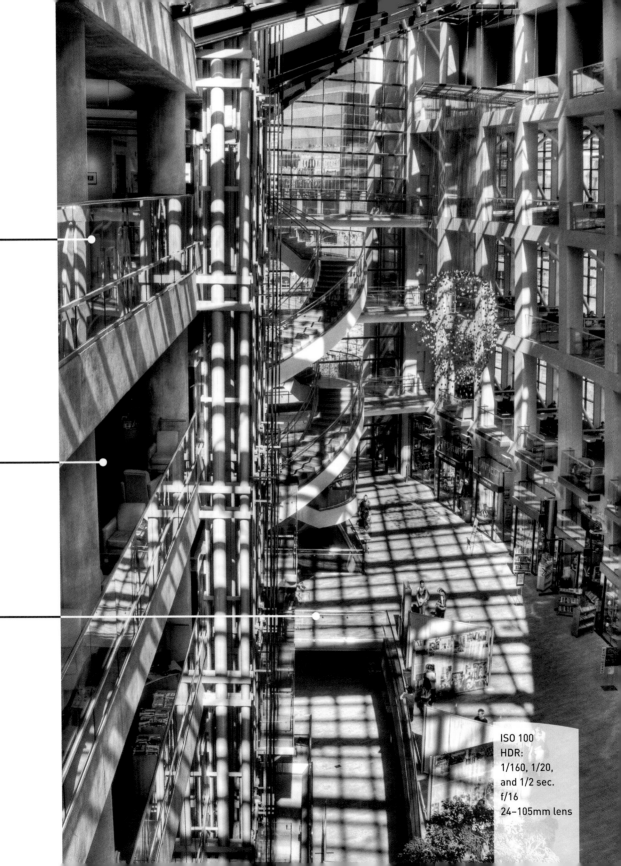

ISO 100
HDR:
1/160, 1/20,
and 1/2 sec.
f/16
24–105mm lens

USING A CUSTOM WHITE BALANCE

Throughout this book, I've discussed several of the white balance settings and when to use them. One white balance setting I haven't covered in detail is the Custom setting. Sometimes the presets on your camera won't be 100 percent accurate. For example, you might use the Daylight setting outside on a sunny day, but the color and quality of the light will be different at noon than they will be at 7 p.m. The Daylight white balance setting will get you to a good starting point, but you'll need to go through a few simple steps to achieve as much accuracy as possible.

The only piece of equipment you need to do this, other than your camera, is something you can point your camera at to measure the temperature of the light. These devices come in many shapes, sizes, and prices; one inexpensive option is a basic 8-by-10-inch 18 percent gray card. You can find these at most camera stores and they don't cost very much—plus they do the job well. But you don't need to purchase anything to set this up—you can always use a plain white piece of paper, or anything with a plain white surface. The color won't be as accurate, but it should get you really close.

SETTING UP A CUSTOM WHITE BALANCE USING A GRAY CARD

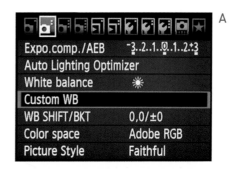

A

1. Place the gray card in the light you will be photographing your subject in. Position the card in front of the camera so that it fills the entire frame, focus manually, and use a balanced exposure. Then press the Shutter button and take a picture.

2. Next, press the Menu button and use the Main dial to get to the second shooting tab. Use the Quick Control dial to scroll down to the Custom WB menu item (**A**), and then press the Set button.

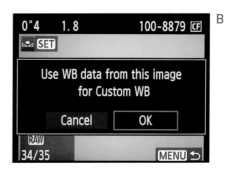

B

3. Use the Quick Control dial to scroll to the photo of the gray card you just took. Press the Set button and select OK (**B**).

4. If your white balance is not already set to Custom, you will get a reminder on the next screen. If this happens, press the Set button and set your white balance to Custom (see Chapter 1 for detailed instructions on changing the white balance).

Now your camera should have the proper white balance for the light you are currently working in. Don't forget to change it when you move to a location with different lighting!

USING THE CUSTOM SETTINGS MODES (C1, C2, AND C3)

 The 7D has three different customizable camera user settings: C1, C2, and C3. These are useful if you frequently find yourself shooting in the same environment with the same settings. They allow you to completely customize a shooting setting any way you like and then record those settings as a preset.

One example of when you may want to use these settings is when shooting HDR. It doesn't matter where I am, what lens I'm using, or what time of day it is; I always use the same starting point. I set the ISO to 100, shoot in Av mode, set the drive mode to High-speed continuous shooting, and make sure that Auto Exposure Bracket mode is turned on. I can record all of these settings in one of the custom settings, and they will be ready any time I want to photograph a series of images for HDR.

Another useful preset to create is one for using the Movie shooting mode. I like to have a good starting point for all of the movies I record, and I don't want to make a silly mistake like forgetting to turn sound recording on, shooting at too high a shutter speed, or using the wrong movie-recording size. Setting up a preset and using a customized camera user setting will guarantee that I won't make any of those mistakes. It also allows me to jump straight into movie shooting without having to think about my settings.

Manual Callout

For a complete list of all the camera user settings that can be registered, please turn to page 224 in your user's manual.

SETTING UP YOUR OWN CUSTOM SHOOTING MODES

1. First make all of the adjustments to the camera that you want in your custom shooting mode. For example, you might set the camera to Av mode, ISO 100, Daylight white balance, and RAW+JPEG image quality.

2. Press the Menu button and use the Main dial to get to the third setup tab.

3. Use the Quick Control dial to highlight the Camera User Setting option (**A**), and then press Set. Select Register and press Set again.

4. Choose which mode dial you would like to register, C1, C2, or C3 (**B**), and then press Set.

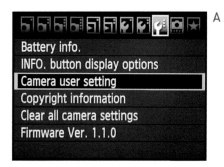

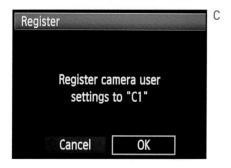

5. Use the Quick Control dial to select OK (**C**), then press Set one last time.

6. When you want to use a setting, just rotate the Mode dial to that custom setting (C1, C2, or C3) and begin shooting.

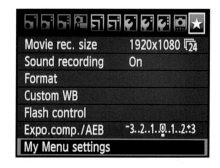

THE MY MENU SETTINGS

You may find that you are constantly going back and forth in the menu to change some of the same settings over and over. Instead of going into the menu to hunt for the one item that you need to change but that you have misplaced (this happens to me all the time), take advantage of the 7D's simple solution to help you keep a few of those settings in one place and make them easier to find—the My Menu tab.

Under the My Menu tab, you have the option to register up to six different menu options and custom functions. To give you an idea of what this looks like, take a look at what I currently have registered in the My Menu tab (**Figure 10.1**). I usually select menu items that I use frequently so that

FIGURE 10.1
This is what the My Menu settings look like on my 7D.

I can quickly make changes to those settings. I do change these from time to time, but the majority of them stay put (for example, the Format menu item is one that will always remain in place).

CUSTOMIZING YOUR MY MENU SETTING

1. Press the Menu button and use the Main dial to select the tab to the far right (the star). Select the My Menu settings option, and press Set.

2. Highlight the Register menu item (**A**), and press Set.

3. Use the Quick Control dial to scroll through the available menu items (**B**); when you see one that you want to add, press the Set button and confirm that you want to add it by selecting OK.

4. Continue adding the items that you want until you have selected your favorites (up to six of them).

5. You can sort your menu items as you see fit or, if you change your mind, you can delete them individually or all at once.

6. If you want the My Menu tab to be the first menu tab that appears each time you go into the menu on your LCD Monitor, enable the Display From My Menu item (**C**).

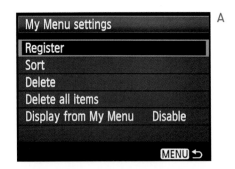

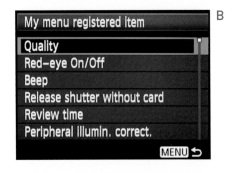

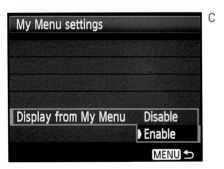

CUSTOM CONTROLS

Setting the 7D's custom controls, located in the Custom Functions menu tab, is a great way to change the buttons and knobs on your camera to your own specifications. You might find that there are some default buttons you don't use very often while you are shooting. If so, there just might be a different setting for those buttons that would make them more useful for your shooting style.

SETTING THE CUSTOM CONTROLS

1. Press the Menu button and use the Main dial to scroll to the Custom Functions tab, and then use the Quick Control dial to highlight the C.Fn IV: Operation/Others item (**A**). Press the Set button.

2. Use the Quick Control dial to select C.Fn IV-1 (Custom Controls) (**B**). Press the Set button.

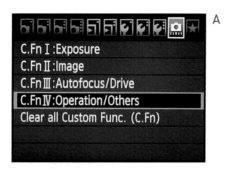 A

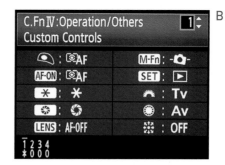 B

3. Next, use the Main dial to highlight the item you woud like to change. For this example I'll show how to add a function to the Multi-Controller (**C**).

4. Press the Set button and use the Main dial to select AF Point Direct Selection (**D**), and then press the Set button once again. Now I can change the focus point in my viewfinder while shooting by toggling the Multi-Controller.

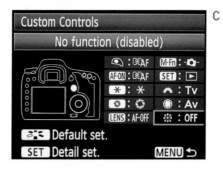 C

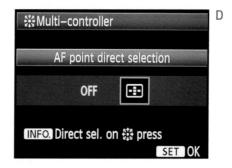 D

You are free to change any of the settings however you like. I recommend scrolling through all of the items to see what they can do. But don't worry f you get things moved around so much that you can't remember what you changed the buttons to—you can always set them back to their default settings by pushing the Picture Style Selection button on the back of your camera when you are in the Custom Controls menu screen.

TETHERING TO A COMPUTER

If you're photographing in an environment where you can be close to your computer while you are shooting, you might find tethering to be a useful feature. When you tether your 7D to a computer, you can instantly view your shots on your computer monitor, and you can even make changes to the camera settings and actually control the camera from the computer.

I find this a very handy feature to have when I'm working in my studio. When my camera is set up on a tripod, it's easy to tether it to a laptop because the camera isn't moving around. But even if you require more mobility, all you need is a USB cable long enough to reach your computer. So, let's get started!

TETHERING YOUR 7D TO A COMPUTER

1. Connect your camera to the computer with the interface cable (mini-USB to USB) that came with your 7D. Also make sure that the Canon utilities software is installed on your computer.

2. Turn the camera on, and open the EOS Utility application. Click the Camera settings/Remote shooting option (**A**). A new window will appear that allows you to adjust the settings on the camera and even take photos (**B**).

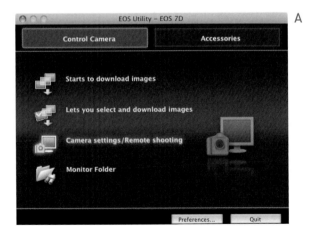 A

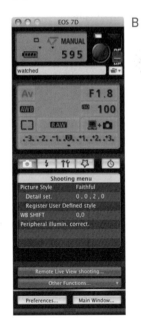 B

3. Click the Preferences button on the bottom left of the window. Here you can choose a destination folder (**C**), change the file-name, and make changes to many other settings.

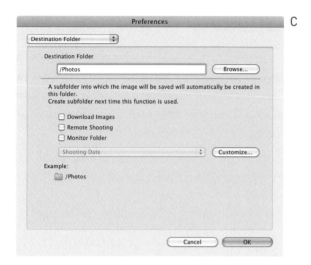

4. When you take a photo, you'll see it appear as a preview on the screen (**D**). This preview will auto-matically change to the current photo each time you press the Shutter button. (If you don't see the preview, click the Other Functions button and select Quick Preview.)

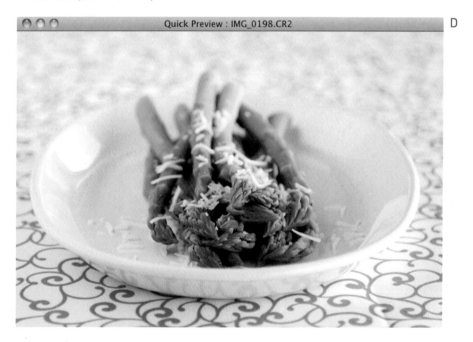

5. You can also shoot in Live View mode and view a live preview of your image on your computer screen by clicking the Remote Live View shooting button near the bottom of the shooting window.

LET'S GET CREATIVE

To finish off this chapter, I'm going to give you a few more shooting tips, mostly fun ways you can play around with light to get some really neat results. Photography wouldn't have as much appeal to me if it weren't for all the exciting ways to use light, along with the different settings on my camera. These are just a few of the hundreds of ways you can experiment with your camera.

THE "SWIRLY FLASH"

It's no secret that I don't like to use the built-in flash. The light is harsh and flat, and when you photograph people in a dark setting, such as indoors or at night, it's too easy to get a background that is dark and underexposed.

So when I'm in a situation in which I have no choice but to use the flash on my camera, I like to change some of the settings to give my snapshots a different look. I drag the shutter, setting it much slower than normal, usually between 1/15 and 1/4 of a second, and spin the camera on axis with the subject while the shutter is open. This keeps the person mostly frozen and well-lit while creating an interesting blur of lights in the background (**Figure 10.2**).

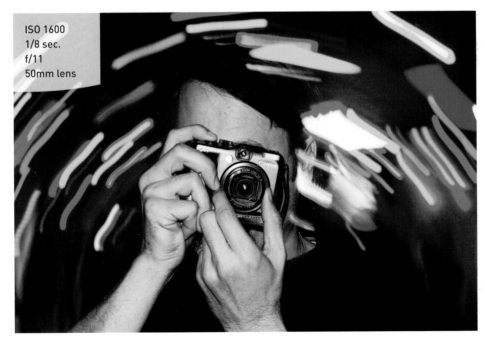

ISO 1600
1/8 sec.
f/11
50mm lens

FIGURE 10.2
By using a slow shutter speed with the built-in flash, you can create fun and unique photos of your friends.

I like to call this technique my "party trick" because when I'm in a room full of people, I'll use this method to take a quick portrait, and often it's something that they haven't seen done before. This technique is not limited to DSLR cameras, and I frequently show people how to set up their point-and-shoot cameras to do it. I find that it adds a unique look to an otherwise boring snapshot. One quick tip: This type of image usually works best when there are a lot of lights behind your subject, such as the lights from a Christmas tree.

CREATING THE "SWIRLY FLASH" EFFECT

1. Set your camera to Tv mode and start with a shutter speed somewhere between 1/15 and 1/4 of a second.

2. Press the built-in flash button on the front of your camera.

3. Point the camera and center your subject in the frame. Start with the camera slightly tilted, and then press the Shutter button to take a photo and spin the camera so that the subject stays centered in the image.

4. If your flash is too bright, press the Flash Exposure Compensation button on the top of the camera and use the Quick Control dial to move the exposure value (EV) to the left. Take another photo and preview your results.

5. If the background is too dark or too bright, you'll want to adjust your ISO setting. The higher the ISO number is, the more ambient light you'll bring into the background.

6. If you have too much or too little blur in the background, adjust the shutter speed (a slower shutter speed for more blur, and a faster shutter speed for less blur).

7. Keep adjusting the settings until you find that "sweet spot." It will be different for each environment, and there's no single right way to do it. Just have fun with it!

LIGHT PAINTING

Another fun technique that's worth trying is light painting (**Figure 10.3**). For this, you'll need a dark environment (nighttime is best), your camera on a tripod, and some semi-powerful flashlights or other light source. Shine your flashlight on your subject to light it, and in effect you'll "paint" the light that will show up on your image.

But you don't have to paint the light on something for it to show up—if it's dark enough you can stand in front of the camera and move the light source to make shapes or spell something out. A fun item to use for this effect is a sparkler (a type of handheld firework that emits sparkles)—just set your camera up on a tripod outdoors at night and have someone run around the frame holding a sparkler, and you'll create shapes and streaks that can look really cool. You could also use small flashlights or

LED lights. In **Figure 10.4** I used a small LED flashlight with a green gel over it to add a different color to the writing.

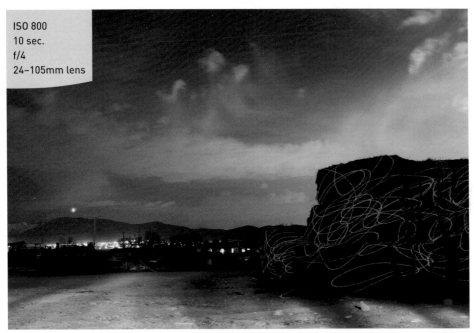

ISO 800
10 sec.
f/4
24–105mm lens

FIGURE 10.3
For this photo-
graph, I used a long
exposure while my
friend scribbled
the haystacks with
a laser pointer
and I "painted"
the ground with a
powerful LED flash-
light. I added small
blue and green gels
on the flashlight
to add color to the
image.

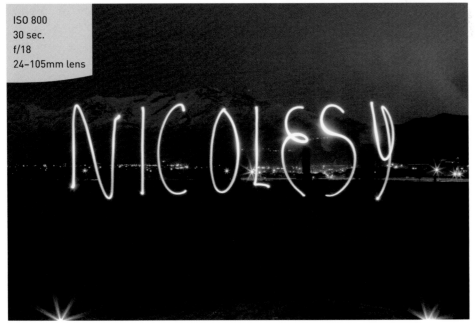

ISO 800
30 sec.
f/18
24–105mm lens

FIGURE 10.4
I photographed
this image with the
help of my friend
dav.d. That's me
writing with a small
LED flashlight. The
original photo was
backwards, so I
flipped the image
horizontally using
editing software.

1. Place your camera on a tripod in a dark environment, preferably nighttime or a darkened room.

2. If your environment is extremely dark, set your camera to the Bulb shooting mode with a large aperture. If you have some ambient light in your scene, set your camera to Av mode and use an aperture that is large enough to capture the light from your light painting but small enough to give you a fairly slow shutter speed—several seconds is usually a good place to start.

3. Using a cable release or one of the self-timer drive modes, press the Shutter button. If you are using Bulb mode, you'll need a cable release in order to hold the shutter open for the duration of your light painting.

4. With the shutter open, use a flashlight, a sparkler, or any other type of powerful light source to create your image. The creative possibilities are endless!

HIGH DYNAMIC RANGE (HDR)

In Chapter 5, I discussed how to use HDR for landscape photography. But HDR doesn't need to be limited to landscapes. In fact, you can photograph almost anything that is not moving and achieve some great effects. **Figure 10.5** is the interior of a library photographed just before noon. The light shining through the windows added contrast to the scene, but by creating an HDR image, I was able to retain a lot of detail in both the highlight and shadow areas of the image.

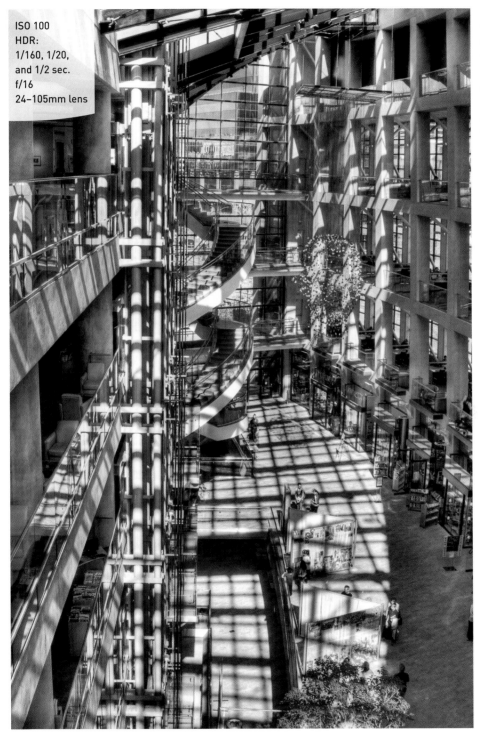

ISO 100
HDR:
1/160, 1/20,
and 1/2 sec.
f/16
24–105mm lens

FIGURE 10.5
This is an HDR image of the interior of a building. Notice that you can still see details in the shaded and sun-filled areas of the scene.

CONCLUSION

As you've gone through each chapter in this book, I hope you've found new ways to use your camera to get some really great shots. Photography is a mix of both technical skill and creativity, and the more you challenge yourself and step outside of your comfort zone, the more you'll improve as a photographer. You'll also find yourself thinking less about the shots you take and relying more on your instincts to create photographs.

As I close, I would like to leave you with a few last pieces of advice. You could read every photography book you can get your hands on, and while you would definitely soak up tons of information, you shouldn't forget to take the time to really look at photography. And I mean a *lot* of photography—lots and lots and lots. View images on the Internet, in the library, or in art galleries, and open up your mind to absorb as much visual information as you can. And, of course, get out and make your own photographs. Take what you've learned and put it to use. Try to see light *all* the time, not just when you're holding your camera. Break all the rules, don't limit yourself, and definitely don't let other people's opinions of you or your work define you or your photography. And lastly, don't be afraid to mess up, because you will! *Every* photographer takes bad photos—you just don't always see our mistakes.

But the most important thing to remember while taking pictures is to have fun! We're photographers because it's our passion and we want to create memories and beautiful images that will be around for generations to come. The way I see it is that, good or bad, *everyone* is a photographer—some of us just take it to the next level. As for me…I'm a photo geek and proud of it.

Chapter 10 Challenges

Many of the techniques covered in this chapter are specific to certain shooting situations that may not come about very often. It's a good idea to practice them a few times so that when the situation does present itself you will be ready. Here are a few challenges to get you started.

Set a custom white balance

Set your camera to whatever white balance seems appropriate for your environment (if you are in the shade, select the Shade white balance setting). Take a quick photo of something in that setting. Then take a gray card or white piece of paper and follow the directions in this chapter for setting a custom white balance. Take another photo and compare its color with the first image.

Customize your camera

If you have a camera setting that you use frequently, set it up and then register it as one of the camera user settings (C1, C2, or C3). Also, go into the custom controls and play around with the different options to see if any of them fit your shooting style better than the default selections. Lastly, if there are several menu items that you frequently use, be sure to set them up to show in the My Menu tab.

Try something new!

Take a shot at some of the last few creative tips included at the end of the chapter. Try photographing a person using the "swirly flash" method, or grab some flashlights and create a light painting image. Use your imagination and try to come up with your own creative techniques using different light sources. There's no right or wrong way to do it—just experiment with your settings and different types of lights, and be sure to have a good time in the process.

Share your results with the book's Flickr group!

Join the group here: flickr.com/groups/canon7dfromsnapshotstogreatshots

INDEX